THE SPANISH SONG COMPANION

THE SPANISH SONG COMPANION

Devised and translated by

JACQUELINE COCKBURN
& RICHARD STOKES

with an Introduction and Notes by
GRAHAM JOHNSON

LONDON
VICTOR GOLLANCZ LTD
1992

First published in Great Britain 1992
by Victor Gollancz Ltd
14 Henrietta Street, London WC2E 8QJ

Translation, arrangement and endnotes
© Jacqueline Cockburn and Richard Stokes 1992

Introduction and notes on the composers
© Graham Johnson 1992

ISBN 0 575 04674 0

ACKNOWLEDGEMENTS

Material by the following authors is copyright and reprinted by
permission of the copyright holders mentioned:

Rafael Alberti: *Rutas*, *Pregón*, *Las doce*, *El pescador sin dinero*,
  Coplilla, *Cuba dentro de un piano*, © Agencia Literaria Carmen
  Balcells, Barcelona.
Clementina Arderiu: *Anacreòntica*, © Edicions 62, Barcelona.
Josep Carner: *Cançó incerta*, © Ed. Selecta, Barcelona.
Nicolás Guillén, *Chévere*, *Canto negro*, © Agencia Literaria Latino-
  america, Havana.
Clara Janés: *Primeros pasos*, © Clara Janés.
Gregorio Martínez Sierra: *Oración de las madres*, *Canción
  andaluza: el pan de ronda*, © Catalina Martinez de la Cotera,
  Madrid.
Ildefonso Pereda Valdés: *Canción de cuna*, © Barreiro y Ramos,
  Montevideo.
Josep María de Sagarra: *Romanç de Santa Llúcia*, © Joán de
  Saggara.
Paul Valéry: *La fausse morte*, *L'insinuant*, *Le sylphe*, *Le vin perdu*,
  Les pas, © Editions Gallimard, Paris.

Despite every effort, we have been unsuccessful in tracing the
copyright holders of the following poems:

Ramón Cabanillas: *Aureana do Sil*.
Josep Janés: 'Damunt de tu només les flors', 'Aquesta nit un mateix
  vent', 'Jo et pressentia com la mar', 'Fes-me la vida transparent'.
Juan Ramón Jiménez: *Pastoral*, 'Llueve sobre el río'.
Fernandez Néstor Luján: *Punto de Habanera*.
Père Ribot i Sunyer: *Sant Martí*.

Typeset at The Spartan Press Ltd,
Lymington, Hants
Printed in Great Britain by
St Edmundsbury Press Ltd, Bury St Edmunds, Suffolk

To Ian and Lynne

CONTENTS

ACKNOWLEDGEMENTS

Our warmest thanks to Dr Pepe Catalán for his tireless efforts in elucidating the thorniest textual problems and his helpful suggestions throughout. Thanks are also due to Alicia de Benito Harland for her careful checking of the typescript.

TRANSLATORS' NOTE

The texts printed here are for the most part those to be found in the collected works of each poet, without the composers' occasional alterations. Where the song consists of selected verses from the original poem, we print the composer's and not the poet's version. The poet's name has only been given when the authorship is beyond dispute; when it has not been possible to trace the original poem, as in the Italian poems of the Marquesa de Bolaños, for example, we have attempted to reconstruct the versification from the score. Orthography in poems from different centuries has not been standardised; when the year of composition is known, it is given beneath the title of the song.

We have not explained the significance of a poem when it forms part of a novel, play or short story, as is the case with Obradors's setting from *Don Quijote*, Turina's from *Fuente Ovejuna* and Vives's from *La gitanilla*; but we have provided explanations of Spanish words and concepts that might be unfamiliar to English readers, and these have been placed at the end of the relevant poem to facilitate understanding.

As far as possible we have observed in translation the Spanish line order and have sought to render the sense and tone of the poem without any slavish adherence to the original rhymes and rhythm.

Jacqueline Cockburn
Richard Stokes

INTRODUCTION

IN SEARCH OF SPANISH SONG

Sunlight, energy and high spirits on tap from the armchair travel shop – that is what many of us expect Spanish music to be, and it is undeniable that a well-conducted package tour can be enormous fun. Francis Poulenc wrote that the wrought-iron railings in the Spain evoked by Emmanuel Chabrier's rhapsody *España* had come from a large Parisian department store. Poulenc, for whom Paris was more glamorous than any Mediterranean city, meant this as the sincerest of compliments: how delicious to wave to Spain from the safety of a French balcony, the most colourful and amusing details pointed out by a guide knowledgeable about the antics of the locals. Chabrier's panoramic tour is one of the best of its type, a *tour de force* in fact. On holiday in Granada in November 1882, the composer took a great deal of trouble to note down a number of genuine folk melodies and dances, which eventually found their way into his work. For all its French polish, and whatever the provenance of its wrought-iron railings, *España* is a masterful musical travelogue by an Auvergnat whose distinctive home region, in both geographical and spiritual terms, is closely related to Spain. Other French composers have also had a hot-line to Iberia: Claude Debussy through the friendship of Albéniz and Falla (and they, in technical terms, also learned a great deal from him) and Ravel whose Basque blood gave him incomparable honorary Spanish credentials. Occasionally even composers of Lieder have succeeded in grasping the Spanish nettle: Schumann's respect and affection for the idea of Spain are obvious in a number of works, but it was Hugo Wolf who found the country's authentic voice through listening intently to the modulation of its poetry, albeit in German translation. Some of the religious songs in his *Spanisches Liederbuch* sound profoundly Spanish without a hint of bolero rhythm or imitation guitar accompaniment.

It is all very well to pay tribute to the composers who have made a genuine effort to understand Spain, but all too soon we find ourselves at the lower end of the musical market where much less trouble has been taken to paint in authentic Spanish tones – and where the colours of folk and fake all too easily run into each other. Most composers and performers amiably patronise Spain by reducing it to an all-purpose *España* with a musical landscape flattened into a set of Hollywood–Andalusian mannerisms. The film-set Spanish villas of Beverly Hills were built to upstage their neighbours' palaces in Tudor style, and the muzak of Spain competes with 'Greensleeves' in the humdrum shopping malls that have brought California to London's North Circular Road. Of course, real Spanish music, like genuine Spanish architecture, has little to do with the clichés of fans, fandangos and flashing eyes – stereotypes which are harmless enough but which represent Spain as inaccurately as Beefeaters at the Tower of London incarnate Britain. And even if these extravagantly dressed yeomen are typically English (and it must be a disappointment for those who value colourful eccentricity to discover they are not), a perspicacious visitor to London might ask about the garb of the Scottish, Welsh and Irish. In exactly the same way, Castile, Andalusia, Catalonia, Galicia and the Basque country have their own styles and customs as well as their own spoken languages; it would be very surprising if their music did not also have its own voice.

When I first went to Barcelona fifteen years ago to rehearse for recitals with Victoria de los Angeles, I was rather proud of my performance of Granados's 'El majo tímido'. The wayward rubato I employed in the introduction and postlude was choice evidence (or so I thought) of my understanding of things Iberian. At our first rehearsal I went at the piece with real torero fire, or looking at it from the other side of the fence, like a bull at a red rag. Madame de los Angeles drew a veil, or rather threw a wet blanket, over the whole enterprise. 'Why do you play this music as if it were from the South, when it comes from Castile?' she asked with gentle pity. Like all first-time visitors, I needed a geography lesson and I was extremely fortunate that my teacher was not only a great singer, but someone who was born in Catalonia of a Castilian mother and an Andalusian father – an embodiment of three of the main ingredients that constitute this peninsula of many nations. I learned that regional differences make an *enormous* difference in Spanish music. I had read about the stylised courtships of Majo and Maja, but in this rehearsal I found that Granados's portrait of Goya's Madrid was painted with a stiffer brush than that employed by, say, Albéniz in his *Iberia* suite for piano, which is inspired by the Moorish musical freedoms of Andalusia. In the *Tonadillas* of Granados the strongest passions are always controlled by the dignity and pride of madrileñismo, a feeling for the complicated etiquette and flirtation of eighteenth-century Madrid. In musical terms this means that rhythms need to be taut and controlled to suggest the arrogance and tension of those exaggeratedly formal courtships. After a few minutes with Victoria de los Angeles, I realised that my first way of playing the song – stewing in the juice of my own Hispanic misconceptions – was the result of a vulgar generalisation: many of my received ideas about this music had come from the Spanish parodies and imitations that have long been part of the musical vocabulary of northern Europe.

Thousands of visitors to Spain have likewise been chastened to find that the truth about the country is both more subtle and more interesting than they had first thought. I needed a lesson in the flesh to discover Granados – and the flesh is a matter of some import in Spain. From Chabrier's letters we learn that the sway and wiggle of the ladies' bottoms were an even greater source of rhythmic inspiration than his folksong researches. Indeed it seems that Spain yields its most exciting secrets to physical, rather than intellectual, examination. When visitors find themselves south of the Pyrenees, the wrought-iron railings of musicology (manufactured by the Spaniards themselves, but seldom exported to us) melt in the heat. It is American musicologists with their close proximity to a Spanish-speaking world in their own hemisphere, who have contributed the most to international understanding of Spanish music. Gilbert Chase, whose book *The Music of Spain* (1941) remains the standard work on the subject, and his fellow American Robert Stevenson whose authoritative researches in Spanish and Latin American musical studies are justly celebrated, are only two names in a large community of English-speaking scholars who have worked tirelessly in this field. But most attempts to fence or to tidy the overgrown and enchanting garden which is musical Spain and to compartmentalise Spanish music into manageable areas seem, for listeners and most performers at least, somewhat pointless, a losing battle; it is not an irrelevant task, but when confronted with the sensual heat of the moment, it seems so. Nowhere does this apply more than in the field of Spanish song which is a veritable jungle of exotic hybrid blooms flowering on age-old trees. Almost everything in the overgrown garden, if we only knew what to call it, or where to find it, seems lovely. Lazy nights spent in the gardens of Spain have always appealed to the hedonist, but the musical botanist trained in the more ordered ways of the north finds the profuse disorder a source of disquiet.

What is the key to this garden and an understanding of its glories? We hope that *The Spanish Song Companion* will open a gate for English-speaking visitors at least; its primary task is to reveal the beauties of

Spanish poetry, and to clear the pathway to the words, the lyrics which all great songs need as the centrepiece of their flowering. This book cannot aspire to be anything like a comprehensive catalogue of Spanish vocal music; rather is it a representative anthology of Spanish lyrics – for the most part about love – which can pleasurably be read as such in its own right. We hope that singers and accompanists will also add it to their studio bookshelves: even the mainstream Spanish song repertory is uncharted territory for most professional artists from the point of view of a detailed knowledge of the texts. The distance of the Manzanares from what has come to be regarded as the French–German mainstream of song, can make the foreign performer rather travel-sick. A few English-speaking musicians have been fortunate enough to have picked up pointers from Spanish colleagues; some have worked in Spain itself and others have found native-born coaches and have begun to discover the country through the sound of the language. But the majority of my colleagues are thoroughly in the dark about this sunlit repertoire. The confusion surrounding (or at the very least, the incomplete knowledge of) this body of music has much to do with the quixotic workings of Spanish printing presses (which sometimes seem to be windmill-driven) and the unpredictable availability of printed music. A lot of indifferent material has been published, and a lot of remarkable music exists only in yellowing manuscripts in the private possession of certain favoured artists. Many works are allowed to go out of print, and so-called definitive editions are peppered with misprints and mistakes; there is seldom anything written to help the outsider fathom much about the work's genesis or its first performance. Like my various fruitful and enlightening encounters with Victoria de los Angeles, information of this kind is more easily found through personal contact. Spain is the last great bastion of the oral tradition; it can also be unkindly characterised as the land of siesta and procrastination. It may also be observed that in the fields of musical and literary studies, Spanish scholars and libraries are somewhat possessive of their research materials and resist the invasion of foreigners on to their turf.

Of course these generalisations could well be said to go hand in hand with my youthful misconceptions of the Granados style, but most English-speaking visitors to Spain have encountered maddening in-efficiency with anything to do with paperwork – and music, before it can come to life in a performance, is nothing more or less than paper. It goes without saying that I have also found unbelievable generosity, when dealings are personal and face-to-face. The late Walter Legge told me that he had to fly to Spain to extract a long-promised programme from a celebrated singer; letters, telephone calls and telegrams were to no avail.

This anecdote is typical of the old-fashioned Spanish pace of life which is wary of twentieth-century innovations and which regards a visit as a more natural and courteous way of seeking information than a telephone call. And this in turn may be an explanation of why there seems to be a disinclination to make an efficient industry, by international standards, of the dissemination of music and musical knowledge. I believe that the Spaniards themselves have not made it easy for us to penetrate their secrets – the island mentality with which we British people are only too familiar, can also be said to apply to a peninsula. In Spain, Franco's interminable dictatorship was another factor inimical to openness, free exchange of information and imaginative publishing initiatives. The age which attempted to stifle the works of a major poet like Lorca (and thus render stillborn the settings that might have been made by contemporary Spanish composers) must be held responsible for a general malaise in many fields of scholastic endeavour, and for the lethargy of state-controlled publishing monopolies.

Some of the most widely performed Spanish songs, Falla's *Canciones populares* and Montsalvatge's *Canciones negras* for example, were published in France, England or America. Is their success the cause or effect of their publication outside Spain, I wonder? Most Spanish songs are launched unheralded and badly marketed into foreign lands where they remain unknown. The outsider, the English-speaking singing student who attempts to find and learn songs off the beaten track, must rummage haphazardly through whatever scores happen to be available, unguided as to what is good music, and usually unaware of what the poems mean. It may be that *The Spanish Song Companion* will generate a new demand for printed music which could improve the distribution and accessibility of the repertoire – for although the majority of the songs in this volume are still in print, others are sadly unavailable to the general public at this time. In England, the young artist may have been fortunate, as were the authors of this book, to consult the baritone Frederick Fuller, doyen of performers of Spanish and Latin-American music – but it is extremely rare to encounter such expertise among English-speaking singing teachers. The average soprano or mezzo will continue to concentrate on her French and German songs at the expense of the other great repertoires of the world, and fudge her way through the old familiar Spanish repertory, where 'something showy for the pianist' is deemed a suitably up-beat way to end a recital. Spanish song is thus too often relegated to the dessert course on ladies' nights (regrettably few male singers seem to explore Spanish song, quite wrongly seeing it as a lady's frippery), where it is usually whipped up from the same few popular recipes. Those gourmets who, in recent years, increasingly sing the praises of the astonishing quality and variety of Spanish food and wines will sympathise with our concern that the riches of Spanish song should be better appreciated.

And the time is now surely right. Spain is closer to us in every respect than ever before – politically, economically and culturally. At this time, there is an almost unprecedented explosion of literary activity in modern Spain, and the chances are that this energy will rub off on song composers who have always had a habit of being friendly with poets. In the musical renaissance that we must hope will be a by-product of Spain's entry into the very fabric of European life in the 1990s, Spanish musicologists, performers, publishers and contemporary composers could initiate the most exciting phase in their nation's musical history since the innovations of Pedrell and his pupils at the end of the nineteenth century. *The Spanish Song Companion* is a contribution to this worthy aim from Spain's English-speaking neighbours and fellow Europeans, and I believe a highly necessary one: it is time to dismantle the barricades that have stood in the way of a deeper understanding of this important body of music. There are now a number of important volumes (one of which, *The Fischer-Dieskau Book of Lieder*, is by one of the authors of this book) which are companions to exploring the German Lieder and French mélodie repertory. S. S. Prawer's *Penguin Book of Lieder* and Pierre Bernac's *The Interpretation of French Song* were pioneering works. In America, Philip Miller's *The Ring of Words* attempted a wide survey of song texts in many languages. The growing tendency for the recording companies to echo on disc the thoroughness and order of printed music's complete editions (something the Germans started but which is now to be found elsewhere) appeals to the enthusiast's collecting instinct. The success of Pierre Bernac's indispensable book devoted to all the Poulenc songs and Richard Wigmore's translations of the complete Schubert Lieder (both published by Gollancz) prove that a growing awareness of song generates the desire for yet more specialised knowledge. The understanding of the Lied and mélodie in the English-speaking world has thus incomparably advanced in the last fifteen years. It now goes without saying that a Liederabend in London should be furnished with good parallel translations and interesting programme notes. Slowly but surely, with full halls and many different programmes, the barrier of a foreign language (in German and French at least) seems less of an issue with both performers and public than it used to be. It is a far cry from Richard Capell's contention in his 1928 study of the Schubert songs, that 'the German language strikes the stranger as uncouth and repellent.'

It is far too long since Spain and Britain were at war for Spanish to have incurred (in recent times, at least) the odium reserved for the languages of enemies and rivals. Spanish simply strikes the English as attractive but unfamiliar and strange. The greatest barrier to the appreciation of Spanish song is still the language. The teaching of Spanish has always been somewhat marginalised in English education and it is no surprise that French and German song seem more accessible to students who have had the chance to learn those languages in school. As Spanish hopefully becomes a more frequent part of the school curriculum (it is already the major foreign language taught in the United States), so will the great beauties of its poetry be more appreciated. In the long term it will also seem more natural and interesting to young people that these poems have found musical settings. It is ignorance of the language, and the lack of a handbook such as this, which has left Spanish vocal music in a rut in English-speaking lands. A major part of preparing any recital is fixing the programme itself, and at a time when recital programmes are increasingly built around themes, what songs are *about* matters more and more. Until now, most singers have been attracted to a new Spanish song for its music alone; as a result the dice have been heavily loaded in favour of quick, exciting and 'entertaining' songs at the expense of many of the most beautiful introverted ones, songs where an understanding of the text is essential to appreciate the full beauties of the work.

The Spanish Song Companion thus aims to be more than a book of translations (as valuable and necessary as these are) – it is also something of a repertoire guide. It aims not only to tell music lovers exactly what their favourite Spanish songs actually mean (after years of only half knowing), but to introduce them to ones that will become new favourites. We hope that readers will find many a beautiful poem that they will then want to hear in a song setting. The singer will be encouraged to go out and find the music, and in the long term the listener will reap the benefit of this when he hears an informed performance. It would be unrealistic to assume that readers will have the printed music for these songs on their shelves – though music lovers will have some of them. Many of these song titles will not be familiar, whereas some of the composers are household names. That is why we have decided not to adopt the alphabetical order that seemed suitable for the quick consultation format of *The Fischer-Dieskau Book of Lieder*. Instead songs can be found under the general heading of their composers' names which, even in the first three general chapters, are presented in the chronological order of their birth. Although the main emphasis in this book is on the piano-accompanied art song, we have judged it important not to ignore certain high points in the music of the thirteenth to the eighteenth centuries. We have made a careful selection of early music, much of it readily available to the singer or student, and all of it encountered at some point by the translators in the modern concert hall or in recorded performances. We have obviously been limited by space (South American song is another omission in a work which could run to many volumes if it aimed at anything like completeness) but we hope that even a glancing knowledge of the medieval and Renaissance music and poetry will enhance a deeper understanding of the conventional Spanish recital repertoire, much of which owes its existence to inspiration from the distant past. It is typical of the homogeneity of Spanish song that a great deal of this very early music sounds perfectly capable of having been written by a Spanish composer of modern times, and that much twentieth-century music can sound very old, particularly when the texts are already familiar from settings from centuries before. And this brings me back to the earlier metaphor of the enchanted and overgrown garden. How are we to separate the herbs from the flowers, the folksong from the art song, the old from the new, the religious from the secular, the Sephardic from the Christian? This is part of the earthy fascination of a musical culture, more isolated than most, and thus preserved intact – a song history more seamless in its continuity than that of any other land. Spanish music relates effortlessly (some might say too easily) to the past. The nationalism which reaffirmed the age-old link between 'art' and 'folk' music, and which was a feature of musical life almost everywhere in Europe at the turn of the century, seemed somehow inevitable in Spain, and immediately fruitful; this was in contrast to a number of other western European countries (including our own) where there was no broad consensus among composers that the folksong revival was really necessary or desirable.

I have long believed that the most intense introduction possible to an unfamiliar European country, short of going to live there, is the study and enjoyment of its song. A song is, after all, a tiny but potent fragment of the land which gave it birth, a cultural stock cube of concentrated strength, and handy for export. Because it is a joint creation of both composer and poet, it has two biographical and historical backgrounds and it can include elements of folklore and sociology quite apart from a range of other artistic disciplines. Cultural and linguistic knowledge softens resistance to things unknown and strange, but it is music itself which helps us leap the emotional gap. When spoken words (even if they are unfamiliar) are turned into sung tone with accompaniment, a miraculous transformation occurs for the musically susceptible listener: something very like love enters the heart as the amalgam of tone and word is poured through the ear. This magic, this inexplicable response to music ('Our climate of silence and doubt invading', as W. H. Auden puts it in his poem 'The Composer'), is one of the things that encourage us to find out more about the song, the new object of our musical affections, perhaps even to discover, with the help of a book such as this, what the poem means. Armed with a more complete understanding based partly on musical instinct and partly on research, we find an ability to forgive, tolerate and ultimately enjoy the 'otherness' of people whose languages and ways of life are new. We can see ourselves and our emotions reassuringly mirrored or stimulatingly challenged by the Spanish people when their poetry is translated for us, partly by the universal language of music, and partly by Richard Stokes and Jacqueline Cockburn.

We musicians stop to hear melodies, and stay to learn meanings. On the other hand those whose instinctive response owes its first allegiance to words, rather than music, can discover through a great musical setting a new depth of meaning in a text they thought they already knew. It is thus that a balance is struck in the marriage of word and tone – one of the most fruitful relationships of all time. In 1992, with the emergence of the single European market, and the great festivals of international sport and trade in Barcelona and Seville, it has an even more crucial significance. We have all long needed the idea of Spain to add zest and colour to our own sun-deprived cultures, but it is no longer good enough for us to treat Spain as an upmarket Disneyland. The five-hundredth anniversary of the discovery of America by Columbus should be marked by a deeper response. As relatively recently as July 1953, *Time* magazine wrote: 'Spain is a land of mystery where the dust of isolation has often settled on men's work and obscured their lives.' To encounter the Spanish literature printed in this book – and better still to hear in the flesh the music that can only be superficially described in it – is to meet, perhaps for the first time, the work, both musical and literary, of many great men and women, obscure for the English speaker only because of the failure of our culture to connect with the real Spain. May the poetry and music that are the subject of this book be the catalyst to this closer connection. May the age-old dust of isolation be blown sky-high by the breath of the singing voice.

Graham Johnson
London, April 1992

I

MONODY AND POLYPHONY

For more than seven hundred years (714–1492) the Arabs occupied
southern Spain. Cordoba, Seville and Granada were all noted for the
magnificence of their courts where poetry and music played a crucial role.
None of this Arab music (the chants and melodies of zejeles and muaxahas)
has come down to us. The chants of the Mozarabic rite have survived as
representative of Christian Spain in this period: San Leandro (*d*.599), San
Isidor (*d*.636), San Ildefonso of Toledo (*d*.667) and San Eugenio (*d*.651)
were composers of chants and monodic allelujahs. These are preserved in
the Azagra Codex. Mozarabic chant was gradually replaced by Gregorian
chant, which led to the liturgical dramas known as mysteries. Profane
chants (wedding songs and bacchanals) have also been preserved, as well as
numerous litanies and elegies.

After about 1140 when the use of Castilian began to spread to replace
Latin and regional Romance dialects, epic chants and *romances* appeared
on a wide variety of historical and religious topics. The emergence of the
Canción culta gave rise to songs of courtly character on pastoral themes, as
well as the age-old preoccupation of love, and a new contemporary
obsession – the crusades. The years of the reign of King Alfonso X 'The
Wise' in Seville (1252–84) are notable for the *Cantigas de Santa María*, a
collection of over four hundred monodic songs devoted to the cult of the
Virgin Mary. The Provençal troubadour Giraut de Riquier (1230–92) also
worked at King Alfonso's court which was remarkable for its cosmopolitan
mixture of Christian, Arab and Jewish poets and musicians.

The rise of polyphony in the thirteenth century, influenced by the Ars
Antiqua in France, was most evident in the cathedrals of Tarragona and
Santiago de Compostela, and later in Toledo and Burgos. The more
polished polyphony of the Ars Nova (also of French origin), gave rise to
the secular vocal and dance music (chansons, baladas, motets, rondos,
virelais, estampidas) in which lie the origins of solo song with instrumental
accompaniment.

The reign of Pedro IV (1336–83) initiated an extraordinary period of artistic activity at the court of Barcelona. The Llibre Vermell contains sacred songs in Latin and Catalan of great historic importance. Pedro's son Juan I continued a flourishing musical tradition which reached its zenith under Alfonso V 'The Magnanimous'. The chapel of the kings of Aragon was famous for its music throughout Europe, and secular works were composed by such outstanding composers as Jacob de Selenches and Gracian Reynaud. In 1443 Alfonso V conquered the Kingdom of Naples and took his court there, never to return to Barcelona. The interaction between Catalan, Italian and Flemish musicians during his reign, and that of his son Ferdinand I of Naples, produced extraordinary polyphonic music. The composers Icart, Oriola and Cornago set Castilian texts in the form of villancicos, *romances* and cosantes which were preserved in various famous songbooks.

Meanwhile in Castile, the reigns of Enrique IV and his sister Isabella who succeeded him were also rich in music. Isabella's consort was Ferdinand of Aragon, and their marriage heralded the inauguration of a united kingdom. 1492 saw the defeat of the Arabs at Granada and their expulsion from Spain. The year of Columbus's discovery of America also witnessed the brutal expulsion of the Jews from the Spanish kingdoms; their Sephardic music had considerable influence on the shaping of Spanish melody. Ferdinand and Isabella had many distinguished composers in their employ (Anchieta, de la Torre, Escobar, Peñalosa and so on). The two monarchs merged their chapels and, in giving preference to Spanish musicians, established the beginnings of a specifically Spanish musical style increasingly free from the pervasive influence of Flanders and Burgundy. Perhaps the most important composer-poet was Juan del Encina whose religious plays were prototypes of the Oratorio and who was considered to be a founder of Spanish theatre. Encina was also renowned for his many villancicos (a popular song with a refrain, often on a Christmas theme).

The performance of music of this period presents something of a problem for the modern concert singer. The compositions in the first two chapters of this book are, strictly speaking, the province of the many expert groups and ensembles who in recent years have specialised, with admirably vivid results, in the field of early music. The presence of a piano on the concert stage would seem to rule this music out of court for recital purposes. And yet I have accompanied Victoria de los Angeles in recitals devoted entirely to Spanish song from the earliest times until the present, something which seemed a perfectly natural way of constructing a Spanish song programme, but would have been out of the question in music from the German or French repertoires. The opening groups of these programmes were all anachronistically accompanied by the piano in very simple arrangements; the simplicity and beauty of the vocal line was gently supported by the piano, here filling in the other voice parts in polyphonic textures, there standing in for the vihuela or guitar. These songs made a profound effect on me because of the beauty of the melodies and the poems – among the most beautiful in Spanish literature; they seemed very obviously to be the seed from which later Spanish song grew, and a necessary part of an evening devoted to an entire retrospective of the form. It is not impossible that non-Spanish singers, and readers of this book, will wish to attempt a similar type of recital in the future. These songs seem simultaneously old and new, and because of this they need not seem incongruous in a wide-ranging recital of this kind. The main scholastic sources of songs from this period are the tomes of the *Monumentos de la música española* (MME in the New Grove), a monument indeed to the labours of Spanish musicology, but not easily accessible to the average singer. The real enthusiast will make his own transcriptions of the treasures buried in these books and others like them – in the relatively recent transcriptions of the vihuela books for example. The less zealous can find a good cross-section of music from this period in the three volumes published by the Union Musical Española. These contain a good deal of the early repertoire sung by Victoria de los Angeles and are published, with simple accompaniments, under the following titles:

Canciones de Andalucia medieval y renacentista, arrangements by José Lamaña, UMV 21222

Canciones españolas del Renacimiento (1440–1600), arrangements by Graciano Tarragó, UMV 20190

Cinco siglos de canciones españolas (1300–1800), arrangements by Lamaña, Tarragó, José Roma and José Subira, UMV 20095

The UMV numbers throughout the text will indicate where (and if) songs printed here are published in this series. Many of them were recorded by Victoria de los Angeles with the instrumental accompaniment of the Ars Musicae of Barcelona. It is interesting that it was the gentlemen of this ensemble, including the late Dr José Lamaña, who were Madame de los Angeles's first teachers and mentors in the 1940s. They set her a syllabus which required her to sing the widest possible range of music, and encouraged her to study Pfitzner and Schoenberg no less assiduously than the early music of her own country. She is the only operatic diva I have known who is enthusiastic and knowledgeable about the music which is normally the province of specialist 'stone-age' (for thus is early music flippantly defined today) singers. It is as if the huge and uninterrupted procession of Spanish composers from the thirteenth century to our own time, is an illustration of a sense of history which T. S. Eliot terms 'a perception not only of the pastness of the past, but of its presence'. But that, in almost every respect, is Spain.

ALFONSO X OF CASTILE AND LEÓN – EL SABIO ('THE WISE') (1221–84)

It is not known how many of the songs and texts of the *Cantigas de Santa María* (a collection of over four hundred songs from which the following are but a few typical examples) were composed by King Alfonso himself. He may have been a gifted poet and musician, but his chief role was as an extraordinary patron of the arts; he was a notable liberal reformer (somewhat at the expense of political stability) whose court combined the artistic and cultural heritages of Christian, Islamic and Jewish life in a dazzling display of enlightened Spanish heterodoxy. Alfonso founded a chair in composition at the University of Salamanca in 1254. Songs from the *Cantigas* were first transcribed and published in 1922 by A. García Solalinde who also issued a further edition in 1930. 'Rosa das rosas' and 'Maravillosos e piadosos', both unaccompanied, are in UMV 21222.

Rosa das rosas e Fror das frores / *Rose of roses*

Rosa das rosas e Fror das frores,	Rose of roses and Flower of flowers,
Dona das donas, Sennor das sennores.	Lady of ladies, Lord of lords.
Rosa de beldad' e de parecer,	Rose of beauty and of charm,
e Fror d'alegria e de prazer,	and Flower of joy and pleasure,
Dona en mui piadosa seer,	Lady of great piety,
Sennor en toller coitas e doores.	Lord enduring grief and pain.
Rosa das rosas e Fror das frores,	Rose of roses and Flower of flowers,
Dona das donas, Sennor das sennores.	Lady of ladies, Lord of lords.
Atal Sennor dev'ome muit' amar,	Such a Lord must I greatly love,
que de todo mal o pode guardar,	for he can shield us from all evil
e pode-ll'os peccados perdóar,	and pardon the sinners
que faz no mundo per maos sabores.	who relish evil in the world.
Rosa das rosas e Fror das frores,	Rose of roses and Flower of flowers,
Dona das donas, Sennor das sennores.	Lady of ladies, Lord of lords.

Santa María, strela do día / Holy Mary, star of day

Santa María, estrella do día,
Móstranos vía
Pera Deus et nos guía,
Da onsadía que lles fazía
Fazer folía mais,
Que non devería.

Holy Mary, star of day,
show us the path
to God and guide us,
give them courage, that they
might no longer stray
in disobedience.

Ca veer faze los errados
Que perder foran per pecados
Entender de que mui colpados
Son mais perdidos son perdoados.

For she shows that those who have erred
through sin were lost,
and shows that the most guilty
are soonest pardoned.

Maravillosos e piadosos / Wonderful and holy

Maravillosos
e piadosos
e mui fermosos
miragres faz
Santa María,
a que nos guia
ben noit' e dia
e nos dá paz.
E dest' un miragre vos contar quero
que en Frandes aquesta Virgen fez,
Madre de Deus, maravillos' e
     fero
por húa dona que foi húa vez

Wonderful
and holy
and most beautiful
are the miracles wrought
by the Virgin Mary,
who guides us
safely by night and day
and gives us peace.
And I want to tell you of a miracle
which that Virgin, Mother of God,
wrought in Flanders – a great and
     wondrous act
on behalf of a lady who once went

a sa eigreja
desta que seja
por nos, e veja-
mo-la sa faz
no Parayso,
u Deus dar quiso
goyo e riso
a quen lle praz.
Aquesta dona levou un menyo,
seu fillo, sigo, que en offreçon
deu aa Virgen mui
     pequenyo,
que de mal llo guardass' e
     d'oqueijon

to her church,
which is given
to us that we might behold
the Virgin's face
in Paradise,
where God bestows willingly
joy and laughter
on whom He pleases.
This woman brought a baby,
her son, with her as an offering,
and she gave him, tiny as he was, to the
     Virgin,
that she might shield him from sickness
     and evil

e lle fezesse
per que dissese
sempr' e soubesse
de ben assaz,
que, com' aprendo
seu pan comendo.
Parouss' en az.

and make him
speak
and always know
what is excellent and good,
and thus teach him
to eat his daily bread.
She halted before Her image.

JACOB DE SELENCHES (*fl*. 1378–95)

Selenches was a French composer (probably born in St Luc near Evreux) who after training in Bruges went to work for a considerable time at the court of John I of Castile. This song was written on the death of Queen Eleanor (wife to John I) in 1382. Selenches was celebrated as a practitioner of an intricate form of the so-called Ars Subtilior. This refinement of Ars Nova used elaborate rhythmic subdivisions and displacements and was an intricate development of the classical ballade style after Machaut.

Fuions de ci / *Let us flee*

Fuions de ci, fuions, povre compaingne;
Chascuns s'en voist querir son aventure
En Aragon, en France ou en Bretaingne,
Car en brief temps on n'ara de nos cure.
Fuions querir no vie bien seüre;
Ne demorons yci eure ne jour,
Puis que perdu avons Alionor.

Car c'est bien drois, rayson le nous
    enseigne,
Puisque la mort tres cruel et obscure
Nous a osté le royone d'Espaingne,
Nostre maestresse, no confort et masure;
Que chascuns ovre leur volunté pure
De bien briefment vuidier de ce contour,
Puis que perdu avons Alionor.

Mais au partir persoune ne se faingne
Que de bon cuer et laialté seüre
Ne prie Dieux que l'ame de li preingne,
Et qu'elle n'ait sa penitence
    dure,
Mais paradis qui de jour en jour dure.
Et puis pensons d'aler sans nul sojor,
Puis que perdu avons Alionor.

Let us flee, poor company that we are,
let each depart to seek his fortune
in Aragon, France or Brittany,
for soon no one will care for us.
Let us flee and seek a surer life;
nor day nor hour let us longer stay,
now that we have lost Alienor.

For reason tells us this course is
    right,
since death so cruel and sombre
has stolen from us the Queen of Spain,
our mistress, solace and refuge;
let each man do as he will
and leave these parts without delay,
now that we have lost Alienor.

But ere we depart, let no one fail
(with good heart and in all loyalty)
to beseech God to take her soul
and that she should not be put to hard
    penance,
but win Paradise which lasts forever.
Let us resolve to flee without delay,
now that we have lost Alienor.

JOHANNES (JUAN) CORNAGO (*fl. c*. 1455–85)

Cornago was one of the Catalan composers who lived and worked in Naples when the Spanish court moved to that realm during the reigns of Alfonso V of Aragon (I of Naples) and his son Fernando I. The majority of his work was composed in Italy. His celebrated mass 'Ayo visto de la mappa mundi' was inspired by a map of the world commissioned by King Fernando, and based on a popular song from Sicily. His courtly love songs, in a melancholic and declamatory style with instrumental interludes, are mostly polyphonic in the manner which derived from French and Flemish influences, and which became something of a Spanish speciality. 'Gentil dama' is in UMV 20190, '¿Qu'es mi vida, preguntays?' in UMV 20095.

Gentil dama, non se gana / Gentle lady, my sole reward

Gentil dama, non se gana	Gentle lady, my sole reward
otro bien en vos mirar	when looking upon thee
sino ver y desear.	is gazing and desiring.
El deleite que se face	The delight thou dost inspire
mirando vuestra beldad	when I behold thy beauty
se destruye y se desface	vanishes and expires
notando vuestra bondad.	when I observe thy virtue.
Ansi que mi fin temprano	Thus my untimely death
non lo tiene que causar	can only be caused by
sino ver y desear.	gazing and desiring.

¿Qu'es mi vida, preguntays? / What, dost thou ask, is my life?

¿Qu'es mi vida, preguntays?	What, dost thou ask, is my life?
Non vos la quiero negar,	I do not wish to deny it thee:
bien amar e lamentar	to love well and lament
es la vida que me days.	is the life thou givest me.
¿Quien vos pudiera servir	Who could have served thee
tambien como [yo] he servido?	as I have served?
¿Mi trabaxado vivir	My troubled life –
Quien pudiera haver sofrido?	who could have suffered so?
¿Para que me, preguntays?	Why me, dost thou ask?
La pena que he de passar,	I must bear the grief,
pues amar e lamentar	for to love and lament
es la vida que me days.	is the life thou givest me.

Pues que Dios / Since God made thee so

Pues que Dios te fizo tal:	Since God made thee so:
graçiosa, dulçe, fermosa,	gracious, sweet, fair,
y mas, honesta,	and more yet, honest,
si te amo desigual,	since I love thee unworthily,
gentil dama valerosa,	gentle, valorous lady,
ava respuessta.	might I have a response?
Respuesta de mi serviçio,	A response to my service –
que vivo vida muriendo	for I live life dying
trasportado en tu figura,	enthralled by thy image –
te demando.	I ask of thee.

Esperando el benefiçio
que me deves dar, doliendo –
te de mi mal y tristura
en que ando.

Pues que ansi nasçiste tal,
en estremo virtuosa,
di: ¿que de cuesta
librarme de tanto mal,
tu, señora, tan fermosa,
con tu respuesta?

I wait for thee
to give me favours; take pity
on the sorrow and sadness
in which I languish.

Since thou wast born so,
wholly chaste,
tell me: what does it cost thee
to free me from such sorrow,
o lady so fair,
with thy response?

ENRIQUE (*fl.* 2nd half of 15th century)

The identity of this composer was once thought to be synonymous with the
Flemish organist Henry Bredemers, but Enrique was probably 'Enricus', a
singer in the service of the Prince of Viana. He set a number of four-part songs;
this canción (in UMV 20190) has a melodic shape and long melismas
characteristic of an earlier age of vocal music.

Mi querer tanto vos quiere / *I adore thee with such love*

Mi querer tanto vos quiere,
muy graciosa doncella,
que por vos mi vida muere
y de vos non tien querella,
tanto sois de mi, querida,
con amor y lealtad,
que de vos non sé que diga,
viendo vuestra honestad,
si mi querer tanto vos quiere,
causalo que sois tan bella,
que por vos mi vida muere,
y de vos non tien querella.

I adore thee with such love,
my gracious lady,
that for thee my life expires
and I do not complain,
so deeply art thou cherished
in love and fealty,
that I can say nothing
when I behold thy modesty.
If I adore thee with such love,
thy great beauty is to blame,
that for thee my life expires
and I do not complain.

JOHANNES (JUAN) URREDA (URREDE, VREDE, WREEDE) (*fl.* 2nd half of 15th century)

There is some controversy as to whether Urreda was Flemish or Spanish by
birth – his music treats Spanish themes in the Franco-Burgundian manner.
Urreda's work was internationally known and admired and appears in Italian

and French manuscripts. In the 1470s he was in the service of García Álvarez de Toledo, Duke of Alba, who wrote this poem. Urreda's setting (originally in three parts) is said to have made use of a popular Spanish tune. The piece became hugely popular, was quoted and parodied by other composers, and appears in two plays by the Portuguese poet Gil Vicente.

Nunca fué pena mayor / There was never greater pain

GARCÍA ÁLVAREZ DE TOLEDO, DUKE OF ALBA

Nunca fué pena mayor	There was never greater pain
Nin tormento tan extraño	nor torment so rare
Que iguale con el dolor	as the suffering
Que rescibo del engaño.	thy deceit causes me.
Y este conocimiento	And this knowledge
Hace mis dias tan tristes,	makes my days so sad,
En pensar el pensamiento	as I think
Que por amores me distes;	of the love thou gavest me;
Me hace haber por mejor	for this I consider
La muerte y por menor daño	death a lesser harm
Que el tormento y el dolor	than the torment and grief
Que rescibo del engaño	thy deceit causes me.

FRANCISCO DE LA TORRE (fl.1483–1504)

De la Torre served Ferdinand V of Aragon for seventeen years as a singer in the choir of the royal chapel. He held minor clerical orders, at one time being responsible for the choir at Seville cathedral. His surviving religious works are highly expressive and his secular works show the influence of Urreda. 'Dime triste coraçon' quotes the folia bass and is in UMV 21222, as is 'Damos gracias a ti, Dios'.

Damos gracias a ti, Dios / We give thanks to Thee, o God

Damos gracias a ti, Dios,	We give thanks to Thee, o God,
Y a la Virgen sin mansilla,	and to the Virgin without blemish,
Porque en el tiempo de nos	that in these our times
España cobró su silla.	Spain recovered her power.
Si los godos olvidando	If the Goths, forgetting
Tus preceptos fenecieron,	Thy precepts, perished,
Nuestro gran rey Don Fernando	our great King Ferdinand
Ganó lo qu'ellos perdieron.	regained what they lost.

Bendito sea solo Dios	Blessed be God alone
Por tan alta maravilla,	for working such a miracle,
Que sin merecello nos	since though we did not merit it,
España cobró su silla.	Spain recovered her power.

Dime, triste coraçon / Tell me, grieving heart

Dime, triste coraçon,	Tell me, grieving heart,
¿por qué callas tu pasión?	why conceal your passion?
Cativo no sé que diga	Enthralled I know not what to say –
A quien sirvo es mi enemiga.	she whom I serve is my foe.
Plázeme con mi fatiga,	I delight in my torment,
Desespero galardón.	despairing of reward.

Pámpano verde / Green vine

Pámpano verde,	Green vine,
razimo alvar;	white cluster;
¿Quién vido dueñas	whoever saw duennas
a tal ora andar?	out at this hour?
Enzinueco entr'ellas	In their midst
entre las donzellas.	let the young girls appear.
Pámpano verde,	Green vine,
razimo alvar;	white cluster;
¿Quién vido dueñas	whoever saw duennas
a tal ora andar?	out at this hour?

JUAN DE ANCHIETA (1462–1523)

Anchieta, a relative of St Ignatius of Loyola, was one of the court musicians of
Queen Isabella, as a singer in her chapel and also as composer – a double role
which seems to have been the normal pattern of the time. He was then
appointed maestro de capilla to her son, the highly musical Prince Juan. After
Isabella's death Anchieta was taken up by Queen Joanna, consort of Philip the
Fair. In her service he visited Burgundy, though he was less influenced by the
complexities of Burgundian music than his contemporary Peñalosa. He visited
the south of England in 1506 on his way home to Spain. Anchieta's music is
well represented in the celebrated *Cancionero de Palacio*, a collection of 550
songs which was probably compiled for the use of the Duke of Alba's
household.

Con amores, la mi madre / With love in my heart, mother

Con amores, la mi madre,	With love in my heart, mother,
Con amores m'adormí.	with love in my heart, I fell asleep.
Así dormida soñaba	While sleeping I dreamed
Lo qu'el corazon velaba,	of what my heart was hiding:
Qu'el amor me consolaba	that love consoled me
Con más bien que merecí.	more than I deserved.
Adormeciome el favor	I was lulled to sleep by the token
Que Amor me dió con amor:	Love bestowed on me:
Dió descanso á mi dolor	my pain was soothed
La fé con que le serví.	by the faith with which I served him.

JUAN DEL ENCINA (1468–1529 or 1530)

Encina was the most celebrated of the musician-poets during the reign of Ferdinand and Isabella, although he was actually attached to the court of the Duke of Alba and served that noble family from 1492 until 1498. This was the most productive time of his life, and most of Encina's musical and literary work dates from this early period. He wrote a series of representaciones, pastoral plays that are the starting point of Spanish secular drama, and there are sixty-two Encina compositions in the *Cancionero de Palacio*. His villancicos successfully combine the learned and popular elements of early Renaissance music and poetry. After his time in the employ of the Alba family, Encina went to Rome where he successfully served a succession of popes. He was ordained a priest in 1519 and travelled to the Holy Land to celebrate his first Mass. He is buried in the choir of León cathedral where he was appointed prior by Pope Leo X. The poem 'Ojos garços ha la niña' found its way, many centuries later, into Robert Schumann's *Spanische Liebeslieder*, under the title 'Blaue Augen hat das Mädchen' (see Appendix). 'Ay triste que vengo' is in UMV 20190 with alternative guitar accompaniment.

Ojos garços ha la niña[1] / The girl has blue eyes

Ojos garços ha la niña:	The girl has blue eyes:
¡quién gelos namoraría!	who would fall in love with them!
Son tan bellos y tan bivos	So fair and alive are they
que a todos tienen cativos,	that they enthrall all men,
mas muéstralos tan esquivos	but they appear so cold
que roban el alegría.	that they steal all happiness.
Roban el plazer y gloria,	They steal both pleasure and delight,
los sentidos y memoria;	senses and memory too;

de todos llevan vitoria
con su gentil galanía.

and they vanquish all
with their sweet elegance.

Con su gentil gentileza
ponen fe con más firmeza;
hazen bivir en tristeza
al que alegre ser solía.

Always with their sweet charm
they inspire great faith,
saddening him
who is wont to be happy.

No hay ninguno que los vea
que su cativo no sea.
Todo el mundo los dessea
contemplar de noche y día.

All who behold them
are made captive.
All desire to gaze
upon them night and day.

    ¹See Appendix for Geibel's translation.

Pues que jamás olvidaros / Since my heart . . .

Pues que jamás olvidaros
no puede mi coraçón,
si me falta galardón,
¡ay qué mal hize en miraros!

Since my heart
can never forget thee –
if I have no reward,
alas that I ever gazed on thee!

Será tal vista cobrar
gran dolor y gran tristura.
Será tal vista penar,
si me fallece ventura.
Mas si vos, por bien amaros,
queréis darme galardón,
no dirá mi coraçón:
¡Ay qué mal hize en miraros!

Such a vision causes
great pain and sadness.
Such a vision brings anguish,
if my fortune fails me.
But if thou, for my great love,
dost wish to reward me,
my heart will no longer say:
alas that I ever gazed on thee!

Ay triste que vengo / Ah, how sad am I

Ay triste que vengo,
vencido d'amor,
maguera pastor.
Más sano me fuera
no ir al mercado,
que no que viniera
tan aquerenciado;
que vengo cuitado,
vencido d'amor,
maguera pastor.

Ah, how sad am I,
though a mere shepherd,
to be overcome with love.
Better by far
to have stayed from the market
and not encountered
such feelings of love.
I am grieved,
overcome with love,
though a mere shepherd.

Con vista halaguera
miréla y miróme,
yo no sé quién era,
mas ella agradóme.
Y fuése y dejóme,
vencido d'amor,
maguera pastor.

Lovingly
I gazed on her and she on me,
I knew not who she was,
but she pleased me well.
She went and she left me –
overcome with love,
though a mere shepherd.

ALONSO DE MONDÉJAR (*fl.*1502–5)

Another composer in the service of Isabella, and later Ferdinand. A small amount of religious music is extant and twelve secular pieces, of which eleven are villancicos in the *Cancionero de Palacio*. The theme of these courtly songs is unrequited love. This piece (originally for three trebles) is a re-arrangement of a setting of the same poem by Francisco Millán.

Míos fueron, mi corazón / *Thine eyes were mine, beloved*

Míos fueron, mi corazón,
Los vuestros ojos morenos.
¿Quién los hizo ser agenos?

Míos fueron, desconocida,
Los ojos con que miráis,
Y si mirando matáis,
Con miraros dais la vida.
No seáis desconocida,
No me los hagáis agenos
Los vuestros ojos morenos.

Thine eyes were mine, beloved,
thy dusky brown eyes.
Who made them cold?

They were mine, ungrateful one,
those gazing eyes,
and though thou dost destroy by gazing,
thou givest life as I gaze upon thee.
Be not remote,
do not gaze upon me coldly
with thy dusky brown eyes.

GABRIEL MENA (*fl.*1511–16)

After serving as a singer in the court chapel of Ferdinand V, Mena (who may be synonymous with one Gabriel de Texerana, also a chapel singer) entered the service of the Admiral of Castile. There are nineteen surviving villancicos in the *Cancionero de Palacio*, some of which quote folk tunes, and all of which reveal a gifted musician and poet. This song is in UMV 20190.

No soy yo quién la descubre / *It is not I who declare*

No soy yo quién la descubre,
esta pena que me dais,
sino vos que me matáis.
¿Cómo se puede encubrir
mal que va tan descubierto,
cómo se puede decir
más claro que verme muerto?
En mi mal no hay más concierto
del que vos, Señora, dais,
pues sois quién me matáis.

It is not I who declare
this grief thou causest me,
it is thou who slayest me.
How can I hide
a grief so stark,
how can this be said more clear,
unless thou seest me dead?
Thou art the sole cause,
Señora, of my grief,
since it is thou who slayest me.

CRISTÓBAL MORALES (1500–53)

By his contemporary Juan Bermudo, Morales was considered to be 'the light of
Spain in music'. Much influenced by Josquin, Morales was in his turn a major
influence on the work of Palestrina. He came from Seville where he received a
superb musical training, and he spent a number of years in Rome in the papal
choir. He also worked in the cathedrals of Toledo and Málaga. A master of
polyphonic style, his vast religious output (at least eight volumes in the
Monumentos de la música española) is balanced by a mere handful of secular
works. This canción amatoria was originally written for three voices, and is in
UMV 21222.

Si n'os huviera mirado / If I had never seen thee

Si n'os huviera mirado
   No penara.
Pero tampoco os mirara.
Veros harto mal ha sido,
Mas no veros peor fuera.
No quedara tan'perdido,
Pero mucho más perdiera
Que viera aquel que n'os viera.
   No penara,
Pero tampoco os mirara.

If I had never seen thee,
   I'd not be grieving,
but then I would not have seen thee.
Simply to see thee gives pain,
but not to see thee would be worse.
I would not be so lost,
but would lose much more
than he who never saw thee.
   I would not be grieving –
but then I would not have seen thee.

THE BEGINNINGS OF
SOLO SONG

The crucial role in world affairs played by Renaissance Spain was personified by its monarch, and his breadth of influence: Carlos I was also Charles V, Emperor of Germany, and Holy Roman Emperor from 1519. The country's central position on the world stage was mirrored by the distinction of Spain's music and musicians, and by the emergence of a new means of personal and courtly communication – the accompanied solo song. One of its principal pioneers was Juan Vasquez who brought a particularly Spanish flavour to the Italian madrigal form. His collections of canciones amorosas, sonetos and villancicos were transcribed for solo voice and accompaniment by players of the vihuela (a plucked instrument of the viol family). The vihuela song was the equivalent of the lute song in Elizabethan England. Vihuela players like Luis de Milán, Mudarra, Pisador, and Daza enriched the repertoire with their books of songs, musical testaments by which they laid their claim to fame and immortality. These books included many transcriptions of other composers' works, as well as original material. Of the many collections, perhaps the most famous of the period was the *Orphenica lyra* by Miguel de Fuenllana. The vocal music of Francisco Guerrero was also of great importance. Outside this tradition, the greatest of the Castilians was someone whose work, like that of many other distinguished Spanish composers, does not fall within the scope of a book devoted to songs: Tomás Luis de Victoria (1545–1611). He was a contemporary of Palestrina and Lassus and compatriot and friend of Saint Teresa of Ávila. With Victoria, Spanish sacred polyphony reached new heights, but it was now an increasingly separate strand in the history of Spanish vocal music. With the vihuela-accompanied song, it was a relatively short step to the emergence of secular drama in music and the dominance of the theatre.

LUIS DE MILÁN (*c*.1500–*c*.1561)

Milán is not to be confused with Francisco Millán who was a singer at Queen Isabella's court, and who contributed twenty-four settings to the *Cancionero de Palacio*. Luis Milán, a much more significant composer altogether, worked for most of his life in Valencia. He was a pioneer of writing for the vihuela and his printed collection *El maestro* (dedicated to King John III of Portugal whose court was exceptionally musical) is a treasure trove not only of music written for that instrument, but of villancicos, *romances*, and even sonetos – settings of Petrarch and other Italian poets. Milán was also a pioneer of using verbal indications of tempo and the use of rubato. The vignette in *El maestro* represents Orpheus playing a six-stringed guitar, rather than an antique lyre. 'Aquel caballero, madre' is in UMV 20190 with alternative guitar accompaniment.

Aquel caballero, madre / *That knight, mother*

Aquel caballero, madre,
que de mí se enamoró,
pena él y muero yo.

That knight, mother,
who fell in love with me,
is grieving and I am dying.

Madre, aquel caballero
que va herido de amores,
también siento sus dolores
porque dellas mismas muero;
su amor tan verdadero
merece que diga yo:
pena él y muero yo.

Mother, that knight
who is wounded with love –
I too feel his pain,
for I die from it too.
His love is so true
that I must speak out:
He is grieving and I am dying.

Toda mi vida hos amé / *All my life I've loved thee*

Toda mi vida hos amé:
Si me amays, yo no lo sé.
Bien sé que teneys amor,
Al desamor y al olvido.
Sé que soy aborrecido
Ya que sabe el disfavor.

All my life I've loved thee:
I know not if thou lovest me.
I know full well thou lovest
indifference and oblivion.
I know that I am scorned
for perceiving this lack of love.

Y por siempre hos amaré:
Si me amays yo no lo sé,
Toda mi vida hos amé:
Si me amays yo no lo sé
Bien sé que teneys amor,
Al desamor y al olvido,
Sé que soy aborrecido,
Ya que sabe el disfavor.

And I shall always love thee.
I know not if thou lovest me.
All my life I've loved thee –
I know not if thou lovest me.
I know full well thou lovest
indifference and oblivion.
I know that I am scorned
for perceiving this lack of love.

ALONSO MUDARRA (*c.*1510–1580)

Like Morales, Mudarra was a musician from the south of Spain, born in
Guadalajara and trained in Seville. He was appointed canon of that cathedral,
and for thirty-four years was a leading light in its musical life. In 1546 he
published a tablature book of vihuela and guitar music including a number of
songs with vihuela accompaniment. Among these are settings of the Latin of
Horace, Ovid and Virgil, as well as *romances* in Spanish and Galician. 'Dime a
do tienes las mientes' is in UMV 21222.

Triste estaba el rey David / *King David was forlorn*

Triste estaba el rey David;
Triste y con gran passión,
Quando le vinieron nuevas
De la muerte de Absalón.

Quando le vinieron nuevas
De la muerte de Absalón,
Palabras tristes dezía,
Salidas del coraçón.

King David was forlorn,
forlorn and full of grief,
when news came to him
of Absalom's death.

When news came to him
of Absalom's death,
he uttered words of sorrow
from the depths of his heart.

Dime a do tienes las mientes / *Tell me what thou art thinking*

Dime a do tienes las mientes
pastorcico descuydado,
Que se te pierde el ganado.

Nunca duermo siempre afano
y ansí cómo con fatigas,
Que se me hielan las migas
entre la boca y la mano.

Quanta soldada yo gano
daría triste cuitado,
Por salir de este cuitado.

Tell me what thou art thinking,
careless shepherd lad,
for thy flock is going astray.

I cannot sleep, I always toil,
and so weary am I when I eat,
that the crumbs freeze
between hand and mouth.

All the wages that I earn
I'd give – such is my anxiety –
to rid me of my cares.

Claros y frescos rios / *Cool crystalline streams*

Claros y frescos rios
que mansamente vais
siguiendo vuestro natural camino;
Desiertos montes mios
que en un estado estáis
de soledad muy triste de contino;
Aves, en quien hay tino

Cool crystalline streams
that gently flow along the path
ordained to you by nature;
my deserted mountains
who are constantly
so sad and alone;
birds, whose fate it is

de estar siempre cantando;	eternally to sing;
Arboles que huís,	trees which flourish
y al fin también morís,	only to die,
perdiendo a veces tiempos y ganando;	now losing, now gaining time –
Oídme, oídme juntamente	hear, all hear
mi voz amarga y tan doliente.	my anguished and bitter cries.

Isabel, perdiste la tua faxa / *Isabel, thou hast lost thy girdle*

Isabel, Isabel, perdiste la tua faxa.	Isabel, Isabel, thou hast lost thy girdle.
Hela por do va,	Look, there it is
nadando por el agua.	floating on the water.
Isabel, la tan garrida.	Isabel – thou art so lovely.

DIEGO PISADOR (1509/10–after 1557)

Pisador was born in Salamanca where he took minor orders in 1526. Despite rather a turbulent family background involving much litigation, he found time to publish in 1552 a significant tablature book – *Libro de música de vihuela agora nuevamente compuesta*. There is a great deal of faithfully intabulated Josquin in this collection, as well as motets and works by many other composers, but some of the twenty-two songs and *romances* in the collection are by Pisador himself. 'Porqué es dama' is in UMV 20095.

No me llaméis sega la erva / *Don't call me a reaper*

¡No me llaméis sega la erva,	Don't call me a reaper,
sino morena!	call me a dusky maid!
Un amigo que yo había	A friend that I had
sega la erva me decía.	called me a reaper.
¡No me llaméis sega la erva,	Don't call me a reaper,
sino morena!	call me a dusky maid!

Si te vas a bañar, Juanilla / *If thou goest to bathe, Juanilla*

Si te vas a bañar, Juanilla,	If thou goest to bathe, Juanilla,
dime a cuáles baños vas.	tell me to which baths thou goest.
Si te entiendes d'ir callando,	If thou dost agree to quieten
los gemidos que iré dando,	the moans I shall utter,
de mí compasión habrás:	thou shalt have pity on me:
dime a cuáles baños vas.	tell me to which baths thou goest.

¿Porqué es, dama, tanto quereros? / Why, lady, do I love thee so?

¿Porqué es, dama, tanto quereros?
¿Para qué es, dama, tanto quereros?
Para perderme y a vos perderos.
Más valiera nunca veros.

Why, lady, do I love thee so?
Wherefore, lady, do I love thee so?
To cause perdition, mine and thine.
Better to have never seen thee.

JUAN VASQUEZ (c.1510–c.1560)

Vasquez is a crucial figure in the history of the solo song in Spain. He was born in Badajoz, and spent some time in Madrid and later Seville. His one surviving religious work, the *Agenda defunctorum*, is a formidable achievement, but his great contribution to song was his collection of villancicos for three, four or five voices employing folk melodies or echoes of the medieval cantigas, by which means courtly music was suffused with the sophistication of the Italian madrigal and the natural charm of folksong. The villancicos of Vasquez were intabulated by numerous vihuela players and composers, and it is these versions, for one voice with accompaniment, which bring the Elizabethan lute song to mind as a contemporary phenomenon. We find two of these transcriptions (by Pisador and Fuenllana) at the end of the section. 'Duélete de mí, Señora' and 'Morenica, dame un beso' are in MV 20190.

Duélete de mí, Señora / Pity me, Señora

Duélete de mí, Señora,
Señora, duélete de mí,
que si yo penas padezco
todas son, Señora, por tí.
El día que no te veo,
mil años son para mí,
ni descanso ni reposo,
ni tengo vida sin tí.
Los dias yo los vivo
sospirando siempre por tí.
¿Dónde estás, que no te veo,
alma mía, que es de tí?

Pity me, Señora,
Señora, pity me –
for if I suffer anguish,
I suffer it just for thee.
If one day I see thee not,
a thousand years pass by:
neither rest nor repose
nor life have I without thee.
I live my days
ever sighing for thee.
Where art thou, I see thee not,
my love, what has become of thee?

Morenica, dame un beso / Dusky girl, give me a kiss

– Morenica, dame un beso.
– ¿Cómo es eso?
– Aquesto que has oído.
– ¡Oxe afuera!

– Dusky girl, give me a kiss.
– What dost thou mean by this?
– What thou hast heard.
– Leave me alone!

No seáis tan atrevido,	Don't be so insolent,
mira que no soy quien quiera.	I'm not just any girl.
-- Dame lo que te mando,	– Do as I command,
no seas desagradecida,	don't be so ungrateful,
mira que tienes mi vida	for look, because of thee my life
continuamente penando,	I live in constant pain,
y pues tu me tienes preso.	and thou dost hold me prisoner too.
¡Dame un beso!	Give me a kiss!
– ¡Que de merced te lo pido,	– For pity's sake, I beg thee,
oxe afuera!	leave me alone!

Cómo queréis, madre / How do you expect me, mother

¿Cómo queréis, madre,	How do you expect me, mother,
que yo a Dios sirva,	to serve God,
siguiéndome el amor	when love pursues me
a la contina?	continually?

Del rosal sale la rosa / From the rose-bush springs the rose

Del rosal sale la rosa.	From the rose-bush springs the rose.
¡Oh qué hermosa!	Ah what beauty!
¡Qué color saca tan fino!	How delicate the colour grows!
Aunque nace del espino,	Though stemming from the thorn,
nac'entera y olorosa.	it blossoms fragrant and entire.
Nace de nuevo primor	This flower is born
esta flor.	in fresh beauty.
Huele tanto desd'el suelo,	From the earth
que penetra hasta el cielo	to the sky it wafts
su fuerza maravillosa.	its strong and wondrous scent.

En la fuente del rosel / At the rose-bush spring

En la fuente del rosel	At the rose-bush spring
lavan la niña y el doncel.	the boy and girl are washing.
En la fuente de agua clara	In the clear water of the spring
con sus manos lavan la cara	with their hands they wash their faces.
él a ella y ella a él,	He washes hers, she washes his,
lavan la niña y el doncel.	the boy and the girl.
En la fuente del rosel	At the rose-bush spring
lavan la niña y el doncel.	the boy and girl are washing.

De los álamos vengo, madre / I come from the poplars, mother

De los álamos vengo, madre,
de ver cómo los menea el aire.

De los álamos de Sevilla,
de ver a mi linda amiga,
de ver cómo los menea el aire.

De los álamos vengo, madre,
de ver cómo los menea el aire.

I come from the poplars, mother,
from seeing the breezes stir them.

From the poplars of Seville,
from seeing my sweet love,
from seeing the breezes stir them.

I come from the poplars, mother,
from seeing the breezes stir them.

ENRIQUEZ DE VALDERRÁBANO
(*fl*. mid-16th century)

We know little about this composer's life, apart from the fact he served the
Count of Miranda. The sixteenth-century musicologist Juan Bermudo
commended Valderrábano's 'Libro de música de vihuela intitulado Silva de
sirenas' to aspiring musicians. This work, published in 1547, is a seven-volume
collection of intabulations, the second and third of which contain vocal music
transcribed from the international repertory. The sixth book contains shorter
and simpler songs for voice and vihuela. Valderrábano wrote that 'among
earthly creatures, God placed music with the greatest reason and perfection in
man, and among stringed instruments, in the vihuela.' 'De dónde venís,
amore' is in both UMV 20095 and 20190, and 'Señora, si te olvidare' is in
20190.

De dónde venís, amore / Where hast thou been, my love?

¿De dónde venís, amore?
Bien sé yo de dónde.

Caballero de mesura,
¿dó venís la noche escura?
Bien sé yo de dónde.

Where hast thou been, my love?
I know well where.

Good my lord,
where hast thou been on this dark night?
I know well where.

Señora, si te olvidare / Señora, if ever I forget thee

Sēnora, si te olvidare,
la mi diestra olvide a mí,
ni si jamás me alegrare,
si no el tiempo que llorare,
cuándo esté ausente de tí.

Señora, if ever I forget thee,
may I lose my right hand,
and if ever I am happy,
let it only be when I weep
because I am far from thee.

Péguese a mis paladares
mi lengua y pierda su ser,
cuándo a mí te me olvidares;
que mas valen mis pesares
por tí que ningún placer.

May my tongue cleave to the roof
of my mouth and lose its use,
if ever I forget thee;
I'd sooner feel this pain
for thee than any pleasure.

Dónde son estas serranas / From where do those mountain girls come

¿Dónde son estas
    serranas?
Del pinar de Ávila son.
A la entrada de la ermita
Relumbrando como el sol.
Y decid serranas
    bellas
deste mal si moriré.

From where do those mountain girls
    come?
From the pine groves of Ávila.
At the entrance to the hermitage
they shine like the sun.
And let it be known, beautiful mountain
    girls,
that I shall die from such torment.

LUYS DE NARVÁEZ (fl.1530–50)

Narváez was born in Granada and travelled to Italy and northern Europe in the service of Prince Philip, later King Philip II. He was a celebrated vihuela player, and famed as an improviser on that instrument. In 1538 he published his *Los seys libros del Delphín* which contains almost his entire output, and in which music in variation form is printed for the first time in Spain. Side by side with original music are intabulations of composers like Josquin, the 'Milles regretz' of whom was said to have been a favourite of the Emperor Charles V in Narváez's arrangement. The song given here (in UMV 21222) is one of the two *romances* in *Los seys libros del Delphín*; it survives in three other contemporary Spanish settings, two with vihuela accompaniment.

Paseábase el rey moro / The Moorish King was walking

Paseábase el rey moro
por la ciudad de Granada,
cartas le fueron venidas
como Alhama era tomada.
    ¡Ay de mi Alhama[1]!

The Moorish King was walking
through the city of Granada,
letters had reached him,
telling of Alhama's fall.
    Alas for my Alhama!

Las cartas echó al fuego,
al mensajero matara;
por el Zacatín[2] arriba
subido se había al Alhambra[3].
    ¡Ay de mi Alhama!

He cast the letters into the fire
and slew the messenger;
up through the Zacatín
he climbed to the Alhambra.
    Alas for my Alhama!

Como en el Alhambra estuvo
al mismo punto mandaba
que se toquen sus trompetas,
sus añafiles de plata.
    ¡Ay de mi Alhama!

When he had reached the Alhambra
he at once gave orders
for his trumpets to be blown
and his silver bugles to sound.
    Alas for my Alhama!

[1]*Alhama*. The capture of Alhama (1482), perched on a cliff above Granada, was of
great significance in the fight against the Moors.
[2]*Zacatin*. A place or street where garments are sold.
[3]*Alhambra*. (Arabic: al-hamra = the red.) The palace of the Moorish Kings at
Granada, built mostly in the thirteenth century. Cf. Washington Irving's *Legends
of the Alhambra* (1832).

MIGUEL DE FUENLLANA
(*b*. early 16th century, *d*. after 1568)

Like his contemporaries Antonio de Cabezón and Francisco de Salinas,
Fuenllana was blind. He was famous as a vihuelist, and was even said to be able
to play perfectly on an out-of-tune instrument. Like many performer-
composers of his time, he published a book as a summation of his life's work
and art. This was the *Orphenica lyra*, dedicated to King Philip II. As was the
practice of the vihuelist composers, Fuenllana also wrote for the humble four-
string guitar. Much of the music was borrowed from famous composers of the
past and some of it transcribed from his own contemporaries. Fuenllana took
the trouble to print alongside the instrumental fantasias the original texts of
poems which had inspired them, for he writes that these texts constitute 'the
soul of any composition'. The *Orphenica lyra* also contains valuable prefatory
'avisos y documentos' – a guide to the performing practice of the time. 'Duélete
de mí, Señora', with alternative guitar accompaniment, is in UMV 20190, as is
his transcription of Morales.

Duélete de mí, Señora / *Pity me, Señora*

Duélete de mí, Señora,
Señora, duélete de mí,
que si yo penas padezco
todas son, Señora, por tí.
El día que no te veo,
mil años son para mí,
ni descanso ni reposo,
ni tengo vida sin tí.
Los dias yo los vivo
sospirando siempre por tí.
¿Dónde estás, que no te veo,
alma mía, que es de tí?

Pity me, Señora,
Señora, pity me –
for if I suffer anguish,
I suffer it just for thee.
If one day I see thee not,
a thousand years pass by:
neither rest nor repose
nor life have I without thee.
I live my days
ever sighing for thee.
Where art thou, I see thee not,
my love, what has become of thee?

De Antequera salió el Moro / *The Moor set out from Antequera*

De Antequera salió el Moro,	The Moor set out from Antequera
tres horas antes el día,	three hours before the dawn,
con cartas en la su mano,	with letters in his hand
en que socorro pedía.	in which he asked for help.
El rey que venir lo vido	The King, who saw his approach,
a recibirlo salía,	went out to greet him
con trescientos de caballo	with three hundred horsemen,
la flor de la morería.	the flower of Moorish men.
Tóquense mis añafiles	Let my tuckets sound,
trompetas de plata fina,	my trumpets of fine silver,
júntense mis caballos,	let my horsemen gather
cuántos en mi reino había.	from every corner of my realm!

ESTEBAN DAZA (*fl.*1575)

Little is known of Daza apart from the fact that he worked in Valladolid. His contribution to the remarkable run of vihuela tablatures that characterise sixteenth-century Spanish musical life is entitled *El Parnasso*, a work divided into three books. The first two volumes offer the familiar pattern of intabulations of motets by composers of earlier times. The third volume contains secular songs (a familiar mix of villancicos, *romances*, sonetos and so on) by a variety of composers; it is difficult to say how much original music is contained in this collection – though one of the last of the vihuela tablatures, it is not the greatest of them. Both of these songs are to be found in UMV 20190.

Enfermo estaba Antioco[1] / *Sick was Antiochus*

Enfermo estaba Antioco,	Sick was Antiochus,
príncipe de la Suria,	Prince of Syria,
de Estratonice la reina	for the love of Stratonice,
ferido de amor yacía.	wounded he lay.
¿Que hacéis vos, amada mía,	What hast thou done, my love,
flor de toda la beldad,	flower of all beauty,
que desde el día que os ví,	that from the day I first beheld thee
ya no puedo sosergar?	my peace has fled?
Abrazándola muy fuerte	Holding her so close
el rostro quisola besar,	he sought to kiss her face,
por sus delicados ojos,	from her gentle eyes
lagrimas vieron saltar.	tears began to fall.

[1]Antiochus was the son of Seleucus, King of Syria; he fell so passionately in love with Stratonice, his step-mother, that his father gave her to him to save his life.

Dame acogida en tu hato / *Take me into thy fold*

Dame acogida en tu hato,
buen pastor, que Diós te duela;
cata que en el monte hiela.
Esta noche en tu cabaña
acoge al triste y cuitado,
que de amores lastimado
anda por esta montaña.
Mira que el tiempo se ensaña,
pastorcito, Diós te duela;
cata que en el monte hiela.

Take me into thy fold,
good shepherd, may God bless thee;
behold, the mountain grows bitter cold.
Into thy hut this night
take one who is sad and grieving,
one who, lovelorn,
wanders through the mountains.
Look, the weather worsens,
dear shepherd lad, may God bless you;
behold, the mountain grows bitter cold.

FRANCISCO GUERRERO (1528–99)

Of all Spanish composers, Guerrero had the most extraordinary life story, with the possible exception of the young Albéniz. After study with his elder brother Pedro, and with Morales, he was employed as a singer in Seville cathedral. Morales then recommended him for the post of maestro de capilla at Jaén. On many an occasion it seems that Guerrero's administrative incompetence was excused because of artistic merit and because, as Gilbert Chase tells us, he was a 'veritable saint . . . filled with true humbleness and charity'. It appears that he neglected his duties as far as the care of the choirboys was concerned, and moved back to Seville where the musical life of the cathedral occupied him between his innumerable journeys. He travelled all over Spain and Portugal, and also to Italy – his works were published as far afield as Venice and Paris, and his reputation was assured for two centuries after his death in South America. Like Encina, he visited the Holy Land, but he encountered pirates twice on the homeward journey and was financially ruined by their depredations, spending a spell in debtors' prison. He wrote a best-selling book about his journey to Jerusalem and Damascus, and died of plague as he was preparing to set off on further travels. He composed a prodigious amount of church music (he was particularly strongly attached to the Marian cult), and did not hesitate to turn secular songs into sacred music by the addition of new words. Unlike Morales and his great contemporary Victoria, Guerrero wrote many secular songs to a wide range of texts, including the poetry of Lope de Vega. The uncomplicated accessibility of much of his music anticipates the felicities of eighteenth-century style. 'Dexó la venda' is in UMV 21222.

Dexó la venda, el arco y el aljaba / *He discarded bandage, bow and quiver*

Dexó la venda, el arco y el aljaba,	He discarded bandage, bow and quiver –
el laçivo rapaz, donosa cosa!	a fine thing for that rakish boy to do! –
por tomar una bella mariposa	to catch a pretty butterfly
que por el ayre andava.	fluttering through the air.
Magdalena, la ninfa que mirava	Madeleine, the nymph, observing
su descuydo, hurtóle	his imprudence, stole
las armas y dexóle	his weapons and left him
en el hermoso prado	in the beautiful meadow
como a muchacho	looking like a foolish
bobo y descuydado.	and imprudent boy.
Ya de hoy	Henceforth
más no de amor gala ni pena	Love causes neither joy nor pain,
que el verdadero amor	since the real Cupid
es Magdalena.	is Madeleine.

Si tus penas no pruevo, o Jesús mío / *Without sharing your anguish, dear Jesus*

LOPE DE VEGA

Si tus penas no pruevo, o Jesús mío,	Without sharing your anguish, dear Jesus,
vivo triste y penado.	I live in grief and pain.
Hiéreme, pues el alma ya te é dado.	Wound me, for I have given Thee my soul.
Y, si este don me hizieres,	And if Thou bestowest this gift upon me,
mi Dios, claro veré que bien me quieres.	my God, I shall truly see Thou lovest me.

GINÉS DE MORATA (*fl.* 16th century)

Little is known of Morata apart from the fact that he was a Spaniard resident in Portugal at some time of his life as choirmaster to the chapel of the Duke of Braganza. Twelve canciones and villancicos have survived for three and four voices. Despite the smallness of Morata's output and the biographical uncertainty surrounding his life, his music is considered to be of the highest quality. This song is in UMV 21222.

Aquí me declaró su pensamiento / *It was here he declared his love*

Aquí me declaró su pensamiento.	It was here he declared his love.
Oyle yo cuitada;	I was distressed at what he said;
más que serpiente ayrada	More angry than a snake

diciéndole mil veces: ¡atrevido!	I called him insolent a thousand times!
Y él triste allí rendido.	And there he stood, all forlorn.
Parece que es agora y que le veo	I seem to see him now –
y aunque es ése mi deseo.	and that indeed is my desire.
¡Ay, si le viere yo!	Ah, could I but see him now!
¡Ay tiempo bueno!	Ah, what times we had!
¡Ribera umbrosa!	The shady river bank!
¿Qué es de mi Sireno?	What has come of my Sireno?

JUAN BAUTISTA COMES (1582–1643)

Comes was a choirboy at Valencia cathedral, and was eventually maestro de capilla there after a spell at Lérida. He later went to Madrid to work in the royal chapel. He wrote many pieces for liturgical use which are notable for adventurous choral writing, especially where each of a number of choruses is accompanied by different groups of instruments. His song settings – *romances* and villancicos – are characterised by the alternation of solo voices with choral responses for bigger forces in a manner that suggests the theatre as much as the church. In Spanish song the influence of the vihuela-accompanied song was now decidedly on the wane, and the stage was set for vocal music to be influenced by the operatic innovations of Italian music.

Pajarillo adulator / Flattering bird

Pajarillo que en selvas amenas	Little bird in pleasant woodlands,
los campos te escuchan amante y cantor,	heard by the fields as lover and singer –
bate las alas, suspende la voz,	beat your wings, hush your voice,
porque en vano acredita sus penas	for it is fruitless for one to affirm his pain
quien lisonjas previene al dolor.	who offers flattery to sorrow.
De crédito vive ajena	No one will lend credence
la pena que explica el canto,	to the pain your song proclaims,
si solamente es el llanto	if lament is the sole
interprete de la pena.	indication of your pain.
Tu misma acción te condena,	Your own action condemns you,
pajarillo adulador.	flattering little bird.

JUAN DEL VADO (fl.1635–75)

Vado began life as a violinist in the royal chapel in Madrid, and became organist and music teacher to the King. Very little is known about his life. His most important work is *Libro de misas de facistor* which contains six masses and a series of intricate canonic puzzles as exercises in contrapuntal virtuosity.

Vado wrote little choral music, and this adaptation of Lope de Vega, which was first published in 1935 in a collection of settings of that poet, seems untypical of his work. It can be found in UMV 20095.

Molinillo que mueles amores / Little mill that grinds love

Molinillo que mueles amores,
pues que mis ojos el agua te dan,
no coja desdenes quien siembra favores,
que aunque me sustentan matarme
    podrán.
Muele una vez descanso y contento,
si pueden tenerle mis penas y males.
No digas, molino, que fuiste de viento,
que mueles con agua de lágrimas tales.
Y si me haces aquestos favores,
otros que esperan envidia te dan.

Little mill, you grind love,
since my eyes provide the water,
do not disdain him who sows favours,
for though they sustain me, they can
    kill.
Grind both repose and content
if they can hold my grief and pain.
Do not say you were a windmill,
for you grind with water from tears,
and if you grant me these favours,
others who hope will envy you.

ANONYMOUS SONG SETTINGS

Here are gathered together songs from the periods covered by both Chapters I and II. 'Canción de cuna', 'En esta larga ausencia' and 'Oh qué bien que baila Gil' belong more properly to Chapter III, but are included here for convenience. Most of the songs are printed in the three anthologies of the Union Musical Española:

UMV 20095   'Maria matrem', '¡Ay trista vida corporal!', 'Ay luna que reluces', 'Canción de cuna'

UMV 20190   'Si la noche se hace oscura', 'Pastorcico non te aduermas', 'Pase el agua, Julieta'

UMV 21222   'Sobre Baça estaba el Rey', '¡Ay que non hay!', 'Tres moricas m'enamoran', 'Puse mis amores'

Mariam matrem / The Virgin Mother

Mariam matrem virginem attollite,
Jesum Christum attollite concorditer.
Maria, saeculi asilum, defende nos;
Jesu, totum refugium, exaude nos.
Nam estis nos totaliter diffugium,
totum mundi confugium realiter.

Praise Mary, the Virgin Mother,
and praise Jesus Christ.
Mary, shelter of mankind, protect us,
Jesus, our refuge, hear us.
For you are, in truth, the haven
of the entire world.

¡Ay, trista vida corporal! / Ah, sad corporeal life!

¡Ay, trista vida corporal!
¡O mon crudel tan desigual!
Trista de mi, ¿qué faré?
Lo meu car fill ¿quant lo veuré?

Ah, sad corporeal life!
O world, cruel and so perilous!
Woe is me, what shall I do?
My dear Son, when shall I see Him?

Si la noche se hace oscura / Since night is falling

Si la noche se hace oscura
y tan corto es el camino,
¿cómo no venís, amigo?
La media noche es pasada
y él que me pena no viene,
mi desdicha lo detiene,
que nací tan desdichada.
Házeme vivir penada,
y muéstraseme enemigo.
¿Cómo no venís, amigo?

Since night is falling
and the way is so short,
why delay so long, my friend?
Midnight is past
and he who grieves me stays away –
my misfortune detains him,
for I was born so unfortunate.
How he makes me grieve,
how hostile he grows.
Why delay so long, my friend?

Pastorcico non te aduermas / Shepherd lad, don't fall asleep

Pastorcico non te aduermas,
que mal se repastan tus ovejas.
Son muy malas de guardar,
tiénenme desatinado,
y yo triste, de cansado,
no las puedo repastar.
Cuido que me han de matar
o me mienten mis ovejas.

– Shepherd lad, don't fall asleep,
thy sheep have nowhere to graze.
– So hard to tend are they,
they make me distracted
and sad for lack of sleep.
I cannot tend my sheep.
I fear my flock
shall kill or deceive me.

¿Porqué estás adormico?
Zagal, hágote saber
que si las dejas perder
yo te cuento por perdido.
Ya no me puedo apartar
de guardar a mis ovejas.

– Why dost thou sleep?
Shepherd lad, hear what I say:
if thou dost lose them
I'll give thee up for lost.
– Now I have no choice
but to tend my sheep.

¡Ay, luna que reluces! / Ah, resplendent moon

¡Ay, luna que reluces,
toda la noche m'alumbres!

Ah, resplendent moon,
all night may you light me!

¡Ay, luna tan bella,
alúmbresme a la sierra,
por do vaya y venga!
¡Ay, luna que reluces,
toda la noche m'alumbres!

Ah, moon so fair,
light my way to the mountain,
wherever I come and go!
Ah, resplendent moon,
all night may you light me!

Pase el agua, Julieta / Cross the water, Julieta

Pase el agua, Julieta,	Cross the water, Julieta,
dama pase el agua,	cross the water, lady,
venite vous a moy.	and come to me.
Ju men anay en un vergel,	I've been to the garden
tres rosetas fuy culler,	to gather three roses,
ma Julieta,	my Julieta;
dama pase el agua,	cross the water, lady,
venite vous a moy.	and come to me.

Sobre Baça estaba el Rey / The King was at Baza

Sobre Baça estaba el Rey	The King was at Baza
Lunes después de yantar;	on Monday after dinner;
Miraba las ricas tiendas	he gazed on the tents so richly adorned
Qu'estaban en su real.	that stood within his camp.
Un moro tras una almena	Behind the rampart a Moor
Comenzóle de fablar:	addressed him thus:
Vete el rey Don Fernando	Be gone, King Ferdinand,
Que no queréis aquí envernar.	do not seek to winter here.
Veinte mil moros hay dentro	Twenty thousand Moors are within,
Todos de armas tomar;	all are men-at-arms,
Ochocientos de a caballo	eight hundred cavalry,
Para el escaramuzar.	ready for the fray.

¡Ay que non hay! / Alas, there is no one!

¡Ay que non hay!	Alas, there is no one,
¡Ay que non era!	alas, all is done,
Mas ¡ay, que non hay	and alas there is no one
Quién de mi pena se duela!	to share my grief!
Madre, la mi madre	Mother, my mother,
El mi lindo amigo	my sweet lover
Moricos de allende	by Moors from afar
Lo llevan cativo.	has been seized.
¡Ay que non era!	Alas, there is no one,
¡Ay que non hay!	alas, all is done,
Mas ¡ay, que non hay	and alas there is no one
Quién de mi pena se duela!	to share my grief!
Moricos de allende	By Moors from afar
Lo llevan cativo,	has been seized –
Cadenas de oro,	golden chains,
Candado morisco.	a Moorish gaol!

¡Ay que non hay!
¡Ay que non era!
Mas ¡ay, que non hay
Quién de mi pena se duela!

Alas, there is no one,
alas, all is done,
and alas there is no one
to share my grief!

Dindirindín / Dindirindin

Dindirindín dindirindín dirindaina,
dindirindín.

Dindirindin dindirindin dirindaina,
dindirindin.

Yu me leve un bel maitín
Matineta per la prata,
Encontré lo ruiseñor
Que cantaba so la rama
Dindirindín.

Early one morning
I set out across the meadow
and met a nightingale
singing on a branch.
Dindirindin.

Dindirindín dindirindín dirindaina,
dindirindín.

Dindirindin dindirindin dirindaina,
dindirindin.

Ruiseñor, le ruiseñor
Faite-me aquesta embaixata
Y dígalo a mon ami,
Que yuya so maritata
Dindirindín.

Nightingale, o nightingale,
bear this message
and tell my friend
that I'm already married.
Dindirindin.

Dindirindín dindirindín dirindaina,
dindirindín.

Dindirindin dindirindin dirindaina,
dindirindin.

Tres moricas m'enamoran / Three Moorish maids bewitched me

Tres moricas m'enamoran en
    Jaén:
    Axa, Fátima y Marién.

Three Moorish maids bewitched me in
    Jaén,
    Axa, Fatima and Marien.

Díxeles: ¿Quién sois, Señoras,
de mi vida rrobadoras?
Cristianas qu'eramos moras de Jaén:
    Axa, Fátima y Marién.

To them I said: who are you, ladies,
who robbed me of my life?
Christians we are, once Moors from Jaén:
    Axa, Fatima and Marien.

Yo vos juro all Alcorán
en quien, señoras, creeis,
que la una i todas tres
m'aveis puesto en grande afán;
¿dó mis ojos penarán
pues tal verén
    Axa, Fátima y Marién?

I swear to you by the Koran
in which, ladies, you believe,
that each and every one of you
has filled me with commotion;
Where can I bring my grieving eyes
to catch a glimpse of you,
    Axa, Fatima and Marien?

De las sierras donde vengo / From the mountains, whence I come

De las sierras donde vengo,
Ví tal hato y tal placer:
Allá me quiero volver.

¡Oh qué sierras, oh qué prados!
¡Oh qué fuentes, qué lugar!
Dichosos son los cuidados
Que se saben emplear.
Quien no se sabe mudar,
Nunca debiera nacer:
Allá me quiero volver.

From the mountains whence I come
I saw such plenty, such pleasure –
I long to return there.

Ah what mountains, ah what fields!
Ah what springs, what a realm!
Fortunate are they
who tend that land.
He who cannot move on
should never have been born.
I long to return there.

Puse mis amores / I gave my love

Puse mis amores
en Fernandillo.
¡Ay! que era casado
¡mal me ha mentido!

Digasme el barquero,
barquero garrido,
en cuál de aquellas barcas
va Fernandillo.

El Traydor era casado
mal me ha mentido.
¡Ay! que era casado
¡mal me ha mentido!

I gave my love
to young Fernando.
Alas, he was married
and deceived me cruelly!

Tell me, boatman,
handsome boatman,
in which of these boats
has sweet Fernando gone?

The traitor was married
and deceived me cruelly.
Alas, he was married
and deceived me cruelly!

En esta larga ausencia / In this long absence

LOPE DE VEGA

En esta larga ausencia,
donde mi desengaño y tu memoria
acaban mi paciencia,
comienza mi dolor la triste historia,
discurso de una vida
bien empleada, pero mal perdida.
   Aquí, donde se viste
de dos albas el sol en noche oscura,
eternamente triste,
ausente de tu luz serena y pura,
vive mi alma asida
al cuerpo triste de quien eres
   vida.

   In this long absence
where my disillusion and memory of you
sorely try my patience,
my anguish begins its sad tale –
the record of a life
well spent but badly wasted.
   Here, where the sun is dressed
in two dawns in dark night –
eternally sad,
absent from your serene and pure light,
my soul still lives, cleaving
to my wretched body, which you infuse
   with life.

Canción de cuna / *Lullaby*

(from the tonadilla *El Gurrumino*, 1762)

Duérmete, hijo de mi alma,
duérmete un poco,
porque si no duermes
llamaré al coco.
A la rorro, rorrorró,
bendita sea la madre que te parió.

Go to sleep, my darling boy,
go to sleep awhile,
for if you don't sleep
I'll call the bogey-man.
Hush-a-bye, hush-a-bye,
blessed be the mother who bore you.

Duérmete, hijo de mi vida,
que el coco viene,
y se lleva a los niños
si no se duermen.
A las rorro, rorrorró,
bendita sea la madre que te parió.

Go to sleep, my dearest boy,
for the bogey-man is coming,
and he carries off children
if they don't go to sleep.
Hush-a-bye, hush-a-bye,
blessed be the mother who bore you.

¡Oh qué bien que baila Gil! / *Ah! How well Gil dances*

¡Oh qué bien que baila Gil
con las mozas de Barajas
la chacona[1] a las sonajas
y el villano al tamboril!
Fué a Barajas Gil llamado
de las mozas del lugar
porque dicen que en bailar
es hombre muy afamado.
Gran contento ha dado Gil
a las mozas de Barajas.

Ah! How well Gil dances
with the girls of Barajas –
the chaconne to the tambourine
and the country dance to the tabor!
Gil was summoned to Barajas
by the girls of the village,
for they say
he's a most renowned dancer.
Gil has given great satisfaction
to the girls of Barajas.

[1]*Chacona*. A stately dance in triple time, which appears to have been imported into Spain from Mexico in the late eighteenth century.

III

SONG IN THE THEATRE: TONADILLA AND ZARZUELA

At the beginning of the seventeenth century, the new Italian style pioneered by Caccini and Monteverdi, recitative and melody with simple chordal accompaniment, swept through Spain. This led to the rise of theatrical music and the birth of the zarzuela and various other forms which are really opera by other names. In 1629 Lope de Vega's *La selva sin amor* was set as an opera and in 1660 a totally sung theatrical work was given – *Celos aun del aire matan* with music by Juan de Hidalgo (1612–85) and a libretto by Calderón de la Barca. Operas (or rather fiestas de música, fiestas de teatro, fiesta cantada or comedias armónicas) were given in Madrid and were written by such composers as Juan Navas (1659–1709), and José Durán. Navas also wrote songs and sonatas, as did José Marín (1619–99) among many others, but opera reigned supreme. It was during this period that the guitar, born of the clumsier and less versatile vihuela and the lute, emerged as the Spanish instrument par excellence. In the eighteenth century Spain, like other European countries, was invaded by Italian opera. The consequent decline in Spanish musical fortunes coincided with political eclipse and the Bourbon rule of Spain. Composers like Antonio Literes and José de Nebra (1702–68) cultivated a new type of villancico to rival the Italian cantata, but the onslaught of Italian taste was confirmed by the ascendancy of the Italian castrato Broschi, known as Farinelli (1705–82), who every night for ten years sang the same four arias by the German composer Hasse to the melancholic King Philip V. This unlikely passage in the history of performers and their royal patrons is exquisitely told in Sacheverell Sitwell's essay 'The King and the Nightingale' in *Southern Baroque Art*. Mention should also be made here of a giant of instrumental writing, the harpsichordist Domenico Scarlatti (1685–1757), without whose name no history of musical Spain is complete.

It was perhaps a lack of royal patronage which effected the decline of the influence of Italian music and the emergence of the tonadilla escénica from about 1760 onwards. This was a form unique to Spain, a type of vocal intermezzo performed between the acts of plays. The original tonadilla was a solo song interpolated into a play by an actor with guitar accompaniment. The tonadilla escénica grew from these humble beginnings into a miniature opera about twenty minutes long, with complicated plots and a small cast of characters. These were usually drawn from working-class life, particularly the poor but proud majos and majas immortalised by Goya. The popularity of these works was enormous: one single archive in Madrid has preserved two thousand works. As time went on, the tonadilla lost its essentially Spanish and concentrated character and became nothing less than a comic opera in the Italian manner. This led to its decline. It is worth mentioning the tonadillas of Manuel García (father of Pauline Viardot and Maria Malibran, and a famous singing teacher); Georges Bizet's exploitation of Spanish colour in *Carmen* (the composer knew the García family in Paris) owes much to Manuel's work. The piano music and songs later composed by Granados are a conscious tribute to, and evocation of, the world of the tonadilla of the late eighteenth century.

It is hardly surprising that for much of the nineteenth century, in a country exhausted and poverty-stricken by the vicissitudes of the Napoleonic Wars, musical life was at a low ebb. The wife of Fernando VII was a princess of Naples and court patronage firmly installed Rossini as the country's musical idol. Spain seemed immune to the influences of Viennese classicism and the new Romantic movement. Composers like Arriaga, Saldoni and Sor wrote in the bel canto manner without being able to rival Bellini and Donizetti. As a reaction against Italian music the zarzuela moderna came into being, fresh and unpretentious comic operas, simple in music and libretto. These began as one-act pieces, but by the middle of the century were ambitious works in three or four acts. In these pieces, the spirit of the tonadilla from the previous century was born again, but despite the musical felicities in the many works produced by such composers as Valverde (of *Clavelitos* fame), Barbieri, Caballero, Jiménez, Vives and so on, it remained something of a second-rate genre in comparison to the musical developments elsewhere in Europe.

All the songs in this chapter, with the exception of those by Literes and Sor, are to be found in a volume entitled *Spanish Songs of the 18th Century ('Tonadillas escénicas')* published by the International Music Company, New York City (No. 1332). The editor of this collection was the eminent Spanish musicologist José Subira (1882–1980), who more than anyone was responsible for bringing some of the best music from forgotten tonadillas back into the modern concert hall. Subira made certain musical modifications to facilitate the separate performance of these songs with piano – they were after all part of larger works – but unlike composers like Obradors and Nin who sometimes used tonadilla items as a basis for their elaborately accompanied songs, Subira's versions are those of an imaginative musicologist rather than a composer, and they avoid a virtuosic twentieth-century slant. The titles of these pieces are also his, but are useful for recital purposes. In 1970 Subira published a series of twenty-four complete tonadillas of varying kinds, all in piano-accompanied versions and including the complete tonadillas from which the following songs were taken. The UMV numbers given in the commentaries refer to the Union Musical Española publication numbers of these works, with the exception of the references for the Literes songs, and one by Laserna, which refers to the volume entitled *Cinco siglos de canciones españolas*.

ANTONIO LITERES (1673–1747)

In combining a career as church music composer with that of a composer for the stage, Literes followed in the tradition of the mentor of his early years, the maestro de capilla of the royal chapel in Madrid, Sebastián Durón. Three stage works of Literes have survived, and this song is taken from *Acis y Galatea*, a so-called zarzuela, without spoken interludes. Literes had the reputation of being the most gifted of the court composers and undertook a number of important commissions from as far afield as Lisbon. As well as much church music (including three four-part masses) he composed a number of secular cantadas humanas. The subtitle of his zarzuela *Los elementos* – 'opera armónica al estilo italiano' – is proof of the ascendancy of the Italian musical style in this period. This song is in UMV 20095.

Confiado jilguerillo / Trusting little linnet

(from *Acis and Galatea*)

Confiado jilguerillo	Trusting little linnet,
mira como importuna	see how love and fortune
de tu estado primero	so untimely did unseat you
te derribó el amor y la fortuna,	from your first high place,
y el viento que tan ufano presumiste	and the air you once so proudly assumed
aún no le hallaste cuando le perdiste.	is now so lost as never to be found.
Si de rama en rama	You flitted once from bough to bough,
si de flor en flor	from flower to flower,
ibas saltando, bullendo, cantando.	hopping, quivering, singing –
¡Dichoso quien ama las ansias de amor!	lucky is the one who yearns for love.

Ibas saltando, ibas saltando,	You flitted hopping,
bullendo y cantando.	quivering and singing –
¡Dichoso quien ama las ansias de amor!	lucky is the one who yearns for love.
Ibas saltando, bullendo y	You flitted hopping, quivering and
cantando.	singing –
¡Dichoso quien ama las ansias de amor!	lucky is the one who yearns for love.
Advierte que aprisa	Notice how quickly
es llanto la risa	laughter turns to weeping
y el gusto dolor,	and pleasure to sorrow,
es llanto la risa	laughter to weeping
y el gusto dolor.	and pleasure to sorrow.
¡Ay, Ay!	Ay, ay,
es llanto la risa	laughter turns to weeping
y el gusto dolor.	and pleasure to sorrow.
¡Ay, Ay!	Ay, Ay!

LUIS MISÓN (*d*.1766)

Misón was of Catalan origin. He was erroneously credited with the invention of the tonadilla escénica in 1757 – rather was it a form of music that evolved gradually. It began life as a topical musical interlude, inserted between acts of a play, no more than twenty minutes in length and conceived for the moment and thus quickly out of date. The tonadilla was written for a varying, but always small, number of solo singers and on different topics – Subira lists 'amorous, patriotic, historical, autobiographical, magical, allegorical, and based on local customs'. This was something so intrinsically Spanish in conception, that composers began to see the composition of tonadillas as the best escape from the overweening influence of Italy. Misón was not above composing an Italian intermezzo, however, when the occasion demanded it. He was a flautist in the royal chapel (he wrote a number of sonatas for flute and strings), but his main claim to fame was his tonadillas, more than eighty of which survive. This song is taken from *Una mesonera y un arriero* (1757), UMV 21516.

Seguidilla[1] *dolorosa de una maja*[2] *enamorada*	/	*Sad seguidilla of a maja in love*

A los montes me salgo	I make for the mountains
Por ver si encuentro un alma	to see if I can find a soul
Que se duela de mi tormento.	to console me in my anguish.
¡Ay de mi! Que me muero,	Woe is me! I am dying!
Pues se marchó y	For he has gone away,
No viene mi amargo dueño.	my bitter lover, never to return.

[1]*Seguidilla*. A dance in 3/8 or 3/4 time, faster than the Bolero and often accompanied by castanets. The tonality is usually major.
[2]*Maja*. The glamorously dressed female companion of the majo – see page 83.

JOSÉ CASTEL (*fl.* 1761–81)

This song is taken from Castel's tonadilla *La gitanilla en el coliseo* (1776), UMV 21385, a work which is rare in the tonadilla genre for its use of a chorus. Nothing is known of Castel, but more than fifty of his works survive, some of them to texts by Ramón de la Cruz, a crucial figure in furnishing composers with texts drawn from the lives of ordinary Spanish people. Works by the more popular tonadilla composers, and Castel is no exception, were now regularly finding their way to the newly-built opera houses of South America.

Canción de la gitana habilidosa / *Song of the clever gypsy girl*

Yo, zeñorez, zoy gitana,	I, gentlemen, am a gypsy girl,
como lo publica el traje.	as my costume proclaims.
Y zalgo a ezte coliseo	And I mount this stage
a hacer miz habilidadez.	to display my skills.
Digo la buenaventura.	I tell fortunes.
He eztudiado muchaz artez.	I have studied many arts.
Y a lo que ez hechicería,	And in matters of wizardry
no he encontrado quien me gane.	have never met my match.
Vaya, zeñorez, den me por	Come, gentlemen, give me in God's
Dioz	name,
una limozna e compación.	alms and pity.
Yo me contento en la ocación	I shall content myself on this occasion
que cada uno me de un doblón[1].	with a doubloon from each of you.
Vaya, queridoz, vaya por Dioz!	Come, my dears, in God's name!
Una limozna e compación.	Alms and pity!
Aquí habrá muchoz curiozoz	There will be many spectators here,
que me pidan novedadez,	asking me for the latest news,
y yo pretendo moztraroz	and I shall try to show you
lo que paza en variaz partez.	what is happening in other parts.
Mirarán laz diverzionez	You shall see the entertainments
que por otroz zitioz hacen,	enjoyed in other places,
por zi con la nueva idea	and shall perhaps with these new notions
ze divierten ezta tarde.	be entertained this evening.
Oigan, zeñorez, haja atención.	Give ear, gentlemen, attention please!
Verán que cozaz de admiración,	You shall see some remarkable things,
que miz juguetez zon de primor.	for my performance is without compare.

[1]*Doblón*. A gold coin, originally double the value of a pistole.

PABLO ESTEVE (d.1794)

In a composing career of thirty-five years, Esteve was an immensely popular master of the tonadilla genre. He wrote over four hundred works, often to his own texts, and fought tirelessly to establish the dignity of a profession which, because of its theatrical associations, seemed to many a dishonorable means of making a living compared to the serious métier of church music. Esteve was a pugnacious character altogether; he had a celebrated fall-out with 'La Caramba' – María Fernández, queen of the tonadilla interpreters – and was put in prison for libelling important society figures. He made a habit of inserting his own music into productions of theatrical works (the operas of Piccini for instance) from other countries. This song is from the solo tonadilla *El juicio del año* (1779), UMV 21386.

Canción satírica de pronósticos / Satirical song of the fortune-tellers

Habrá de varias frutas grandes cosechas,	There shall be rich harvests of various fruits,
Pero excederá a todas la de las brevas.	but figs shall be most plentiful of all.
En las fiestas los tragos harán prodigios,	Drink will work such wonders at fiestas
Tanto que hombres humanos serán divinos.	that men will become gods.
Habrá recreos, habrá comedias y maravillas	There will be entertainment, plays and wondrous things,
Por esas tierras e irán todas las cosas de esta manera.	and that shall be the pattern throughout these lands.
¿No es verdad, esto? Mucho que sí.	Is this not so? Of course.
Todos atiendan. Silencio.	Attention, one and all. Silence.
Oid, que aun tengo mucho que referir.	Give ear, for I still have much to tell.
Habrá entre petimetras y peluqueros,	Between stylish ladies and their hairdressers
Por cobrar los peinados, algunos pleitos.	there will be disputes about the cost of coiffures.
Vendrán de Cataluña, Cádiz, Valencia,	From Catalonia, Cádiz and Valencia
Varias rosas muy lindas de espinas llenas.	shall come many roses with many thorns.
Habrá dolores y reumatismos,	There will be pains and rheumatism,
Mil constipados y tabardillos;	countless colds and sunstrokes,
Y los gustos del mundo serán los mismos.	and all tastes shall be identical.
¿No es esto cierto? Mucho que sí.	Is this not certain? Of course.
Tras este augurio, voy a concluir,	With this forecast I shall conclude,
Y mis defectos todos suplid.	and may everyone make allowance for my defects.

ANTONIO ROSALES (c.1740–1801)

From 1762 on, Rosales wrote 150 or so tonadillas, a number of them to the libretti of Ramón de la Cruz. Despite his talents and enthusiasm, he never rose above the rank of músico secundario in the elaborate hierarchy of the Spanish theatres. His works are a successful mix of Spanish folk melodies and dances and some of them remained popular up until the Napoleonic era. This song is sung by the tenor Tuno in the tonadilla *El recitado*, UMV 21378, a work in four short scenes with three characters. It is a parody of the all-pervasive Italian operatic style which threatened the livelihood of Spanish composers at this time as much as it was to undermine the careers of German-speaking composers (including Schubert) in the following generation.

Canción contra las madamitas gorgoriteadoras	*Song against warbling madames*
Yo, señores míos, soy un tuno tal que tuno Más tuno no lo encontrarán. A todas las niñas me gusta embromar; Con pimienta a unas, y a otras con sal. Aquellas que en todo más gracia me dan Son las que más suelen gorgoritear. ¡Ay! Es esto primura, ¡Ah! Que tiene su aquel y es esto garganta Que pide un cordel.	I, gentlemen, am a rogue amongst rogues, a greater rogue you'll never meet. I like to tease all the girls, some with sauce and some with wit. Those who afford me most amusement are those who are wont to warble most. Ah! What elegance! Ah! It has that certain something – namely a throat crying out for a rope.
Yo, cierta madama la voy ahora a ver. La quiero, la adoro con todo mi aquel. Es muy primorosa, filigrana es, Pues canta italiano y viste a la dernier. Del gusto a lo chiaro quiere algo aprender, Y yo de su estilo quiero algo coger. ¡Ah! ¡De fijo, de fijo! ¡Ah! Con ello saldré. Agur, caballeros, después volveré.	I am now off to see a certain lady. I love her, I adore her with all my heart. She's very delicate and fine, since she sings Italian and dresses à la mode. She wishes to learn something of the popular style and I to catch something of her manner. Ah! Indeed, indeed! Ah! In this I shall not fail. Farewell, gentlemen, I'll be back later!

JACINTO VALLEDOR Y LA CALLE (1744–c.1809)

Like Rosales, Valledor had atrocious luck in turning his talent and success into a financially viable way of life. He was the well-educated scion of a famous theatrical family, and married Gabriella Santos, a famous interpreter of tonadillas. He was successful enough in the Barcelona theatres in the early 1780s, but after he was seconded to Madrid (it was the capital's right to requisition promising 'provincial' artists) he found himself in the shadow of Esteve, and was never able to achieve a well-paid job in the theatre. He ended his life in straitened circumstances. Twenty-five tonadillas by Valledor survive, a few of them among the most successful works in the genre. This song is from *El apasionado* (1768), which is not published by UME. The more celebrated tonadilla *La cantada vida y muerte del General Malbrú* is UMV 21528.

Canción de tímida / A bashful girl's song

Quiero cantaros, señores míos,	Gentlemen, I wish to sing
Cuatro palabras por divertiros.	a few words to amuse you.
Mas si no logro lo que pretendo,	But if I fail in my efforts,
Disimuladme como discretos,	pardon me, like the discreet folk you are,
Que ya se ve que claro está	since it is quite evident
Que cierto es que no sé más.	that I simply don't know any more.
Si no les gusta, luego me iré;	If you don't like it, I shall go away;
Mas porque callan, proseguiré.	but since you keep silent, I'll proceed.
Sepan, señores, que la otra tarde	Know, gentlemen, that the other evening
Tuve el capricho de ir a pasearme.	I suddenly wished to go for a stroll.
Cuando ya estaba muy peripuesta,	Then when I was all dressed up,
Veo que suben por la escalera.	I see folk coming up the stairs.
Llaman por mi. Yo voy allá a ver quien es.	They call me. I go to see who it is.
Y claro está . . . Mas no les digo lo que pasó.	And of course . . . But I'll not tell you what happened.
Me da vergüenza. Así soy yo.	I am ashamed to. That's the way I am.

VENTURA GALVÁN (GALBÁN) (*fl.* 1762–73)

Galván was a comic actor turned composer, well known in the field of tonadilla and zarzuela composition by 1762. He collaborated with Ramón de la Cruz on the zarzuela *Las foncarraleras* (1772). The song printed here is from Galván's most famous tonadilla, *Los Vagabundos y ciegos fingidos* (*The Vagabonds and the false blind men*), UMV 21377. The piece, a depiction of low life in Madrid, is in six short sections with a small amount of spoken dialogue. This song is the third item in the tonadilla, and was originally shared between 'Ella' and 'Prima' – a couple of nameless 'currutacas modestas' (in reality anything but modest) of the type to be immortalised by Granados in his Goya-inspired *Tonadillas*.

Seguidillas del oficial cortejante / *Song of the courting officer*

Un oficial de guerra fué mi cortejo	An officer was my lover
Y en muy pocas semanas quedó sin resto.	and in very few weeks he was broke.
Ya se ha marchado, pero tengo el consuelo	Now he has gone, but I am consoled
Que va pelado, que va pelado.	that he left without a sou.
¡Qué bueno será el señor oficial!	How nice for the officer!
Pero tengo el consuelo que va pelado.	But I am consoled that he left without a sou.
¡Pobrecito! Y qué contento quedaría!	Poor fellow! How happy he must have been!
En la gente de guerra es evidente	With soldiers it's apparent
Que está siempre el bolsillo convaleciente.	that their purses are always poorly.
¡Ay, qué bueno será el señor oficial!	Ah, how nice for the officer!
Está siempre el bolsillo convaleciente.	Their purse is always poorly.
Pero con todo, no faltan oficiales que son garbosos.	But for all that, officers can be generous.
Y más vale un *te daré* de algunos oficiales	And a promise from some is worth more
Que dos *toma* de un paisano.	than two gifts from a civilian.

BLAS DE LASERNA (1751–1816)

Laserna was certainly one of the most prolific and successful of the 'tonadilleros'. At his height he was contracted to write sixty-three tonadillas a year, and he eventually succeeded Esteve as musical director at the Teatro de la Cruz. He wrote more than five hundred works in this genre as well as a great deal of other music. The disruption of the peninsular war had a terrible effect on his earnings, and he was reduced to working as a copyist and writing in the very Italian manner which he had worked so hard throughout his career to supplant in favour of authentic Spanish traditions. The song entitled 'Seguidillas majas' is taken from *El majo y la Italiana fingida* (1778), UMV 21379, a tonadilla which parodies Italian opera, and has a role for a singer posing as an Italian girl – there is even an 'Arieta' with an Italian text nonsensical in the worst traditions of bel canto opera. 'El jilguerillo con pico de oro', from the tonadilla *Los amantes chasqueados*, is in UMV 20095. Laserna's celebrated 'Tirana del Trípili', quoted by Mercadante in his *I due Figaro* of 1829, was to play its part in spreading the sound of what the world soon took to be typical Spanish music. Granados was to use the same piece as the inspiration for 'Los Requiebros', the opening piece of the *Goyescas* for piano. Five of Laserna's pieces appear in Joaquin Nin's *Classiques espagnols du chant* of 1926.

Canción del jilguerito con pico de oro / *The little golden-beaked linnet*

El jilguerillo con pico de oro
canta sonoro
y todo es trinar.
Ah, cruza la selva de rama en
   rama,
y a la que ama buscando va.

The little golden-beaked linnet
sings melodiously,
trilling all the time.
Ah, he flies over the forest from branch to
   branch
in search of the one he loves.

Seguidillas¹ majas² / *Seguidillas majas*

Aunque el aire de majas no le tenemos,
También hay italianas con resalero.
Mire usté qué regarbo.
Mire usté qué gracejo.
Mire usté qué columpio.
Mire usté qué poleo.
¡Vaya usté a la . . . . ! Toma!
Don Estafermo; que aunque el aire de
   majas no le tenemos,
Hay también italianas con resalero.

Though we don't resemble majas,
there are Italian girls of wit and charm.
Look, how graceful!
Look, how winsome!
Look, what swaying!
Look, the proud gait!
Go to the . . . . ! Take that!
Don Estafermo; for though we don't
   resemble majas,
there are Italian girls of wit and charm.

Aunque el aire de majas no le
   tenemos,
Sígame pronto si imito yo a las majas con
   desahogo.

Though we don't resemble majas, come
   quick
and see if I don't imitate those majas with
   ease.

Mire usté qué chulada
Mire usté qué meneo.
Mire usté qué atractivo.
Mire usté qué portento.
¡Vaya usté a la . . . . ! Toma!
Don Estafermo; y aunque soy
   italiana,
Por mi salero, yo me igualo
A las majas de fundamento.

Look, what cheek!
Look, what a wiggle!
Look, what charm!
Look, what promise!
Go to the . . . . ! Take that!
Don Estafermo; and though I'm an
   Italian girl,
through my wit and charm I'm the equal
of any true maja.

¹*Seguidilla*. A dance in 3/8 or 3/4 time, faster than the Bolero and often
accompanied by castanets. The tonality is usually major.
²*Maja*. The glamorously dressed female companion of the majo – see page 83.

El Trípili¹ / *The Trípili*

Tres mil veces cada día
me acuerdo que me quisiste,
y tres mil veces me acuerdo
que lo que fué ya no existe.

Three thousand times every day
I remember that you loved me,
and three thousand times I remember:
what used to be is now no more.

Con el trípili, trípili, trápala,	With a trípili, trípili, trápala,
esta tirana² se canta y se baila.	this tirana is sung and danced.
Anda, chiquilla, anda, salada,	Go, pretty one, go, witty one,
que estás robándome el alma.	for you're stealing from me my soul.
Yo soy como aquella piedra	I'm like that stone
que está en medio de la calle;	in the middle of the street –
todos se meten con ella	everyone meddles with it,
sin meterse ella con nadie.	without it meddling with anyone.
Con el trípili, trípili, trápala,	With a trípili, trípili, trápala,
esta tirana se canta y se baila.	this tirana is sung and danced.
Anda, chiquilla, anda, salada,	Go, pretty one, go, witty one,
que estás robándome el alma.	for you're stealing from me my soul.

¹*Trípili*. An ancient song and dance.
²*Tirana*. An Andalusian dance in 6/8 time; it is usually accompanied by the guitar and danced by a man waving his hat or handkerchief and a woman waving her apron. The words usually took the form of four-line *coplas*.

JOSÉ PALOMINO (1755–1810)

Palomino was a violinist in the royal chapel from an early age and was an equally precocious and successful tonadilla composer – indeed this song from *El canapé*, a short solo tonadilla in four numbers, UMV 21388, was composed when he was fourteen years old. At the age of nineteen, Palomino emigrated to Lisbon where he had a distinguished career as a composer of theatre and chamber music, as well as being a celebrated violin teacher. In the wake of the Napoleonic invasion he was forced to leave Lisbon and accepted a post in Las Palmas where he died two years later. This song is also to be found in UMV 20095.

Canción picaresca / *Picaresque song*

Un canapé he comprado	I bought a sofa
esta mañana,	this morning,
y me ha contado	and it told me
todo lo que pasaba	all that befell
con su dueña primera,	its first owner,
que era madama de cierto cortejante	the lady of a certain suitor
muy cortejada.	who wooed her greatly.
No solo quien descubre	It is not only maids
son las criadas,	who talk,
pues hasta los asientos	since even chairs
todo lo parlan.	tell all.

Mi canapé me ha dicho	My sofa informed me
todas las faltas y sobras	of all the misdeeds and excesses
que había en la otra casa,	that took place in the other house,
lo que dicen y hacen	what suitor and lady
galán y dama.	said and did.
Y en especial	And especially
si encima de él se sentaban.	if they sat down on him.
Yo voy a referiros	I am going to tell you
lo que pasaba	what happened
entre aquel currutaco	between that beau
y su madama.	and his lady.
Mas como ya es hoy tarde,	But since it's already late,
lo haré mañana.	I shall do it tomorrow.

FERNANDO FERANDIERE (*fl.*1771–?1816)

Like Palomino, Ferandiere was a violinist. It is possible that he was of Portuguese birth, and it seems that he may have lived for a time in Cádiz. Ferandiere was almost exclusively a composer of music for guitar, or chamber music for guitar and other instruments in many different combinations. The treatises he published in 1771 and 1799 contain his only surviving music and are evidence of a fine musicological mind aware of the differences between popular and classical guitar music, and the possibilities inherent in the guitar as a concert instrument. This song is taken from Ferandiere's only tonadilla, *La consulta*, UMV 21360.

Minueto en alabanza de la música seria	*Minuet in praise of serious music*

Vamos a lo serio, vamos a lo fino,	Let us strive for the serious, let us strive for the fine,
Que esto se introduce hasta el corazón.	since this reaches the very heart.
Hiere blandamente, endulza lo airado,	It wounds one gently, soothes anger,
Suspende el cuidado, mitiga el dolor,	relieves care, softens pain,
Suspende el dolor.	assuages grief.

MARIANO BUSTOS (*fl.*1790)

The Municipal Library of Madrid has about two dozen tonadillas by Bustos. Like many of his contemporaries he attempted to establish himself as maestro compositor on the retirement of Esteve in 1790. This powerful post was filled by Pablo de Moral. This song comes from the tonadilla *La necedad*, UMV 21384.

Canción contra los violetistas / *Song against false erudites*

¡Oh! Violetistas greco-latinos, anglico-
itálicos, seudo eruditos!
Chitón! y callad! Que jamás ha visto el
orbe
Tan esteril porfiar, como el vuestro,
violetistas,
Negando la necedad, como el vuestro,
violetistas.
Uno delira, otro
patea
Y a otro se le hinchan todas las venas.
No hay que discutir, pues quien más
sabe
Es más tonto entre los de ese redil.

Juzgáis dislate lo que yo os digo,
Insignes zánganos enfurecidos.
¡Chitón! y callad! Que sois un ejemplo
vivo,
Aunque os pese de verdad, que sois un
ejemplo vivo,
De que en este pobre mundo abunda la
necedad.
Lo que yo afirmo es evidente
Y será un simple quien me lo niegue.
La cosa es así, y si no
tenéis
Enmienda a un más habréis de sufrir.

Oh, Greco-Latin, Anglo-Italian pseudo-
erudites!
Hush and be silent! For the world has
never seen
such sterile persistence as yours,
erudites,
denials of folly, such as yours, false
erudites.
One of them raves, another stamps his
feet
and another puffs himself up with pride.
There's no two ways about it, since he
who knows most
is the silliest sheep in that pen.

You consider what I tell you to be absurd,
you notorious, ranting drones.
Hush and be silent! For you are a living
example,
though the truth hurts, you are a living
example
that stupidity is rife in this poor
world.
What I say is self-evident,
and whoever denies it is a simpleton.
That's the way it is, and unless you make
amends
you'll have to suffer even more.

MANUEL PLÁ (*d*.1766)

Plá was born of a Catalan family in Torquemada in the province of Palencia. This song (published in UMV 20095 as well as the International Music collection) comes from the religious play *La lepra de Constantino*, and he is also known for his tonadilla for two voices *El soldado*, UMV 21539. Plá was an accomplished oboist, as were his two brothers Juan and José who made their names as players in foreign courts.

Seguidillas religiosas / *Religious seguidillas*

Tres personas en una
Te muestra el cielo,

Heaven shews us
three persons in one,

Que en tres personas caben	and in three there is room
Muchos misterios.	for many mysteries.
Y aunque se oculten	For though they be hidden,
Está en Roma la Sede	in Rome is the Holy See
Que los promulgue.	to attest to them.
Sé fiel a tres virtudes	Be faithful to three virtues
En este mundo,	in this world:
Caridad, Esperanza	charity, hope
Y Fé del justo,	and the faith of the just –
Si es que pretendes	if you wish
Hallar eterna gloria,	to find eternal glory
Tras de tu muerte.	after your death.

FERNANDO SOR (SORS) (1778–1839)

Sor, a famous guitar virtuoso, was also a composer of a great deal of vocal and chamber music. He was born in Barcelona, and educated in the monastery of Montserrat; he had composed his first successful opera by the age of nineteen. Sor fought against the Napoleonic invasion and composed a number of patriotic songs, but his decision to work for the French authorities after the Spanish defeat made it necessary for him to flee Spain in 1813. Thereafter he lived mainly in Paris, although he travelled as far afield as Russia – and England, where his success was compared in the press with that of the Waverley novels of Scott. His ballets made him famous throughout Europe, but playing the guitar was more central to his fame, as was his *Méthode pour la guitare*, a treatise which is still thought remarkable. The songs printed here are twelve of the twenty-five or so *Seguidillas boleras* for various vocal combinations with guitar or piano. In accompanying the songs so far given in this book, the piano can do valiant service as a surrogate (for vihuelas, guitars, vocal and instrumental combinations or orchestras), but with the seguidillas of Sor we find ourselves on the threshold of authentic piano-accompanied song.

Seguidillas / Seguidillas

Cesa de atormentarme / Cease tormenting me

Cesa de atormentarme,	Cease tormenting me,
cruel Memoria,	cruel Memory,
acordándome un tiempo	reminding me of a time
que fuí dichoso.	when I was happy.
Y aún lo sería	I should still be so,
si olvidarme pudiera	could I but forget
de aquellas dichas.	that happiness.

De amor en las prisiones / Shackled by love

De amor en las prisiones
gozosa vivo. ¡Ay!
Y sus dulces cadenas
beso y bendigo. ¡Ay!

Y el verme libre
más que el morir me fuera
duro y sensible. ¡Ay!

Shackled by love
I relish life. Ah!
And its sweet chains
I kiss and bless. Ah!

And to see myself free –
more difficult and grievous
than death that would be. Ah!

Acuérdate, bien mío / Remember, my love

Acuérdate, bien mío,
cuando solías
buscar las ocasiones
para las dichas.

Y ahora mudable
huyes aún de las mismas
casualidades.

Remember, my love,
how you were wont
to seek out occasions
for happiness.

And now, inconstant,
you even flee
those very opportunities.

Prepárame la tumba / Prepare me my tomb

Prepárame la tumba,
que voy a expirar
en manos de la madre
de la falsedad.

No siento tanto
el morir como hallarme
en tales brazos.

Prepare me my tomb,
for I am about to die
in the arms of the mother
of falsehood.

I do not so much mind
death as finding myself
in such arms.

¿Cómo ha de resolverse? / How can anyone resolve?

¿Cómo ha de resolverse
para embarcarse
aquel que desde lejos
ve tempestades?

How can anyone resolve
to set sail
who from afar
descries storms?

Muchacha, y la vergüenza / Your shame, my girl

Muchacha, y la vergüenza,
¿dónde se ha ido?
'Las cucarachas, madre,
se la han comido.'

Your shame, my girl,
where has it gone?
'The cockroaches, mother,
have eaten it up.'

Muchacha, mientes,	You lie, my girl,
porque las cucarachas	for cockroaches
no tienen dientes.	don't have teeth.

Si dices que mis ojos / If you say that my eyes

Si dices que mis ojos	If you say that my eyes
te dan la muerte,	are slaying you,
confiésate y comulga,	confess and receive the Sacrament,
que voy a verte.	for I shall come and see you.
Porque yo creo	Since I believe
me suceda lo mismo	the same will befall me,
si no te veo.	if I do not see you.

Seguidillas del Requiem eternam / Seguidillas of the Requiem eternam

Los canónigos, madre,	Canons, mother,
no tienen hijos;	don't have sons,
los que tienen en casa	what they do have at home
son sobrinitos.	are little nephews.
Ay, madre mía,	Ah, mother,
un canónigo quiero	I want a canon
para ser tía.	so as to be an aunt.

El que quisiera amando / The lover who wishes

El que quisiera amando	The lover who wishes
vivir sin pena	to live without grief
ha de tomar el tiempo	must take things
conforme venga.	as they come.
Quiera querido;	Love and be loved,
y si te aborrecieren,	and should they shun you,
haga lo mismo.	do the same.

Si a otro cuando me quieres / If when you love me

Si a otro cuando me quieres	If when you love me
la mano le das,	you give your hand to another,
cuando ya no me quieras,	when you no longer love me,
¡di qué le darás!	what will you give then, pray?
No fuera mala	It would not be bad
el que yo me muriera	if I were indeed to die
por un canalla.	for a rascal.

Las mujeres y cuerdas / Women and guitar strings

Las mujeres y cuerdas de la guitarra, es menester talento para templarlas.	Women and guitar strings – talent is needed to tune them.
Flojas no suenan, y suelen saltar muchas si las aprietan.	When slack they don't sound, and many snap when you tighten them.

Mis descuidados ojos / My unwitting eyes

Mis descuidados ojos vieron tu cara. ¡Oh qué cara me ha sido esa mirada!	My unwitting eyes beheld your dear face. Ah, how dear it has cost me, that glance!
Me cautivaste, y encontrar no he podido quien me rescate.	You captivated me, and I have found no one to free me.
Ya tomarán mis ojos a buen partido, para no verte siempre, no haberte visto.	Now my eyes will firmly resolve, so as not to see you forever, never to have seen you.
Pues tienes cosas que sólo debe verlas él que las goza.	For you have things which only he should see who enjoys them.
De mi parte, a tus ojos diles que callen, porque si les respondo quieren matarme.	Tell your eyes from me to be silent, for if I respond to them they seek to kill me.
Y es fuerte cosa que ha de callar un hombre si le provocan.	And it is hard for a man to be silent, when provoked.

IV

ISAAC ALBÉNIZ
(1860–1909)

During much of the nineteenth century, Spanish opera audiences were enslaved by lightweight and unexceptional music, much of it imitating the French and Italian styles. In the last decades of the century, however, there was a new spirit at work, a move to free Spain from the musical domination of Italy; performers and composers – and consequently also the public – began to be aware of the glories of Spain's musical heritage. This reformation of the nation's musical life, nothing less than a new dawn of national consciousness, was led by the Catalan composer and teacher Felip Pedrell (1841–1922). It was Pedrell's aim to revivify the sacred music of Spain and establish a national opera. Although these aims were not fulfilled in exactly the way Pedrell would have wished, in the late 1860s and 70s were born the three composers – Albéniz, Granados and Falla – who, under Pedrell's guidance, would usher in an exciting new phase in the country's musical history.

The inclusion of the songs of Isaac Albéniz in an anthology such as this may seem perverse – it cannot be denied that his rarely performed vocal music stands so far in the shadow of his towering achievements as a composer of piano works that 'crumbs from the table' may not be an inappropriate way to describe them. But Albéniz is such an important figure in the revival of nationalism in Spanish music in the last decade of the nineteenth century that his sallies into song have an interest of their own and a possible place in certain recital programmes.

The facts of his life are astonishing. Albéniz was born in Catalonia on 29 May 1860, and gave his first public concert at the age of four. His father, with an eye to exploit his son's potential, made the boy practise to the exclusion of other studies. At six he was refused admission to the Paris Conservatoire, it is said because of unruly behaviour. Isaac went back to Spain and the life of a travelling piano prodigy. In 1868 the family moved to Madrid. Inspired by the writings of Jules Verne, the boy took to the road on his own initiative in improvised concert tours throughout the country; his adventures en route included being robbed by highwaymen. In Cádiz he embarked as a stowaway on a ship, and was put ashore at Buenos Aires where he gave numerous concerts and made a great deal of money. Albéniz then moved on to Cuba (by this time he was still only thirteen years old) where he happened to encounter his father; Albéniz senior, amazed by the boy's financial success, let him go his own way. The money ran out in New York where he worked as a dock porter, and as a vaudeville turn, playing the piano with his back turned to the instrument. Further highlights in this picaresque life include visits to England, Germany and Brussels, and study with Franz Liszt in Weimar. The turning point was in 1883 when Albéniz began to study in Barcelona with Felip Pedrell, who gently revealed to the wandering nomad the glories of his Spanish musical heritage. Albéniz married and settled down, and gave up concert life in favour of composing. For a period he lived in Paris and taught at the Schola Cantorum; apart from a link with Debussy, he was close to Chausson, Fauré, Bordes, Dukas and many others. His greatest achievement, the four books of the suite *Iberia* for piano, dates from the last years of his life. Albéniz died in his prime, his health probably undermined by the strenuous travels of his youth.

Albéniz's creativity in vocal music was blighted by an arrangement (which he himself called 'the pact of Faust') with the rich British banker Francis Money-Coutts: the composer received a generous stipend in return for being a non-resident house musician to milord. Coutts had grandiose literary pretensions as a librettist and Albéniz slaved away at a number of Coutts operas including the galumphing *Henry Clifford* (performed in 1895 in Barcelona) and the much more successful *Pepita Jiménez* (1896). It is one of the anomalies of his life that Albéniz, a great Spanish nationalist composer, should have composed a number of songs in English – all to Coutts texts of course: the cycle entitled *To Nellie*, and four songs published in Paris in the last year of his life and dedicated to Fauré. These songs have reasonably demanding piano parts, which is not the case with either of the two song sets in this book, both of which date from the composer's late twenties – before he had given up his concert career, and before he had encountered the influence of the French composers. With the exception of the fifth song, which has something of Schubert's 'Ungeduld' about it, the *Cinco rimas de Bécquer* display an astonishing lack of pianistic rhetoric; they refuse to upstage a vocal line which seems uninventive in itself. Perhaps this is because the 'songs' were originally intended to be recitations of Bécquer's text, accompanied by piano – a genre found in Schubert, Liszt, Schumann, and even Reynaldo Hahn.

There are two editions of the work (only the songs are available today, UMV 39060), and it seems that the recited version was the original.

Seis baladas italianas / *Six Italian songs*

MARQUESA DE BOLAÑOS
(1887)

1. *Barcarola* / *Barcarole*

Tacita è l'onda, tranquillo il mar,
E s'ode il canto del marinar.

La luna ascosa in bianco vel,
D'amor gli sguardi rinvia dal ciel:
Resta Natura e s'ode sol
Il remo lieve del barcaiuol.

Deh! Tutto tace; non far rumor.
La notte parla mistero e amor.

The waves are hushed, the sea is calm,
and the song of the sailor is heard.

The moon, hidden in a white veil,
sends back loving glances from heaven:
nature is at rest, only the gentle strokes
of the boatman's oars are heard.

Ah, all is silent! Make no sound.
Night speaks of mystery and love.

2. *La lontananza* / *Distance*

Lungi, o cara, da te, chi mi
consola?
Il mio pensiero teco ognor soggiorna.
E se il chiamo non ode e a me
s'invola.
Non ode la mia voce, più non
torna.
Deh! Che farò qui abbandonata e
sola:
Lungi, o cara, da te, chi mi
consola?

Se de bei di passati al cor mi viene
Dolcissima talor la rimembranza,
Non fia ch'abbian conforto le mie pene.
Dura troppo è per me la lontananza!

E sempre il mio pensier a te s'invola . . .
Ma lungi, o Dio, da te chi mi
consola?

Far from you, my love, who can console
me?
My thoughts are always with you.
And if I call them, they do not hear and
vanish,
they do not hear my voice and return no
more.
Ah, what shall I do here, abandoned and
alone:
far from you, my love, who can console
me?

And if sometimes the sweetest memories
of happy days steal back into my heart,
even this does not quieten my grief.
The distance is too much for me to bear!

And my thoughts always fly to you . . .
But far from you, o God, who can console
me?

3. *Una rosa in dono* / *The gift of a rose*

Ecco un bel fior,
Le foglie ha porporine,

Behold – a beautiful flower.
Its leaves are purple

D'amor favella al cor.
E più in April
Spande soave odore
E appare più gentil.
L'accetta in don,
E leggi in questa imago
I miei desir qual son.
Ei sembra dir
Del tuo fedele
Ardenti sono per te i sospir.
Tal rosa ognor – interprete
    leggiadro –
Di me ti parli al cor.

and it speaks to the heart of love.
And then in April
it sheds a sweet scent
and appears more lovely still.
Accept it as a gift,
and from this image
learn what I desire.
It seems to say
how ardent are the sighs
of your beloved.
May such a rose – my graceful
    interpreter –
always speak of me to your heart.

4. *Il tuo sguardo / Your gaze*

Colmo egli è di dolcezza!
Incanta ed innamora!
E all' alma dolce ebbrezza
Infonde e il cor ristora!
Se la nera pupilla
Mesta mi figgi in viso,
L'amorosa scintilla
D'angelo par d'Eliso.

It brims with sweetness!
It charms and inspires love!
And into the soul it instils
gentle rapture and heals the heart!
If your dark eyes
stare at me in sorrow,
their loving sparkle
resembles an angel's from Elysium.

Sia rubello od avaro,
Mesto egli sia o sereno,
Sempre il tuo sguardo è caro
E amor suscita in seno!
Se mi guardi, mi bei
E insiem mi fai soffrir.
Viver, mio ben, vorrei
D' un tuo sguardo e morir!

Whether rebellious or unyielding,
sad or serene,
your gaze is ever dear to me
and awakens love in my heart!
If you gaze at me, you make me happy
and wretched simultaneously.
I'd fain, my love, live
for one glance from you, and die!

5. *Morirò / I shall die*

Qual fiorellin novello
Che all' aura spande il suo soave odor
E il verde praticello
Adorna solo un giorno e poi s' en muor –
Così la vita mia
Qui sulla terra breve passerà,
E il cor la pena ria,
Figlia d' amor, non mai ti narrerà.

Just as that fresh little flower
which sheds its sweet scent in the breeze
and adorns the green meadow
for a single day, then dies –
so shall my life
pass swiftly here on earth,
and my heart shall never tell,
daughter of love, of its bitter pain.

Morirò come il fiore,
Dopo aver l' aura piena di sospir,
Ma lieta pur in core
Di non aver turbato il tuo gioir.
E quando in breve, o Dio,
D'amor consunta e di dolor sarò,

I shall die like the flower,
having filled the air with sighs,
yet happy in my heart
not to have spoiled your joy.
And when shortly, o God,
I shall be consumed with love and grief,

Mandando a te, ben mio,
L' ultimo mio sospiro . . . morirò!

I'll send you, my sweet,
my final sigh . . . and die!

6. *T' ho riveduta in sogno* / *I saw you again in a dream*

Avvolta in bianco celestial splendore
Ti vidi l' altra notte, angelo mio.
Eri si bella e si spiravi amore
Che ti credetti un Angelo di Dio!

I saw you last night, my angel,
clad in white, celestial splendour.
You were so fair and inspired such love,
I believed you were an angel from God!

Ah! Eternamente io ti credea perduta,
Ma in sogno pur ben mio t' ho riveduta!

Ah! I had believed you lost for ever,
but I saw you again in a dream, my sweet!

Io piangeva d' amor, e lieve intanto
La tua morbida mano rasciugava
Quel mio dirotto, ahi! troppo dolce
    pianto,
Che le gote consunte m' irrigava.

I wept with love, and meanwhile
your soft and gentle hand dried
my distraught yet too sweet
    tears,
which watered my wasted cheeks.

Ah! In eterno non sei dunque perduta,
Se l' altra notte in sogno t' ho veduta!

Ah! So you are not lost to me for ever,
since I saw you in a dream last night!

Favellasti d' amor, diletta mia,
E il suon della tua voce mi parea
Soavissima del Cielo un' armonia
Che in giù dall' alte sfere a me scendea.

You spoke to me of love, my sweet,
and your voice sounded
like gentlest heavenly harmony,
descending to me from on high.

Ah! Se, dolce amor mio, non sei perduta,
Deh! Riedi quale in sogno t' ho veduta!

Ah! If, my sweet, you are not lost,
ah, return as I saw you in my dream!

Rimas[1] *de Bécquer* / *Bécquer songs*

GUSTAVO ADOLFO BÉCQUER

(1889)

'*Rimas*. Literally 'rhymes'. Bécquer called his published edition of some 100 poems 'Rimas' ('Verse') to indicate their modest nature.

I.

Besa el aura que gime blandamente
las leves ondas que jugando riza;
el sol besa a la nube en occidente
y de púrpura y oro la matiza;
la llama en derredor del tronco ardiente
por besar a otra llama se desliza
y hasta el sauce inclinándose a su
    peso
al río que le besa, vuelve un beso.

I.

The breeze, softly moaning, kisses
the gentle waves it ripples in jest;
the sun kisses the cloud in the west,
tingeing it with purple and gold;
the flame slips round the burning tree
to kiss another flame
and even the willow, bowing beneath its
    weight,
returns the river's kiss.

2.

Del salón en el ángulo oscuro,
de su dueña tal vez olvidada,
silenciosa y cubierta de polvo,
veíase el arpa.

¡Cuánta nota dormía en sus cuerdas,
como el pájaro duerme en las ramas,
esperando la mano de nieve
que sabe arrancarlas!

¡Ay!, pensé; ¡cuántas veces el genio
así duerme en el fondo del alma,
y una voz como Lázaro espera
que le diga 'Levántate y anda'!

3.

Me ha herido recatándose en las sombras,
sellando con un beso su traición.
Los brazos me echó al cuello y por la
    espalda
partióme a sangre fría el corazón.

Y ella prosigue alegre su camino,
feliz, risueña, impávida, ¿y por qué?
Porque no brota sangre de la herida,
porque el muerto está en pie.

4.

Cuando sobre el pecho inclinas
la melancólica frente,
una azucena tronchada
me pareces.

Porque al darte la pureza
de que es símbolo celeste,
como a ella te hizo Dios
de oro y nieve.

5.

¿De dónde vengo? . . . El más horrible y
    áspero
de los senderos busca;
las huellas de unos pies ensangrentados
sobre la roca dura,
los despojos de un alma hecha jirones
en las zarzas agudas,

2.

In a dark corner of the room,
by its mistress perhaps forgot,
covered in dust and silent
stood the harp.

In its strings what notes lay dormant,
like in a bird asleep on the boughs,
awaiting the touch of a snowy hand
to call them forth!

Ah, I thought, how often genius
sleeps thus in the depths of the soul,
awaiting, like Lazarus, a voice
to bid it: 'Rise and go!'

3.

Concealed in the dark she wounded me,
sealing with a kiss her betrayal.
She flung her arms around my neck, and
    from the back
cold-bloodedly pierced my heart.

And cheerfully she went her way,
happy, smiling, impassive. And why?
Because no blood gushes from the wound,
because the dead man is on his feet.

4.

When on my breast you lean
your melancholy brow –
a broken lily
you seem.

For when He gave you purity,
its celestial symbol,
God made you thus
of gold and snow.

5.

Whence do I come? . . . The most
    hideous and harsh
of paths seek out;
the print of bleeding feet
on the hard rock,
the remains of a soul lacerated
on the sharp brambles

te dirán el camino
que conduce a mi cuna.

¿Adónde voy? El más sombrío y
    triste
de los páramos cruza,
valle de eternas nieves y de eternas
melancólicas brumas.
    En donde esté una piedra solitaria
sin inscripción alguna,
donde habite el olvido,
allí estará mi tumba.

will tell you the way
to my cradle.

Whither do I go? The most sombre and
    sad
of deserts traverse,
the valley of eternal snows and eternal
melancholy mists.
    Where there is one solitary stone
devoid of all inscription,
where oblivion abides –
there will be my tomb.

Chanson de Barberine / Barberine's song

ALFRED DE MUSSET

(1897)

Beau chevalier qui partez pour la guerre,
        Qu'allez-vous faire
        Si loin d'ici?
Voyez-vous pas que la nuit est profonde,
        Et que le monde
        N'est que souci?

Vous qui croyez qu'une amour délaissée
        De la pensée
        S'enfuit ainsi,
Hélas! hélas! chercheurs de renommée,
        Votre fumée
        S'envole aussi.

Beau chevalier qui partez pour la guerre,
        Qu'allez-vous faire
        Si loin de nous?
J'en vais pleurer, moi qui me laissais dire
        Que mon sourire
        Etait si doux.

Handsome knight setting out for war,
        what will you do
        so far from here?
Can you not see that the night is deep
        and the world
        is naught but care?

You who believe that an abandoned love
        can escape the mind
        in this way,
alas, alas, you who seek fame –
        your smoke
        will vanish too.

Handsome knight setting out for war,
        what will you do
        so far from us?
I shall weep, who told myself
        that my smile
        was so sweet.

V

ENRIQUE GRANADOS
(1867–1916)

The songs of Granados are the first in Spanish music where the piano, long an established part of the song tradition in the rest of Europe, is permitted to enter into an important role in its own right. With Granados, the guitar, the natural accompanying instrument of the Spanish people, is supplanted by the piano which becomes the unashamed partner of the voice. Not only was he a remarkable pianist, but from the vantage point of his own irreproachable Spanish nationalism, Granados drew on a synthesis of musical influences outside Spain, including the piano music (and song accompaniments) of such composers as Schumann. With his very different younger contemporary Manuel de Falla, who from time to time also used the piano in an elaborate, if rather more French-inspired fashion, Granados helped provide Spain with its own answer to Lieder and mélodies, a new tradition underpinned by the instrument common to the songs of France and Germany, yet with a vocal line founded firmly on Spanish vocal traditions.

The facts of Granados's life are as simple as his end was tragic. He was a Catalan, born in Lérida on 29 July 1867. After studies in Barcelona (with Pedrell among others), illness prevented him from going to Paris to study. When he eventually got there, he was too old for entry into the Conservatoire. This was possibly an advantage in that the influence of France is less felt in Granados than many Spanish composers. He taught the piano with distinction in Barcelona, wrote a successful zarzuela and numerous piano pieces, but it was 1914 before he achieved international recognition in Paris with a performance of his masterpiece, the piano suite *Goyescas*. He was encouraged to expand this work into an opera which was successfully performed in New York in 1916 ('La maja y el ruiseñor', the best known aria from this work and sometimes found in concerts, is to be found at the end of this chapter). An invitation to perform for President Wilson delayed the composer's departure for home with fatal results. He sailed in HMS *Sussex* which was torpedoed in the English Channel on 24 March 1916. The composer was picked up by a lifeboat, but died in a futile attempt to rescue his wife whom he saw struggling in the sea.

Granados said, 'I am not a musician but an artist.' He was in fact an excellent painter and was obsessed with the work of Francisco Goya, several of whose works he owned. If Andalusia was the chief inspiration of Albéniz, Granados found himself powerfully (though not exclusively) drawn to the eighteenth-century Madrid of Goya and Ramón de la Cruz – the epoch of the great tonadillas. In the wake of his Paris success with his piano pieces, the *Colección de tonadillas*, settings of the Valencian journalist Fernando Periquet, were premièred in that same city in 1916. Three of the twelve songs (Nos 1, 2 and 6) were dedicated to the celebrated Catalan soprano Maria Barrientos. Of the twelve songs, only one, 'El majo olvidado', is written in the bass clef, and suitable for male singer. This was dedicated to the Spanish-American baritone Emilio de Gogorza. The International Music Edition of these songs fails to print the long piano introduction to 'La Maja de Goya'; in fact this is meant to be background music for the singer to recite the story of Goya's mistress, the Duchess of Alba – a long poem outlining the painter's prowess in getting the better of the cuckolded Duke. The UME edition of the single song (UMV 32540) and the complete collection (UMV 21082) print this music with short cues for the speaker, but here we give the full text of this rarely encountered hybrid piece of spoken–sung theatre. It is of course perfectly permissible to sing the song without the recitation, but Victoria de los Angeles always insisted on my playing the long introduction nevertheless. For obvious practical reasons, it is extremely unusual to hear in the concert hall the optional cor anglais obbligato of the first of the three 'Maja dolorosa' songs. 'Las currutacas modestas' is strictly speaking written as a duet, but Madame de los Angeles has often performed it as a solo, singing the top line and allowing the piano to fill in the missing harmonies.

The *Canciones amatorias* (UMV 19807) were performed in public before the *Colección de tonadillas*. They were given their first performance in 1913, as part of the debut recital, in Barcelona, of the eminent Catalan soprano Conchita (Concepcio) Badía. Two of the songs are dedicated to her. Like the *Tonadillas*, they look back to a Spain of the past, in this case a much earlier Spain than that of eighteenth-century Madrid. The poems are modern yet somehow reminiscent of the vihuela songs and pastorellas of the sixteenth century. Even the piano style of Granados loses the confident swagger of low-life Madrid, and returns to a somewhat more folksong-inspired idiom, although there is controversy that Granados's manuscripts of these songs differ considerably from the so-called revised version by Rafael Ferrer. Of all the modern Spanish composers, it is perhaps Granados who would benefit most from a scrupulous new edition of his works. The first of the two so-called *Canciones españolas* (UMV 21676) continues the Madrid theme – the Retiro is a famous park in that city and a place for flaunting and flirting. The 'aching in the head' experienced by the poor husband is the emerging horns of cuckoldry. The second of these posthumous songs (UMV 20991) is sung by a beautiful serrana – a gypsy girl from the mountains, and transports us to the Andalusia where the Granados songs never otherwise venture.

Because of his celebrated affection for old Madrid, it is all too easy to forget that our composer was first and foremost Enric Granados – a Catalan: the two final songs in this chapter have Catalan texts. They are the best evidence we have of Granados's participation in modernisme (an Iberian equivalent of the art nouveau movement where dream, sensual imagery and nostalgia, as well as a feeling for urban life, are grist to the mill of the creative artist) which was prevalent in Catalonia at the turn of the century, and which embraced many facets of art. Barcelona owes its unique architectural appearance to buildings by modernista architects such as Gaudí, Domènech y Muntaner and others.

Colección de tonadillas / *Collection of tonadillas*

FERNANDO PERIQUET

1. *Amor y odio* / *Love and hate*

Pensé que yo sabría	I thought I would know
ocultar la pena mía	how to hide my sorrow –
que por estar en lo profundo	since it was so deep in my heart
no alcanzara a ver el mundo:	no one would ever see
este amor callado	this secret love of mine
que un majo[1] malvado	which a wicked majo
en mi alma encendió.	kindled in my soul.
Y no fue así	But it was not so,
porque él vislumbró	for he perceived
el pesar oculto en mí.	the grief hid within me.
Pero fue en vano	But it was in vain
que vislumbrara	he perceived it,
pues el villano	for the villain
no mostrose ajeno	was not averse
de que le amara.	to my loving him.
Y esta es la pena	And this is the sorrow
que sufro ahora:	I suffer now:
sentir mi alma llena de amor	my heart brims with love

por quien me olvida,
sin que una luz alentadora
surja en las sombras de mi vida.

for a man who forgets me,
and there is no ray of hope
to brighten the gloom of my life.

[1]*Majo*. The word, and its feminine form maja, was used to describe the working-class population of Madrid in such areas as Lavapiés at the end of the eighteenth century. At the other end of the social scale from Señor, a majo is usually stereotyped as boisterous, ostentatious, physically attractive and a little arrogant.

2. *Callejeo* / *I have paced the streets*

Dos horas ha que callejeo,
pero no veo,
nerviosa ya, sin calma,
al que le di confiada el
    alma.

For two hours I have paced the streets,
but I cannot see,
anxious and agitated,
the man to whom I trustingly gave my
    soul.

No vi hombre jamás
que mintiera más
que el majo que hoy me engaña;
mas no le ha de valer,
pues siempre fui mujer de maña.
Y si es menester,
correré sin parar tras él, entera
    España.

I never met a man
more full of lies
than the majo who now deceives me;
but it won't help him,
for I was always a cunning woman.
And if need be
I'll pursue him the length and breadth of
    Spain.

3. *El majo discreto* / *The discreet majo*

Dicen que mi majo es feo.
Es posible que sí que lo sea,
que amor es deseo
que ciega y marea.
Ha tiempo que sé
que quien ama no ve.

My majo, they say, is ugly.
And maybe it is so,
for love is an urge
that blinds and bewilders.
I have long since known
that lovers are blind.

Mas si no es mi majo un hombre
que por lindo descuelle y asombre,
en cambio es discreto
y guarda un secreto
que yo posé en él
sabiendo que es fiel.

But though my majo is not a man
who excels or dazzles with good looks,
he is discreet
and keeps the secret
I confided to him,
since I knew he was faithful.

¿Cuál es el secreto
que el majo guardó?
Sería indiscreto
contarlo yo.
No poco trabajo costara saber
secretos de un majo con una
    mujer.
Nació en Lavapiés[1]. ¡Eh, ¡eh! ¡Es
un majo, un majo es!

What is the secret
my majo kept?
It would be indiscreet
Of me to tell.
No little effort is required to discover
the secrets between a majo and a
    woman.
He was born in Lavapiés. Oh yes!
He's a majo, a real majo!

[1]*Lavapiés*. A district in the East End of Madrid.

4. *El majo olvidado* / *The forgotten majo*

Cuando recuerdes los días pasados
piensa en mí, en mí.
Cuando de flores se llene tu
    reja[1]
piensa en mí, piensa en mí.
¡Ah!

Cuando en las noches serenas
cante el ruiseñor
piensa en el majo olvidado
que muere de amor.

¡Pobre del majo olvidado!
¡Qué duro sufrir!
Pues que la ingrata le dejó,
no quiere vivir.
¡Ah!

Were you to recall bygone days,
think of me, of me:
were your window to be filled with
    flowers,
think of me, think of me.
Ah!

Were on still nights
the nightingale to sing,
think of the forgotten majo
dying of love.

Poor forgotten majo!
How intense his suffering!
Since the ungrateful girl left him,
he does not wish to live.
Ah!

[1]*Reja*. A window, adorned and protected by a grille. Courtship traditionally took place at such windows, as we see in 'El majo tímido', where the woman is seated behind the grille.

5. *El majo tímido* / *The timid majo*

Llega a mi reja y me mira
por la noche un majo
que, en cuanto me ve y suspira,
se va calle abajo.
¡Ay qué tío más tardío!
¡Si así se pasa la vida,
estoy divertida!

Si hoy también pasa y me mira
y no se entusiasma
pues le suelto este saludo:
¡Adiós Don Fantasma!
¡Ay qué tío más tardío!
¡Odian las enamoradas
las rejas calladas!

At night there comes to my window
a majo to gaze on me;
the moment he sees me and sighs,
he sets off down the street.
Lord, what a dithering fellow!
If he spends life like this,
I've had my fun!

If today he comes again and looks at me
and doesn't warm up,
then I'll greet him with:
Hello, Don Fantasma!
Lord, what a dithering fellow!
Girls in love detest
a silent window!

6. *El mirar de la maja* / *The maja's gaze*

¿Por qué es en mis ojos
tan hondo el mirar
que a fin de cortar
desdenes y enojos
los suelo entornar?
¿Qué fuego dentro llevarán
que si acaso con calor

Why do my eyes
have so deep a gaze,
that to suppress
scorn and anger
I must lower my lids?
Such fire dwells within,
that if I chance to gaze

los clavo en mi amor
sonrojo me dan?
Por eso el chispero[1]
a quien mi alma dí
al verse ante mí
me tira el sombrero
y díceme así:
'Mi Maja, no me mires más,
que tus ojos rayos son
y ardiendo en pasión
la muerte me dan.'

passionately at my love,
they make me blush.
And so the chispero
to whom I gave my soul,
when meeting me
pulls down his sombrero
and says:
'My maja! Look on me no more,
for your eyes flash like lightning
and, burning with passion,
destroy me.'

[1]*Chispero*. A Madrilenian ruffian.

7. *El tra la la y el punteado / Tra la la and the plucked guitar*

Es en balde, majo mío,
que sigas hablando,
porque hay cosas que contesto
yo siempre cantando.
Tra la la . . .
Por más que preguntes tanto,
tra la la . . .
en mí no causas quebranto
ni yo he de salir de mi canto,
tra la la . . .

It is pointless, my majo,
to go on talking,
for some things I answer
only in song.
Tra la la . . .
However much you question,
tra la la . . .
you'll not interrupt me
nor shall I cease my song,
tra la la . . .

8. *La maja de Goya / Goya's maja*

Recitado

To be spoken

De Goya sabréis sin duda,
Que fué un pintor sin igual;
Pero no que fué un gallardo
Y desenvuelto galán.

You will know, of course, that Goya
was a painter without compare,
but not that he was a bold
and brazen gallant.

Por su estudio desfilaron,
Desde la manola audaz
Hasta la dama tapada,
A quien Goya hizo inmortal.

They all passed through his studio,
from the audacious Madrid girl
to the veiled lady
whom Goya made immortal.

Era ingenioso, y valiente
Hasta la temeridad . . .
Mezcla de señor y majo
De torero y militar . . .

He was witty and valiant
to the point of temerity . . .
A mixture of noble and majo,
bullfighter and soldier . . .

En fin, era Goya, y Goyas
Hizo Dios uno y no más.
Caballero cual nadie
Amador tierno y audaz . . .

In short, he was Goya, and of Goyas
God made only one:
a gentleman like none other,
a tender and audacious lover . . .

Y lo que ocurrió á aquel hombre
Ahora mismo a escuchar vais;

And what happened to that man
you are even now about to hear;

Que los hombres de estos tiempos
Oigan, comparen y ¡en paz!

*   *   *   *

A una dama, gran señora
Y muy famosa beldad,
Allá, junto al Manzanares[1],
Enseñóla Goya á amar.

Cierta mañana de Julio
De limpidez estival
Goya y la dama del cuento
Dialogaban á la par.

El, que en todo era un artista,
Mirábala con afán,
En ese traje sin traje
Único que Dios nos da.

Rompen de pronto el silencio
Tres golpes que fuera dan
Y una voz que dice firme:
Abrid á quien no esperáis.

Y antes de que la sorpresa
Permitiera razonar
Cedió al empuje la puerta
Y un hombre asomó la faz.

Sólo pudo la cabeza
La hermosa dama tapar:
El resto de sus encantos
Quedaron en libertad.

Goya interpuso su cuerpo
Entre ella y su gavilán,
Que era el marido celoso,
Como ya se supondrá.

– ¿Que queréis? – pregunta Goya –
   – La hembra que me arrebatáis.
– ¿Es vuestra? el pintor replica.
   – La ley me la dió por tal.

– Si es vuestra – le arguye Goya,
Bien hacéis si la buscáis;
Mas ved que la hembra que escucha
No ha sido vuestra jamás . . .

   – Lo veré – dice el celoso;
– No el rostro – dice el galán –
Que si es vuestra, en viendo el cuerpo
Sabréis si es la que buscáis.

may the men of those times
lend ear and, in peace, compare!

*   *   *   *

A woman, a grand lady
and most celebrated beauty,
down by the Manzanares
was taught by Goya to love.

On one clear summer
morning in July,
Goya and the lady of this tale
were together talking.

He – ever an artist –
was gazing on her with desire,
as she wore her suit, her birthday suit,
the only one God gives us.

Suddenly the silence was broken
by three knocks from outside
and a voice firmly saying:
open for one you were not expecting.

And before surprise
allowed him to reason,
the door was pushed open
and a man showed his face.

Only her head
could the fair lady cover,
the rest of her charms
remained at large.

Goya placed his body
between her and her hawk –
who was the jealous husband,
as might have been supposed.

'What do you want?' asks Goya.
   'The woman you've snatched from me.'
'Is she yours?' the painter replies.
   'The law gave her to me as such.'

'If she is yours', argues Goya,
'You do well to seek her;
but look – the woman who is listening
has never once been yours . . .'

   'I shall see', says the jealous man;
'Not the face', replies the gallant,
'for if she's yours, by seeing the body
you'll know if it's the one you seek.'

Y así fué; que el gran celoso Dió una vuelta y otra más En torno de aquel desnudo De belleza excepcional.	And thus it was; the big jealous man walked round her once and once again, around that nude of exceptional beauty!
Hasta que no hallando nada Que le hiciese sospechar, Saludó, y al salir dijo: – Me equivoqué; perdonad.	Till finding nothing to arouse his suspicion, he bowed and said as he was departing: 'I was mistaken, I beg your pardon.'
Y así se salvó la dama De aquel marido tenaz Que nunca supo cual Goya De la belleza gozar.	And thus the lady was saved from that tenacious husband who, unlike Goya, did not know how to savour beauty.
Porque hay maridos que tienen Cerca de sí una beldad, Y no saben detallarla Si por ella preguntáis.	For husbands there are with a beautiful woman, whose details they cannot enumerate, if ever they are asked.
Eso hizo Goya, aquel Goya Majo, artista y militar, Que á los hombres dominaba Y á las hembras mucho más.	This is what Goya did, Goya the artist, the majo, the soldier, who was wont to dominate men – and women so much more.

Cantado	*To be sung*
¡Yo no olvidaré en mi vida la imagen de Goya gallarda y querida! No hay hembra ni maja o señora que no le recuerde con envidia ahora! Si yo hallara quien me amara como el amó no anhelara ni buscara más venturas ni dichas yo.	As long as I live I shall not forget the gallant and beloved image of Goya! There's no woman – maja or lady – who does not think of him fondly today! If I could find someone to love me as he loved, I'd neither covet nor crave greater fortune or happiness.

¹*Manzanares*. The river which runs through Madrid.

9. *La maja dolorosa 1* / *The grieving maja No. 1*

¡Oh muerte cruel! ¿Por qué tú, a traición, mi majo arrebataste a mi pasión? ¡No quiero vivir sin él, porque es morir, porque es morir así vivir!	O cruel death! Why didst thou treacherously snatch away my majo from my desire? Without him I have no wish to live, for it is death, it is death to live thus!
No es posible ya sentir más dolor: en lágrimas deshecha ya mi alma está.	It is not possible to feel greater pain: my heart is dissolved in tears.

¡Oh Dios, torna mi amor,
porque es morir, porque es morir
así vivir!

Oh God! Restore to me my love,
for it is death, it is death
to live thus!

10. *La maja dolorosa 2* / *The grieving maja No. 2*

¡Ay majo de mi vida,
no, no, tú no has muerto!
¿Acaso yo existiese
si fuera eso cierto?
¡Quiero, loca,
besar tu boca!
Quiero, segura,
gozar más de tu ventura.
¡Ay! de tu ventura!

Ah, majo of my life,
no, no, you have not died!
How could I go on living
if this were true?
Demented, I desire
to kiss your mouth!
I want, reassured,
to relish your fortune more,
ah, your fortune!

Mas, ¡ay!, deliro, sueño:
mi majo no existe.
En torno mío el mundo
lloroso está y triste.
¡A mi duelo no hallo consuelo!
Mas muerto y frío
siempre el majo será mío
¡Ay! Siempre mío!

But alas! I rant and dream
my majo lives no more.
The world all around me
is weeping and sad.
For my grief I find no solace!
But though dead and cold
my majo will ever be mine,
ah, ever be mine!

11. *La maja dolorosa 3* / *The grieving maja No. 3*

De aquel majo amante
que fue mi gloria
guardo anhelante
dichosa memoria.
El me adoraba
vehemente y fiel.
Yo mi vida entera
di a él.
Y otras mil diera
si él quisiera,
que en hondos amores
martirios son flores.
Y al recordar mi majo amado
van resurgiendo ensueños
de un tiempo pasado.

That loving majo
who was my glory
I remember with
breathless happiness.
He adored me
ardently and loyally.
My whole life
I gave to him.
And a thousand more I'd have given,
if he had so wished:
for when love is deep,
torments are sweet.
And when I remember my beloved majo,
dreams of former days
come flooding back.

Ni en el Mentidero[1]
ni en la Florida[2]
majo más majo
paseó en la vida.
Bajo el chambergo
sus ojos vi
con toda el alma
puestos en mí.

Neither in Mentidero
nor La Florida
did a finer majo
ever walk forth.
Beneath his sombrero
I saw his eyes
fixed on me
with all his soul;

Que a quien miraban
enamoraban,
pues no hallé en el mundo
mirar más profundo.

whoever they gazed on
was filled with love for him.
I have nowhere in the world
seen so profound a gaze.

Y al recordar mi majo amado
van resurgiendo ensueños
de un tiempo pasado.

And when I remember my beloved majo,
dreams of former days
come flooding back.

> ¹*Mentidero*. A small eighteenth-century square in Madrid – now the entrance to
> the Calle del León.
> ²*Florida*. The district around the church of Antonio de la Florida in Madrid,
> where Goya painted in the cupola his frescos of the Miracle of Saint Anthony.

12. *Las currutacas modestas* / *The modest belles*

Decid qué damiselas se ven por ahí
que luzcan así.
Al vernos a las dos no hay quien no diga:
Dios que os bendiga.

Tell me what local girls there are to see
as elegant as we.
Seeing the two of us, all call out
'God bless you!'

Porque hace falta ver
el invencible poder
de que goza una mujer
cerca nacida de la Moncloa¹
o la Florida.

For you should see
the invincible power
which women have
when they're born near Moncloa
or La Florida.

Pues diga usté
si en tierra alguna
vióse otro pie
tan requechiquitito,
¡Olé!
Y pues nuestra abuela²
murióse tiempo ha
toda modestia sobra ya
¡Ja ja!

Just you tell me
if in another land
you have seen another foot
as dainty as this one,
olé!
And since our granny
died some time ago,
what's the point of modesty?
Ha! Ha!

> ¹*Moncloa*. The district in Madrid around the square of La Moncloa.
> ²*Abuela*. Grandmother. 'No tiene abuela' is a popular euphemism for a braggart.
> While alive, the grandmother would give praise, but after her death the individual
> must praise himself.

Canciones amatorias / *Songs of love*

1. *Descúbrase el pensamiento* / *Let me unveil the thought*

Descúbrase el pensamiento
de mi secreto cuidado,
pues descubrir mis dolores,
mi vivir apasionado;
no es de agora mi pasión,

Let me unveil the thought
of my secret love,
and reveal my anguish,
my life of suffering;
my passion is not new,

días ha que soy penado.
Una señora a quien sirvo
mi servir tiene olvidado.

Su beldad me hizo suyo,
el su gesto tan pulido
en mi alma está esmaltado.
¡Ah! ¡Ay de mí!
Que la miré, que la miré
para vivir lastimado,
para llorar y plañir
glorias del tiempo pasado.
¡Ah! Mi servir tiene olvidado.

already I've suffered endlessly.
I am servant to a lady
who has forgotten my servitude.

Her beauty enthralled me,
and her shining face
is set in my soul.
Ah! Woe is me
who gazed on her
only to live in grief,
to weep and lament
glories of times gone by.
Ah! She has forgotten my servitude.

2. *Mañanica era* / *Daybreak*

Mañanica era, mañana
de San Juan' se decía al fin,
cuando aquella diosa Venus
dentro de un fresco jardín
tomando estaba la fresca
a la sombra de un jazmín;
cabellos en su cabeza,
parecía un serafín.
Sus mejillas y sus labios
como color de rubí
y el objeto de su cara
figuraba un querubín;
allí de flores floridas
hacía un rico cojín,
de rosas una guirnalda
para el que venía a morir,
¡ah!, lentamente por amores
sin a nadie descubrir.

Daybreak – the morn
of Saint John dawned at last,
when that goddess Venus
in a cool garden
was taking the air
beneath jasmine shade;
with her tresses
she resembled a seraph.
Her cheeks and lips
were the colour of ruby,
and her expression
that of a cherub.
From blossoming flowers
she fashioned a rich cushion,
a garland of roses
for one who came to die
a slow death for a love, alas,
he would reveal to none.

'St John's day is 24 June, Midsummer day.

3. *Llorad, corazón* / *Weep, heart*

LUIS DE GÓNGORA

Lloraba la niña
(y tenía razón)
la prolija ausencia
de su ingrato amor.
Dejóla tan niña,
que apenas creo yo
que tenía los años
que ha que la dejó.
Llorando la ausencia
del galán traidor,
la halla la Luna

The girl was lamenting
(and with reason)
the prolonged absence
of her ungrateful lover.
He left her so young,
that I believe she was scarcely
as old as the years
since he left her.
Lamenting the absence
of her faithless lover,
she is found by the moon

y la deja el Sol,	and left by the sun,
añadiendo siempre	ever heaping
pasión a pasión,	suffering on suffering,
memoria a memoria,	memory on memory,
dolor a dolor.	anguish on anguish.
Llorad, corazón,	*Weep, heart,*
que tenéis razón.	*for you have reason.*

4. *Mira que soy niña* / *Look, I am but a child*

Mira que soy niña. ¡Amor, déjame!	Look, I am but a child. Love, let me be!
¡Ay, ay, ay, que me moriré!	Ah, for I shall die!
Paso amor, no seas a mi gusto extraño,	Gently, love, thwart not my desire,
no quieras mi daño.	do not wish me harm.
Pues mi bien deseas,	Since you wish me well,
basta que me veas	suffice it to see me
sin llegárteme.	without drawing near.
¡Ay, ay, ay, que me moriré!	Ah, for I shall die!
No seas agora por ser atrevido,	Do not now be forward for the sake of it.
¡ay! Sé agradecido	Ah! Be grateful
con la que te adora,	to the one who adores you,
que así se desdora	lest you tarnish
mi amor y tu fe.	my love and your faith.
¡Ay, ay, ay que me moriré!	Ah, for I shall die!

5. *No lloréis, ojuelos* / *Don't cry, little eyes*

No lloréis, ojuelos,	Don't cry, little eyes,
porque no es razón	for it is not right
que llore de celos	to cry with jealousy
quien mata de amor.	if you kill with love.
Quien puede matar	She who can kill
no intente morir,	should not seek to die,
si hace con reir	if she can do more with laughter
más que con llorar.	than with tears.
No lloréis, ojuelos,	Don't cry, little eyes,
porque no es razón	for it is not right
que llore de celos	to cry with jealousy
quien mata de amor.	if you kill with love.

6. *Iban al pinar* / *Going to the pine grove*

LUIS DE GÓNGORA

Serranas[1] de Cuenca[2]	Mountain girls of Cuenca
iban al pinar,	were going to the pine grove,
unas por piñones,	*some for pine nuts,*
otras por bailar.	*others to dance.*

Bailando y partiendo	The fair highland girls
las serranas bellas,	dance, dividing
un piñon con otro,	one nut with another,
si ya no es con perlas,	if not with pearls,
de Amor las saetas	merrily deflecting
huelgan de trocar,	the arrows of Cupid,
unas por piñones,	*some for pine nuts,*
otras por bailar.	*others to dance.*

Entre rama y rama	Between the branches,
cuando el ciego dios	when the blind god
pide al Sol los ojos	begs the sun for eyes
por verlas mejor,	to see them better,
los ojos del Sol	you will see them treading
las veréis pisar,	on the eyes of the sun,
unas por piñones,	*some for pine nuts,*
otras por bailar.	*others to dance.*

¹*Serrana*. A woman from the 'sierra' or mountain range.
²*Cuenca*. The medieval town is situated romantically on the rocky spur of
S. Cristóbal and cut off from the Serranía de Cuenca by the deep defiles of the
Júcar and the Huecar – both rivers are overhung by the old walls and towers of the
town.

7. *Gracia mía / My graceful one*

Gracia mía, juro a Dios	My graceful one, I swear to God,
que sois tan bella criatura	you are so fair a creature,
que a perderse la hermosura	that were beauty to be lost
se tiene de hallar en vos.	it would be found in you.

Fuera bien aventurada	My life would be blessed
en perderse en vos mi vida,	to be lost in you,
porque viniera perdida	for it would be lost
para salir más ganada.	to emerge enriched.

¡Ah! Seréis hermosuras dos	Ah, you would be two beauties
en una sola figura,	within one form,
que a perderse la hermosura	for were beauty to be lost,
se tiene de hallar en vos.	it would be found in you!

En vuestros verdes ojuelos	In your little green eyes
nos mostráis vuestro valor	you show us your worth,
que son causa del amor	for they inspire love;
y las pestañas son cielos,	and your eyelashes are heavens,
nacieron por bien de nos.	created for our delight.

Si al Retiro me llevas / If you take me to the Retiro

Si al Retiro me llevas	If you take me to the Retiro
entre tanto galán,	amid so many gallants,
por la noche no digas	do not at nightfall say

que te sientes muy mal.
Que el marido que enseña
la que debe guardar,
no es extraño que diga
que le duele el frontal.

that you are feeling ill.
For a husband who parades
her whom he should guard,
may quite easily complain
of an ache in the head.

Canto gitano / Gypsy song

¡Ay madrecita de mis entrañas,
me han robao a mi gitana!
Me pongo triste, madre del alma
porque pierdo mi serrana.

Oh dear mother of my heart,
they've stolen my gypsy lass.
Mother of my soul, I'm sad,
for I've lost my mountain lass.

Serranica de mi vida,
a tí no te duele el alma.
¡Ay madrecita de mis entrañas,
me han robao a mi gitana!

Dear mountain lass of my life,
your soul knows no distress.
Oh dear mother of my heart,
they've stolen my gypsy lass.

¡Ay madrecita de mis entrañas,
yo no sé lo que me pasa!
Sin mi chiquilla me vuelvo loco,
y el corazón se me abrasa.

Oh dear mother of my heart,
I don't know what's befallen me!
Without my girl I'm going mad,
and my heart is on fire.

Serranica de mi vida,
el tuyo no siente nada.
¡Ay madrecita de mis entrañas,
me han robao a mi gitana!

Mountain lass of my heart,
your heart is feeling nothing.
Oh dear mother of my heart,
they've stolen my gypsy lass.

Elegia eterna / Eternal elegy

APEL.LES MESTRES

El papalló no li ha dit mai:
no gosa revelar-li son mal;
però glateix d'amor per una rosa
que idolatra a la brisa matinal.

The butterfly never told her —
he dares not reveal his pain;
but quivers with love for a rose
who adores the morning breeze.

La brisa matinal enamorada
per la boira es desviu
i la boira perduda i afollada,
decandint-se d'amor, adora el riu,
adora el riu.

The morning breeze, in love
with the mist, suffers too,
and the mist, lost and crazed,
languishes with love,
adoring the river.

Mes, ai!, el riu enjogassat fugia,
enjogassat, de penyal en penyal.
La boira enamorada el riu seguia,
i a la boira la brisa matinal.

But oh!, the playful river ran
from rock to rock.
The lovelorn mist pursued the river
and the morning breeze pursued the mist.

En tant, vegent-se abandonada i
    sola,
s'ha desfullat la flor,
i al damunt d'aquell tronc sense corol·la
s'atura el papalló, clou l'ala, i mor.

Meanwhile, seeing herself abandoned and
    alone,
the flower shed her petals;
alighting on that stem without corolla,
the butterfly folds his wings and dies.

L'ocell profeta / *The prophet bird*

ISABEL MARÍA DEL CARME CASTELLVÍ I GORDON

Canta, aucell aimat!
Canta, aucell profeta!
L'aire és suavitat
i la nit discreta.
Ah! Joia de mon cor,
ta cançó és la vida.
Canta la veu d'or.
Canta, canta ma cançó exquisida.

Ah, gentil aucell,
mestre en poesia.
Diu l'amor novell
quan s'escola el dia:
Ah! Vola per ma nit
fosca d'enyorança.
Deixa al fons del pit,
deixa, deixa, somnis d'esperança.

De l'amor ardit
ma tardor s'omplena;
l'hora d'infinit
nova llum ofrena.
Ah! Porta per l'espai
l'amorosa troba.
Canta, ardent i gai,
canta, canta una aubada nova.

Sing, beloved bird!
Sing, prophet bird!
The air is soft
and the night discreet.
Ah! Joy of my heart,
your song is my life.
Let your golden voice sing.
Let it sing, sing my exquisite song.

Ah, gentle bird,
master in poetry.
New love says
when the day fades:
ah! Fly through my night
dark with longing.
Leave in the depth of my heart,
leave, leave those dreams of hope.

With brave love
my autumn is filling;
the infinite hour
offers new light.
Ah! Bear through space
the poem of love.
Sing, ardent and joyful,
sing, sing a new dawn.

La maja y el ruiseñor / *The maja and the nightingale*

FERNANDO PERIQUET

¿Por qué entre sombras el ruiseñor
entona su armonioso cantar?
¿Acaso al rey del día
guarda rencor
y de él quiere
algún agravio vengar?
Guarda quizás en su pecho
oculto tal dolor
que en la sombra
espera alivio hallar,
triste entonando cantos de amor.
¡Ay!
¿Y tal vez alguna flor,
temblorosa del pudor de amar,
es la esclava enamorada
de su cantar?
¡Misterio es el cantar

Why in the dusk does the nightingale
strike up his harmonious song?
Perhaps against the king of day
he holds some grievance
and seeks
to avenge some wrong?
Perhaps in his breast
he conceals such sorrow,
that in the shadows
he hopes to find some relief,
sadly singing songs of love.
Ah!
And perhaps there is some flower,
trembling with the shame of love,
who is enthralled
by his singing?
It is a mystery, this song,

que entona envuelto
en sombra el ruiseñor!
¡Ah!
Son los amores como flor
a merced de la mar.
¡Amor! ¡Amor!
¡Ah! No hay cantar,
sin amor.
¡Ah! ¡Ruiseñor, es tu cantar
himno de amor,
oh, ruiseñor!

which wreathed in shadow
the nightingale sings!
Ah!
Love is like a flower
at the mercy of the sea.
Love! Love!
Ah! There is no song
without love.
Ah! Nightingale, your song
is a hymn to love,
o nightingale!

VI

AMADEO VIVES
(1871–1932)

Younger than Albéniz and Granados, and older than Falla, Vives with his celebrated zarzuelas and impeccable feel for authentic Spanish atmosphere was, in some ways, a throw-back to the composers of the tonadilla in its golden age – his stage music had a similar popularity which, like the best of eighteenth-century theatre composers, was founded on real creative talent and taste. Vives was also a playwright, known for his literary discernment; his main collection of songs is the *Canciones epigramáticas* (1915), UMV 3457, thirteen settings of mainly sixteenth- and seventeenth-century poets including choice items by Góngora, Trillo y Figueroa and Cervantes. Like the Granados *Colección de tonadillas*, written at about the same time, the graceful and tuneful vocal lines of the Vives songs recall the world of the tonadilla, but unlike his eighteenth-century forebears, and unlike Granados who considerably slimmed down his solo piano style for his accompaniments, Vives wrote highly demanding piano parts (particularly for something like the extended Cervantes setting 'La buenaventura') which anticipate the pianistic floridity of Joaquín Nin.

Vives was a Catalan (born near Barcelona on 18 November 1871) and like all his significant contemporaries was a pupil of Pedrell. At the age of twenty he was co-founder of the Orfeo Català, a famous choral society which not only concerned itself with new music and ancient polyphony, but which revived the performance of the Catalan folk music which found its way into Vives's first opera *Artus*. On moving to Madrid, Vives became one of the most famous zarzuela composers of his day, modernising the form by adding elements of French light opera to the time-honoured style. He also wrote more serious operas (of which *Maruxa* was the most popular) but he will perhaps be most remembered for his zarzuela *Doña Francisquita*.

No vayas, Gil, al sotillo / Gil, don't go to the grove

LUIS DE GÓNGORA

No vayas, Gil, al Sotillo,
          que yo sé
quien novio al Sotillo fue,
que volvió después novillo.

Gil, si es que al Sotillo vas,
mucho en la jornada pierdes;
verás sus álamos verdes,
y alcornoque volverás;
allá en el Sotillo oirás
de algún ruiseñor las quejas,
yo en tu casa a las cornejas,
y ya tal vez al cuclillo.
No vayas, Gil, al Sotillo,
          que yo sé
quien novio al Sotillo fue,
que volvió después novillo.

Al Sotillo floreciente
no vayas, Gil, sin temores,
pues mientras miras sus flores,
te enraman toda la frente;
hasta el agua transparente
te dirá tu perdición,
viendo en ella tu armazón,
que es más que la de un castillo.

No vayas, Gil, al Sotillo,
          que yo sé
quien novio al Sotillo fue,
que volvió después novillo.

Mas si vas determinado,
y allá te piensas holgar,
procura no merendar
desto que llaman venado;
de aquel vino celebrado
de Toro no has de beber,
por no dar en que entender
al uno y otro corrillo.
No vayas, Gil, al Sotillo,
          que yo sé
quien novio al Sotillo fue,
que volvió después novillo.

Gil, don't go to the grove,
          for well I know
that every groom who was in the grove
later returned a cuckold.

Gil, if you go to the grove,
you'll lose much of the working day;
you'll see its green poplars
and return a blockhead;
there in the grove you'll hear
the plaint of some nightingale,
and I in your house shall hear the crows
and perchance the cuckoo too.
Gil, don't go to the grove,
          for well I know
that every groom who was in the grove
later returned a cuckold.

To the blossoming grove
don't go, Gil, without due care,
for while you gaze on the flowers,
they will enmesh your brow;
even the limpid water
will speak of your perdition,
when in it you see your frame,
larger than a castle.

Gil, don't go to the grove,
          for well I know
that every groom who was in the grove
later returned a cuckold.

But if you go determined,
resolved to dally there,
try not to dine
on what is known as venison;
and of that famous Toro
wine you must never partake,
so that no one
will gossip about you.
Gil, don't go to the grove,
          for well I know
that every groom who was in the grove
later returned a cuckold.

¡Válgame Dios, que los ánsares vuelan! / Bless my soul, the geese are flying!

FRANCISCO DE TRILLO Y FIGUEROA

Andando en el suelo	Walking on the land
vide un ánsar chico,	I saw a little goose,
y alzando su pico	and raising its beak
vino a mí de vuelo.	it came flying to me.
Dióme un gran consuelo	Great comfort it gave me
de verle alear.	to see it take wing.
El ansar gracioso	The graceful goose
comenzó a picarme,	started to peck me,
y aun a enamorarme	and even to woo me
su pico amoroso;	with his amorous beak;
mas como alevoso	but perfidiously
volvióme a dejar.	he turned and left me.
¡Válgame Dios, que los ánsares vuelan!	Bless my soul, the geese are flying!
¡Válgame Dios, que saben volar!	Bless my soul, how they can fly!
Era tan bonico	He was so pretty
que me dejó en calma,	that he left me calm,
dando gusto al alma	and my soul rejoiced
su agraciado pico,	at his graceful beak,
pues era, aunque chico	for though he was little
grande en el picar.	his peck was large.
Más quisiera yo	I'd sooner
nunca haberle visto,	never have seen him,
pues dulce le asisto	for I treated him gently
y cruel huyó:	and he cruelly fled:
sólo me dejó	he left me alone
que sentir y amar.	to suffer and love.
¡Válgame Dios, que los ánsares vuelan!	Bless my soul, the geese are flying!
¡Válgame Dios, que saben volar!	Bless my soul, how they can fly!

Vida del muchacho / A boy's life

LUIS DE GÓNGORA

Hermana Marica,	Sister Mary,
mañana que es fiesta,	tomorrow is fiesta,
no irás tú a la amiga	you won't go to your teacher
ni yo iré a la escuela.	and I won't go to school.
Pondráste el corpiño	You'll put on your bodice
y la saya buena,	and your best skirt,
cabezón labrado,	embroidered collar,
toca y albanega;	bonnet and hair-net;
y a mí me pondrán	and they'll dress me
mi camisa nueva,	in a new shirt,
sayo de palmilla,	and smock made of woollen cloth
media de estameña;	and stockings made of serge;

y si hace bueno
traeré la montera
que me dió, la pascua,
mi señora abuela,
y el estadal rojo
con lo que le cuelga,
que trajo el vecino
cuando fué a la feria.

Iremos a misa,
veremos la iglesia,
darános un cuarto[1]
mi tía la ollera.

Compraremos dél
(que nadie lo sepa)
chochos y garbanzos
para la merienda;

y en la tardecica,
en nuestra plazuela,
jugaré yo al toro
y tú a las muñecas

con las dos hermanas,
Juana y Madalena,
y las dos primillas,
Marica y la tuerta;

y si quiere madre
dar las castañetas,
podrás tanto dello
bailar en la puerta;

y al son del adufe
cantará Andrehuela:
No me aprovecharon,
madre, las hierbas.

Y yo de papel
haré una librea,
teñida con moras
por que bien parezca,

y una caperuza
con muchas almenas;
pondré por penacho
las dos plumas negras

del rabo del gallo
que acullá en la huerta
anaranjeamos
las carnestolendas;

y en la caña larga
pondré una bandera
con dos borlas blancas
en sus trenzaderas;

y en mi caballito
pondré una cabeza
de guadamecí,
dos hilos por riendas;

y entraré en la calle
haciendo corvetas

and if the weather's good,
I'll bring the cloth cap
your granny gave me
at Eastertide,
and the red ribbon
she wraps around it,
which the neighbour
brought back from the fair.

We'll go to mass,
we'll see the church,
my bird-like aunt
will give us a cuarto.

And with it we'll buy
(let nobody know)
sweetmeats and chick-peas
to eat at tea;

and at sundown
in our little square,
I'll play at bullfighting
and you with dolls

with your two sisters,
Juana and Madalena,
and your two little cousins,
Mary and the one-eyed girl;

and if mother wants
to give us castanets,
you can dance to them
in the doorway;

and to the sound of the tambourine
Andrehuela shall sing:
the potion, mother,
did me no good.

And I with paper
shall make a livery,
dyed with blackberries
to make it beautiful,

and a hood
with many a merlon,
and as a crest I'll set
two black feathers

from the rooster's tail
that yonder in the orchard
we made orange
at Carnival time;

and on the long pole,
I'll put a flag
with two white tassels
on its plaited cord;

and on my little white horse
I'll put a headdress
of embossed leather,
and two threads for reins;

and I'll enter the street
prancing and leaping,

yo, y otros del barrio,
que son más de treinta;
   jugaremos cañas
junto a la plazuela,
por que Barbolilla
salga acá y nos vea;
   Bárbola, la hija
de la panadera,
la que suele darme
tortas con manteca,
   porque algunas veces
hacemos yo y ella
las bellaquerías
detrás de la puerta.

with others from our district,
of which there are more than thirty;
   and we'll play at sticks
by the little square,
so that Barbolilla
comes out and sees us –
   Barbola, the baker's
daughter,
who gives me
butter cakes,
   because sometimes
she and I
get up to no good
behind the door.

   ¹*Cuarto*. A copper coin.

Madre, la mi madre / *Mother, ah my mother*

MIGUEL DE CERVANTES

(from *El celoso extremeño*)

Madre, la mi madre,
guardas me poneis;
que, si yo no me guardo,
mal me guardareis.

Mother, ah my mother,
you set your guards upon me,
but if I don't guard myself
you guard me all in vain.

Dicen que está escrito,
y con gran razón,
que la privación
engendra apetito;
crece en infinito
encerrado amor;
por eso es mejor
que no me encerreis:
Que si yo no me guardo,
mal me guardareis.

They say that it is written,
and rightly so, indeed,
that abstinence
feeds appetite;
imprisoned love
increases without end;
better then by far
not to imprison me;
for if I don't guard myself,
you guard me all in vain.

Si la voluntad
por si no se guarda,
jamás le harán guarda
miedo o calidad;
romperá, en verdad,
por la misma muerte,
hasta hallar la suerte
que vos no entendeis:
Que si yo no me guardo,
mal me guardareis.

If inclination
does not guard itself,
never shall fear or rank
be capable of guarding it;
it will break, in truth,
through death itself,
and find the fortune
you fail to understand:
for if I don't guard myself,
you guard me all in vain.

Quien tiene costumbre
de ser amorosa,
como mariposa
se irá tras la lumbre;

Whoever is wont
to be in love,
like a butterfly
will make for the flame –

y aunque más deslumbre
y guardas les pongan,
o aunque más propongan
de hacer lo que haceis:
Que si yo no me guardo,
mal me guardareis.

Y es de tal manera
la fuerza amorosa,
que a la más hermosa
la vuelve en quimera;
el pecho de cera,
de fuego la gana,
la mano de lana,
de ciervo los pies:
Que si yo no me guardo,
mal me guardareis.

however much it dazzle
and however much they guard,
however much they try to do
what you are doing to me:
if I don't guard myself,
you guard me all in vain.

Of such nature
is the power of love,
it turns the fairest
into a shadow of itself:
her breast turns to wax,
her desire to fire,
her hands to wool,
her feet to deer:
so if I don't guard myself,
you guard me all in vain.

El retrato de Isabela / Isabella's portrait

Oyeme tu retrato,
niña Isabela
  salvo ser justo,
  salvo ser propio,
  salvo que hiela.

Linda mata de pelo
peina tu mano,
  salvo ser poco,
  salvo ser corto,
  salvo ser cano.

Con la luz de tus ojos
a todos pierdes,
  salvo que lloran,
  salvo ser bizcos,
  salvo ser verdes.

Con tu boca preciosa
nada compite,
  salvo ser grande,
  salvo ser belfa,
  salvo que pide.

Es tu nariz florero
de fino aroma,
  salvo ser fea,
  salvo ser ancha,
  salvo ser roma.

Tus dientes son alhajas
de fino engarce,

Listen to your portrait,
sweet Isabella —
  but it's fair,
  but it's true,
  but it's numbing.

A fine head of hair
you comb,
  but it's thin,
  but it's short,
  but it's grey.

With the sparkle of your eyes
you captivate all,
  but they water,
  but they squint,
  but they're green.

With your lovely mouth
nothing can compare,
  but it's large,
  but it's thick-lipped,
  but it's demanding.

Your nose is a posy,
of fine scents,
  but it's ugly,
  but it's broad,
  but it's flat.

Your teeth are jewels,
finely chased,

salvo ser pocos,
salvo ser negros,
salvo ser grandes.

Tu cintura embellece
tu linda facha,
   salvo que dobla,
   salvo que tuerce,
   salvo que agacha.

Y el amor que te tengo
me desconsuela,
   porque eres falsa,
   como tu madre,
   como tu abuela.

Este es tu fiel retrato,
niña Isabela.

but they are few,
but they're black,
but they're long.

Your waist is embellished
by your pretty sash,
   but it's crooked,
   but it's twisted.
   but it's awry.

And the love I bear you
grieves me,
   since you are false,
   like your mother
   and your grandmother.

This portrait is true to life,
sweet Isabella.

La buenaventura / Fortune-telling

MIGUEL DE CERVANTES
(from La gitanilla)

– Hermosita, hermosita,
la de las manos de plata,
más te quiere tu marido
que el Rey de las Alpujarras.
   Eres paloma sin hiel;
pero a veces eres brava
como leona de Orán,
o como tigre de Ocaña.
   Pero en un tras, en un tris,
el enojo se te pasa,
y quedas como alfeñique,
o como cordera mansa.
   Riñes mucho y comes poco:
algo celosita andas;
que es juguetón el teniente,
y quiere arrimar la vara.
   Cuando doncella, te quiso
uno de una buena cara;
que mal hayan los terceros,
que los gustos desbaratan.
   Si a dicha tú fueras monja,
hoy tu convento mandaras,
porque tienes de abadesa
más de cuatrocientas rayas.
   No te lo quiero decir . . .;
pero poco importa; vaya,
enviudarás, y otra vez,
y otras dos, serás casada.
   No llores, señora mía;

Fairest lady, fairest lady,
with your hands of silver,
your husband loves you more deeply
than any King of Alpujarras.
   A dove without bitterness you are,
and yet at times you are as fierce
as a lioness of Oran,
or a tigress of Ocaña.
   But in a trice
your fury fades,
and you are then like almond paste
or like a gentle lamb.
   You quarrel much and hardly eat,
and are a little jealous;
your husband's frolicsome
and likes to wield his wand.
   Before you wed you were loved
by a handsome man –
a plague on go-betweens
who spoil pleasures.
   If perchance you had been a nun,
today you'd be in charge of a convent –
for the four hundred lines and more
on your hand make you an abbess.
   I'd sooner not tell you . . .
but never mind, have no fear,
you'll be a widow more than once,
and twice again you'll marry.
   Do not weep, my fair lady,

que no siempre las gitanas
decimos el Evangelio;
no llores, señora; acaba.
　Como te mueras primero
que el señor teniente, basta
para remediar el daño
de la viudez que amenaza.
　Has de heredar, y muy presto,
hacienda en mucha abundancia;
tendrás un hijo canónigo;
la iglesia no se señala.
　De Toledo no es posible.
Una hija rubia y blanca
tendrás, que si es religiosa,
también vendrá a ser perlada.
　Si tu esposo no se muere
dentro de cuatro semanas,
verásle corregidor
de Burgos o Salamanca.
　Un lunar tienes, ¡qué lindo!
¡Ay Jesús, qué luna clara!
¡Qué sol, que allá en los antípodas
oscuros valles aclara!
　Más de dos ciegos por verle
dieran más de cuatro blancas.
¡Agora sí es la risica!
¡Ay, que bien haya esa gracia!
　Guárdate de las caídas,
principalmente de espaldas;
que suelen ser peligrosas
en las principales damas.
　Cosas hay más que
　decirte;
si para el viernes me aguardas,
las oirás, que son de
　gusto,
y algunas hay de desgracias.

for gypsies do not always
bring good tidings;
do not weep, my lady, all shall be well.
　For if you die before
your husband, consolation
for the woe of widowhood
will surely come his way.
　An heiress you'll be, and very soon,
fortune in abundance shall be yours;
your son shall be a canon –
of which church it is not known.
　But not of Toledo, to be sure,
A daughter beautiful and fair
you'll have, and if she becomes a nun,
she too shall fill a prelate's chair.
　If your husband does not die
before a month has passed,
you shall see him mayor
of Burgos or Salamanca.
　You have a mole, oh what delight!
O Jesus! what a resplendent moon!
What a sun, that to the dark
antipodean vales brings light!
　Many a blind man would give
more than four farthings to see it.
Now you are laughing –
thank God for the joke!
　Beware of falls,
especially onto your back
for these are risky
for ladies of quality.
　More things there are that I could tell
　you;
if on Friday you attend me,
you shall hear them – some will tell of
　pleasure
and others of misfortune.

El amor y los ojos / *Love and eyes*

A la sala del crimen
Llevé tus ojos,
Porque son dos ladrones
Facinerosos.
Y cuando entraron,
Se ha quejado el regente
Que lo robaron.

Con los ojos del alma
Te estoy mirando;
Y con los de la cara
Disimulando.
Que este es el modo

To the criminal court
I took your eyes,
for they are two thieves,
atrocious ones.
And when they entered,
the magistrate complained
that they were robbing him.

With the eyes of the soul
I look at you,
and with those of my face
I hide my feelings.
For this is the way

De que nuestro cariño
Se oculte a todos.

¿Sabes qué es lo que quiero
Más que a mi vida?
Pues son tus ojos negros
Que me asesinan.
He de mirarte,
Y con tal que me mires,
Aunque me mates.

that our love
may be hidden from all.

Do you know what I want
more than my life?
I want your dark eyes
which slay me.
I must look at you
and I want you to look at me,
even if it kills me.

VII

MANUEL DE FALLA
(1876–1946)

It was Falla who brought Spanish music into the twentieth century – his knowledge and use of folksong, and his fidelity to the Spanish spirit make him the Bartók or Kodály of Spain. And yet his considerable achievements would not have been possible without the influence of France where he acquired his technique, and his music remained open to the influence of his greatest foreign contemporaries, Stravinsky in particular. After the romantic effusions of Granados, we hear a more acerbic side of the Spanish character – lean and wiry, like the composer himself, and capable of conquering self-indulgence with an iron will. Because his main medium was the orchestra, rather than the piano, the song enthusiast finds slim pickings, numerically speaking, in Falla's output. But the *Siete canciones populares* (published by Eschig and Chester in both high and the original medium keys) remain a touchstone of Spanish song; the synthesis they represent of original art and folklore has held the recital stage more successfully than any of the other folksong arrangements by an array of international composers of the period. Perhaps this is because these songs are not literal transcriptions of folksongs, but what Gilbert Chase calls 'a subtle artistic transmutation of their essential values'. The songs form an anthology of various regions: 'El paño moruno' and 'Seguidilla murciana' come from the region of Murcia, 'Asturiana' is from the north of Spain, and 'Jota' is from Aragon. 'Nana' has the hypnotic melismatic quality of the Moorish south. The Andalusian 'Polo' encapsulates Falla's understanding of the cante jondo, the 'song of depth' and the tragedy of life, half sung and half recited (the 'Ay' in this song is almost shouted at the end) which derives from flamenco traditions.

Falla was born in Cádiz on 23 November 1876 – he was thus an Andalusian though there was Catalan blood on his mother's side. It almost goes without saying that he studied with Felip Pedrell – the progress of Spanish music and the so-called national revival would seem to have been impossible without this great teacher whose own music is all but forgotten. The easiest way for most composers to get on in the Spain of the time was to write zarzuelas, just as in the Vienna of Schubert's time the successful composer of Singspiele was the name that mattered. Falla's ascetic temperament was absolutely unsuited to this kind of work; a brief and unsuccessful stint as a zarzuela composer was followed by a trip to Paris – an expedition which was planned for seven days but lasted seven years. In Paris Falla met his compatriot Albéniz, as well as Debussy, Dukas and Ravel, from whom he absorbed the idea of impressionism, a concept surprisingly adaptable to the depiction of Spanish life through the vivid colour of its folk music. The three songs to texts by Théophile Gautier were written at this time (1909 – published by the International Music Company No. 1350) and represent a uniquely authentic Spanish voice in the mélodie tradition which has always been awash with Spanish pastiche and characterisation. Falla returned to Spain in 1914. His predilection for the Andalusian style in the first part of his career was balanced by a re-discovery of Castilian tradition and neo-classicism in the 1920s (illustrated by the difference between the piano concerto *Noches en los jardines de España* of 1909–15, and the harpsichord concerto (1926) with its echoes of Scarlatti, and its quotation of 'De los álamos vengo, madre'). Relatively unproductive in his later life, Falla moved to Argentina in 1939 and died there in 1946. His last work, the mighty opera *Atlantida*, was never finished. The completion of this task was undertaken by Falla's student and friend Ernesto Halffter whose somewhat controversial definitive version was performed in 1976 after years of work. Halffter also orchestrated the *Siete canciones populares* (1938–45).

The five early songs of Falla, composed between 1899 and 1915, were gathered together in 1980 by the musicologist Enrique Franco in a volume he entitled *Obras desconocidas* (*Unknown Works*), UMV 22236. 'Oración de las madres que tienen a sus hijos en brazos', like Debussy's 'Noël des enfants qui n'ont plus de maisons' which was written in the same year, recoils with horror from the escalating onslaught of the First World War. With the exception of 'El pan de ronda' (an Andalusian song to an improvised poem about a loaf of bread enjoyed in the streets of the town of Ronda in Málaga, and part of a projected cycle that was never completed), the piano writing in these songs shows none of the independence and intricacy of the *Canciones populares* or the Gautier settings. 'Tus ojillos negros' is an early Andalusian song from 1902. For the sake of completeness in the songs of this important composer, we also print the poem 'Psyché', which was set for voice with flute, harp and string trio accompaniment in 1924. The 'Soneto a Córdoba', the last of Falla's solo songs, has a harp accompaniment which can also be played on the piano.

Obras desconocidas / Unknown works

Preludios / Preludes

ANTONIO DE TRUEBA

(?1900)

Madre, todas las noches junto a mis rejas
canta un joven llorando
   indiferencia:
'Quiéreme, niña, y al pie de los
altares séras bendita.'

Esta dulce tonada tal poder tiene
que me pone al oirla triste y alegre;
di por qué causa entristecen y
alegran estas tonadas.

'Hija, lo que las niñas como tú sienten
cuando junto a sus rejas a cantar vienen
es el preludio del poema más
grande que hay en el mundo.

Tornada en Santa Madre la Virgen
   pura,
tristezas y alegrías en ella turnan,
y este poema es, niña, el que ha
empezado junto a tus rejas.'

Mother, each night at my windows
a young man sings tearfully of my
   indifference:
'Love me, my sweet, and at the foot
of the altar you shall be blessed.'

This sweet melody has such power
that hearing it makes me sad and happy;
tell me why such melodies
cause sadness and happiness.

'Daughter, what girls like you feel
when someone sings at their windows
is but the prelude of the greatest poem
that exists in the world.

The pure Virgin became the Holy
   Mother,
sadness and happiness she felt in turn,
and this poem is, my child, the one
which began outside your windows.'

Olas gigantes / Vast waves

GUSTAVO ADOLFO BÉCQUER

(1899–1900)

Olas gigantes que os rompéis bramando
en las playas desiertas y remotas,
envuelto entre la sábana de espumas,
¡llevadme con vosotras!

Ráfagas de huracán que arrebatáis
del alto bosque las marchitas hojas,
arrastrado en el ciego torbellino,
¡llevadme con vosotras!

Nubes de tempestad que rompe el rayo
y en fuego ornáis las desprendidas orlas,
arrebatado entre la niebla oscura,
¡llevadme con vosotras!

Llevadme por piedad a donde el vértigo
con la razón me arranque la memoria.

Vast waves, breaking with a roar
on deserted and distant strands,
shroud me in a sheet of foam,
bear me away with you!

Hurricane gusts, snatching
the tall wood's withered leaves,
dragging all along in dark turbulence,
bear me away with you!

Storm clouds rent by lightning,
with your edges bordered in fire,
snatch me up in a dark mist,
bear me away with you!

Bear me away, I beg, to where vertigo
eradicates my memory and reason . . .

¡Por piedad! ¡Tengo miedo de quedarme
con mi dolor a solas!

Have mercy . . . I dread being left
alone with my grief!

¡Dios mío, qué solos se quedan los muertos! / My God, how lonely are the dead!

GUSTAVO ADOLFO BÉCQUER

(1899–1900)

Cerraron sus ojos
que aún tenía abiertos,
taparon su cara
con un blanco lienzo,
y unos sollozando,
otros en silencio,
de la triste alcoba
todos se salieron.

They closed her eyes
that she still kept open;
they covered her face
with a white linen cloth;
and some with sobs
and others in silence,
from the sad bedroom
all took their leave.

La luz que en un vaso
ardía en el suelo,
al muro arrojaba
la sombra del lecho,
y entre aquella sombra
veíase a intérvalos
dibujarse rígida
la forma del cuerpo.

The light in a glass
burned on the floor,
it cast on the wall
the bed's shadow,
and within that shadow
at times could be glimpsed
the rigid outline
of the body.

Despertaba el día
y a su albor primero
con sus mil ruidos
despertaba el pueblo.
Ante aquel contraste
de vida y misterio,
de luz y tinieblas,
yo pensé un momento:
*¡Dios mío, qué solos
se quedan los muertos!*

Day was awakening
and at its first dawning,
with a thousand noises
the village was awakening.
Faced with that contrast
of life and mystery,
of light and darkness,
I thought for a moment:
*My God, how lonely
are the dead!*

Oración de las madres que tienen a sus hijos en brazos[1] / The prayer of mothers who hold their sons in arms

MARÍA AND GREGORIO MARTÍNEZ SIERRA

(1914)

¡Dulce Jesús, que estás dormido!
¡Por el santo pecho que te ha
    amamantado,
te pido que este hijo mío no sea
soldado!

Sweet Jesus, lying asleep,
by the holy breast that suckled
    you,
I ask that this son of mine
be not made a soldier!

Se lo llevarán, ¡y era carne
    mía!
Me lo matarán, ¡y era mi alegría!
Cuando esté muriendo, dirá: '¡Madre
    mía!'
Y yo no sabré la hora ni el
    día.

¡Dulce Jesús, que estás dormido!
¡Por el santo pecho que te ha
    amamantado,
te pido que este hijo mío no sea
soldado!

They will take him away, and he was my
    flesh!
They will kill him, and he was my joy!
As he lies dying, 'Mother!' he'll
    say,
and I shall know neither the time nor the
    day.

Sweet Jesus, lying asleep,
by the holy breast that suckled
    you,
I ask that this son of mine
be not made a soldier!

[1]Falla's response to the German invasion of Belgium in 1914.

Canción andaluza: el pan de ronda / Andalusian song: Ronda bread

MARÍA AND GREGORIO MARTÍNEZ SIERRA

(1915)

Aunque todo en el mundo
fuese mentira,
¡nos queda este pan!
Moreno, tostado,
que huele a la jara de monte,
¡que sabe a verdad!

Por las calles tan blancas,
tan blancas,
bajo el cielo azul,
vayamos despacio,
partiendo este pan
¡que sabe a salud!

Y aunque todo en el mundo
fuera mentira,
¡esto no lo es!
Vivamos despacio
la hora que es buena
¡y vengan tristezas después!

Even if everything in the world
were a lie,
still we'd have this bread!
Dark, crisp,
with the fragrance of mountain rockrose,
tasting of truth!

Through the white streets,
gleaming so white
beneath the blue sky,
let us walk slowly,
sharing this bread
that tastes of health!

And even if everything in the world
were a lie,
this is not!
Let us live slowly
the hour that is good,
and may sorrows come later!

Tus ojillos negros / Your dark eyes

CRISTÓBAL DE CASTRO

(1902)

Yo no sé qué tienen tus ojillos negros
que me dan pesares y me gusta verlos,
Son tan juguetones y tan zalameros,
sus miradas prontas llegan tan adentro,
que hay quien asegura que Dios los ha
    hecho

What is it about your dark eyes
that makes me sad and happy to see them?
They are so playful and so graceful,
their rapid glances pierce me so,
that you could say that God begot
    them

como para muestra de lo que es lo bueno,
de lo que es la gloria, de lo que es el cielo.

Mas, por otra parte, ¡son tan embusteros!
Dicen tantas cosas que desdicen luego,
que hay quien asegura que Dios los ha
    hecho
como para muestra de lo que es tormento,
de lo que es desdicha, de lo que es
    infierno.

Y es que hay en tus ojos como hay en los
    cielos,
noches muy obscuras, días muy serenos.
Y hay en tus miradas maridaje eterno
de amorcillos locos y desdenes cuerdos,
y entre sus penumbras y sus centelleos
brillantes afanes y tus pensamientos,
como entre las sombras de la noche
    obscura
brillan los relámpagos con su vivo fuego.

Luces que parece que se están muriendo
y que de improviso resucitan luego.
Sombras adorables, llenas de misterio
como tus amores, como mis deseos.
Algo que da vida, mucho que da
    miedo.
Yo no sé qué tienen tus ojillos negros
que me dan pesares y ¡me gusta verlos!

to demonstrate what good is,
what glory is and heaven.

But yet they are so deceitful,
say so much they then deny,
that you could say that God begot
    them
to demonstrate what torment is,
what unhappiness is and hell.

There are in your eyes, as in the
    sky,
very dark nights, very serene days;
and your glances show a constant blend
of foolish love and wise disdain,
and in their shadows and their brightness
dwell bright longing and your thoughts,
as in the shadows of dark
    night
lightning flashes with its living fire.

Lights that seem to fade away
then suddenly quicken once again.
Adorable shadows, full of mystery,
like your love, like my desire.
Something that gives life, much that
    frightens.
What is it about your dark eyes
that makes me sad and happy to see them?

Trois mélodies / Three melodies

THÉOPHILE GAUTIER

(1909)

1. Les colombes / The doves

Sur le coteau, là-bas où sont les tombes,
Un beau palmier, comme un panache vert
Dresse sa tête, où le soir les
    colombes
Viennent nicher et se mettre à couvert.

Mais le matin elles quittent les branches :
Comme un collier qui s'égrène, on les
    voit
S'éparpiller dans l'air bleu, toutes
    blanches,
Et se poser plus loin sur quelque toit.

On the hillside, there where the tombs lie,
a beautiful palm, like a green plume
raises its crown, where at evening the
    doves
come to roost and shelter.

But at daybreak they leave the branches:
like a necklace scattering beads, you see
    them
disperse, all white, into the blue
    air,
and settle on some more distant roof.

Mon âme est l'arbre où tous les soirs, comme elles,	My soul is that tree where each evening, like them,
De blancs essaims de folles visions	white swarms of wild visions
Tombent des cieux, en palpitant des ailes,	fall with fluttering wings from the sky,
Pour s'envoler dès les premiers rayons.	to fly away when day first dawns.

2. *Chinoiserie* / *Chinoiserie*

Ce n'est pas vous, non, madame, que j'aime,	No, it is not you, madam, whom I love,
Ni vous non plus, Juliette, ni vous,	nor you, Juliet, nor you
Ophélia, ni Béatrix, ni même	Ophelia, nor Beatrice, nor even
Laure la blonde, avec ses grands yeux doux.	fair Laura with her large sweet eyes.
Celle que j'aime, à présent, est en Chine ;	She whom I now love is in China ;
Elle demeure avec ses vieux parents,	she lives with her old parents
Dans une tour de porcelaine fine,	in a tower of fine porcelain,
Au fleuve Jaune, où sont les cormorans.	where cormorants dwell by the Yellow River.
Elle a des yeux retroussés vers les tempes,	She has eyes that slant towards her temples,
Un pied petit à tenir dans la main,	a little foot you could hold in your hands,
Le teint plus clair que le cuivre des lampes,	a complexion clearer than a lamp's copper glow,
Les ongles longs et rougis de carmin.	long finger nails of carmine red.
Par son treillis elle passe sa tête,	She looks out from her trellis window,
Que l'hirondelle, en volant, vient toucher,	where a swallow brushes by in flight,
Et, chaque soir, aussi bien qu'un poète,	and each evening, like any poet,
Chante le saule et la fleur du pêcher.	she sings of the peach blossom and willow.

3. *Séguidille*[1] / *Seguidilla*

Un jupon serré sur les hanches,	Her skirt clinging to her hips,
Un peigne énorme à son chignon,	in her chignon an enormous comb,
Jambe nerveuse et pied mignon,	rippling legs and dainty feet,
Œil de feu, teint pâle et dents blanches ;	pale, with fiery eyes and white teeth ;
Alza! olà!	Alza! Ola!
Voilà	Behold
La véritable Manola.	a true street-girl from Madrid.
Gestes hardis, libre parole,	Bold of gesture, free of speech,
Sel et piment à pleine main,	as spicy as salt and pepper,
Oubli parfait du lendemain,	oblivious of the morrow,
Amour fantasque et grâce folle ;	fantastic love and wild grace ;
Alza! olà!	Alza! Ola!
Voilà	Behold
La véritable Manola.	a true street-girl from Madrid.

Chanter, danser aux castagnettes,	She sings and dances to castanets,
Et, dans les courses de taureaux,	and in the bull-ring
Juger les coups des toreros,	considers the bullfighters' thrusts,
Tout en fumant des cigarettes;	while she smokes her cigarettes;
Alza! olà!	Alza! Ola!
Voilà	Behold
La véritable Manola.	a true street-girl from Madrid.

[1]Gautier's poem was inspired by 'La Manola' by Bretón de los Herreros. See Appendix.

Siete canciones populares españolas / Seven Spanish folksongs
(1914–1915)

1. El paño moruno / The Moorish cloth

Al paño fino, en la tienda,	On the delicate fabric in the shop
una mancha le cayó.	there fell a stain.
Por menos precio se vende,	It sells for less,
porque perdió su valor.	for it has lost its value.
¡Ay!	Ay!

2. Seguidilla[1] murciana / Seguidilla from Murcia

Cualquiera que el tejado	People who live
tenga de vidrio,	in glass houses
no debe tirar piedras	shouldn't throw stones
al del vecino.	at their neighbour's.
Arrieros semos;	We are drovers;
¡puede que en el camino,	it may be
nos encontremos!	we'll meet on the road!
Por tu mucha inconstancia,	For your many infidelities
yo te comparo	I shall compare you
con peseta[2] que corre	to a peseta passing
de mano en mano.	from hand to hand,
Que al fin se borra,	till finally it's worn down –
y creyéndola falsa	and believing it false
nadie la toma!	no one will take it.

[1]Seguidilla. A dance in 3/8 or 3/4 time, faster than the Bolero and often accompanied by castanets. The tonality is usually major.
[2]Peseta. Diminutive of pesa = weight. A coin, equivalent to the French franc. It is divided into 100 centimos and has been the unit of value in Spain since 1868.

3. *Asturiana* / *Asturian song*

Por ver si me consolaba,	To see if it might console me
arrimeme a un pino verde.	I drew near a green pine.
Por verme llorar, lloraba.	To see me weep, it wept.
Y el pino como era verde,	And the pine, since it was green,
por verme llorar, lloraba!	wept to see me weeping!

4. *Jota*[1] / *Jota*

Dicen que no nos queremos,	They say we're not in love
porque no nos ven hablar.	since they never see us talk;
A tu corazón y al mío,	let them ask
se lo pueden preguntar.	your heart and mine!
Ya me despido de tí,	I must leave you now,
de tu casa y tu ventana.	your house and your window,
Y aunque no quiera tu madre.	and though your mother disapprove,
Adiós, niña, hasta mañana.	goodbye, sweet love, till tomorrow.

[1]*Jota*. A dance dating from the twelfth century, connected perhaps with the Moor, Aben Jot. Mostly danced in Aragon, but also common in Navarre, Castile and Valencia, the Jota is usually in a fairly fast 3/4 time, and often accompanied by castanets.

5. *Nana* / *Lullaby*

Duérmete, niño, duerme,	Sleep, little one, sleep,
duerme, mi alma,	sleep, my darling,
duérmete, lucerito,	sleep, my little
de la mañana.	morning star.
Nanita, nana,	Lullay, lullay,
duérmete, lucerito	sleep, my little
de la mañana.	morning star.

6. *Canción* / *Song*

Por traidores, tus ojos,	Since your eyes are treacherous,
voy a enterrarlos.	I'm going to bury them;
No sabes lo que cuesta	you know not what it costs,
«del aire».	'del aire',
Niña, el mirarlos	dearest, to gaze into them.
«Madre, a la orilla».	'Mother, a la orilla.'
Dicen que no me quieres,	They say you do not love me,
ya me has querido.	but you loved me once.
Váyase lo ganado	Make the best of it
«del aire».	'del aire'.

Por lo perdido,   and cut your losses,
«Madre, a la orilla».   'Mother, a la orilla'.

7. *Polo*[1] / *Polo*

¡Ay!   Ay!
Guardo una pena en mi pecho   I have an ache in my heart
que a nadie se la diré.   of which I can tell no one.

¡Malhaya el amor, malhaya   A curse on love, and a curse
y quien me lo dió a entender!   on the one who made me feel it!
¡Ay!   Ay!

> [1]*Polo*. A dance, native to Andalusia but probably of Moorish origin, in a
> moderately fast 3/8 time and often syncopated with periodic ornamental phrases
> on words such as 'Ay' and 'Olé'.

Psyché / *Psyche*

G. JEAN-AUBRY

(1924)

Psyché! La lampe est morte; éveille-toi.   Psyche, the lamp is extinguished; awake.
Le jour te considère avec des yeux noyés   Day gazes at you with eyes drowned in
    d'amour,   love
Et le désir nouveau de te servir encore.   and the new desire to serve you again.
Le miroir, confidant de ton visage en   The mirror, secret sharer of your tearful
    pleurs,   face,
Reflète, ce matin, lac pur parmi des   reflects on this morning – a clear lake
    fleurs,   among flowers –
Un ciel laiteux ainsi qu'une éternelle   a milky sky, an eternal
    aurore.   dawn.
Midi s'approche et danse, ivre sur ses   Midday draws near and dances, drunken
    pieds d'or.   on its golden feet.
Tends-lui les bras, sèche tes pleurs; dans Reach out to him, dry your tears; in
    un essor   soaring flight,
Abandonne, Psyché, la langueur de ta   Psyche, abandon the languor of your
    couche.   bed.

L'oiseau chante au sommet de l'arbre; le   The bird sings at the top of the tree; the
    soleil   sun
Sourit d'aise en voyant l'universel   smiles for joy at seeing the whole world
    éveil,   awake
Et le Printemps s'étire, une rose à la   and Spring stretches her limbs, a rose
    bouche.   between her lips.

Soneto a Córdoba[1] / *Sonnet to Cordoba*

LUIS DE GÓNGORA

(1927)

¡Oh excelso muro, oh torres coronadas
de honor, de majestad, de gallardía!
¡Oh gran río, gran rey de Andalucía,
de arenas nobles, ya que no doradas!

¡Oh fértil llano, oh sierras levantadas,
que privilegia el cielo y dora el día!
¡Oh siempre gloriosa patria mía,
tanto por plumas cuanto por espadas!

¡Si entre aquellas ruinas y despojos
que enriquece Genil y Dauro
    baña
tu memoria no fué alimento mío,
nunca merezcan mis ausentes ojos
ver tu muro, tus torres y tu
    río,
tu llano y sierra, oh patria, oh flor de
    España!

Oh lofty wall, oh towers crowned
with honour, majesty and gallantry!
Oh great river, great king of Andalusia,
with your sands noble, if not golden!

Oh fertile plain, oh soaring hills,
favoured by the sky and gilded by the day!
Oh my native land, ever renowned
as much for its pen as for its sword!

If, amid those ruins and remains
which the Genil enriches and the Dauro
    bathes,
your memory did not sustain me,
let my absent eyes never deserve
to see your wall, your towers and your
    river,
your plain and mountains, oh native land,
    oh flower of Spain!

[1]*Córdoba*. With its many mosques and public baths, it was once the spectacular
capital of Moorish Spain and boasted comparison with Baghdad. The magnificent
mosque or mezquita still remains.

VIII

JOAQUÍN NIN
(1879–1949)

Nin was Cuban by birth, and like that other energetic colonial, his contemporary Percy Grainger, his knowledge of, and enthusiasm for, the folksong of his mother country knew no bounds. He shared with the Australian Grainger a number of other characteristics – both men were virtuoso pianists whose folksong arrangements reflect their very individual pianism, and the printed editions of their works are idiosyncratically (but usefully) annotated in loving detail, including pronunciation glossaries and newly minted expression marks bordering on the eccentric.

Nin was born in Havana on 29 September 1879. He was taken to Spain as a child, and followed his piano studies in Barcelona with a six-year period in Paris (1902–8) where he studied with Moszkowski and later at the Schola Cantorum. He eventually taught at that institution as Albéniz had before him. He also held a position in Berlin, and travelled the world as a concert pianist, specialising (and proselytising, as was his way) in the playing of Bach and early Spanish composers on the modern piano; it was perhaps inevitable that he and the famous harpsichordist Wanda Landowska should cross swords in dramatic fashion. In 1923 Nin published twenty *Cantos populares españoles* (Eschig) in two books, as well as two books of *Airs anciens* containing fourteen arrangements of songs by such composers as Esteve and Blas de Laserna. The rather more simple ten *Villancicos españoles* (also Eschig) date from 1932. Nin tended to classify his songs into lengthily justified categories, but they all follow the same pattern – existing vocal lines, whether folksongs or melodies from the tonadilla age, are provided with elaborate and demanding accompaniments. It is instructive to compare, for example, Nin's arrangement of 'El vito' with that of Obradors, the first undoubtedly exciting if the performers manage to bring it off, the second much easier, but actually equally effective in the concert hall.

Joaquín Nin was the brother of Anaïs Nin, famous for her correspondence with Henry Miller and her writings about erotic escapades in Paris, and the father of the composer Joaquín Nin-Culmell (*b.* 1908) who took up residence in the United States. The songs of Nin-Culmell include a large number of folksong arrangements (also Eschig) from Catalonia, Andalusia and Salamanca.

from
Veinte cantos populares españoles / *Twenty popular Spanish songs*
(1923)

Montañesa / From the mountains

Segaba yo aquella tarde
Y ella atropaba la yerba
Y estaba mas colorada, morena y
    salada
Que en su sazón las cerezas.

I was harvesting that afternoon
and she was gathering hay,
and she was most ruddy, dark and
    charming
like cherries in season.

Cuatro pinos tiene tu pinar
Y yo te los cuido,
Cuatro majos los quieren cortar,
No se han atrevido.

Your pine wood has four pines
and I tend them for you,
four majos wish to fell them
but none of them has dared.

Tonada de Conde Sol / Song of Count Sol

Grandes guerras se publican
entre España y Portugale:
pena de la vida tiene
quien no se quiera embarcare.

Great wars are being declared
between Spain and Portugal:
those men risk pain of death
who do not wish to embark.

Al Conde Sol le nombraban
por Capitán generale.
Del Rey se fué a despedir
de su esposa otro que tale.

Count Sol was appointed
field-marshal;
he took his leave from the King
and likewise from his wife.

La Condesa qu'era niña
todo se le va en llorare.
Dime Conde, cuantos años
tienes de echar por alláe.

The Countess, who was young,
dissolved in tears.
Tell me, Count, how many years
do you intend to be over there?

Si a los seis años no vuelvo,
os podréis, niña, casare.
Pasan los seis y los ocho
y del Conde no se oye hablare.

If in six years I do not return,
you may, my beloved, wed.
Six years pass, eight years pass,
and of the Count no word is heard.

Malagueña[1] / *Malagueña*

Cuando salí de Marbella,
hasta el caballo lloraba,
que me dejé una doncella
que al sol sus rayos quitaba.

¡Amores de largo tiempo
qué malos de olvidar son!
Porque han echado raíces
en medio del corazón.

When I left Marbella,
even my horse lamented,
for I left a young girl
who stole the sun's rays.

A long-lasting love
is hard to forget,
for it spreads its roots
deep into the heart.

> [1]*Malagueña*. An Andalusian song originally from Malaga, it can also take the form of an instrumental piece.

Granadina / *From Granada*

Las fatigas del querer
Son las fatigas más grandes,
Porque se lloran cantando,
Y las lágrimas no salen.
Dame con ese puñal,
Y dirás que yo me maté,
Y en el color de la sangre
Verás si bien te quiero.

The torments of love
are the greatest torments,
for they are lamented in song
and the tears do not come.
Strike me with that dagger,
and you will say I killed myself,
and by the colour of the blood
you shall see if I love you truly.

Paño murciano / *Cloth from Murcia*

Diga usted, señor platero,
Cuanta plata es menester
Para engarzar un besito
De boca de una mujer.

Señor platero, he pensado
Que usted sabe engarzar;
Por eso le vengo a dar
Una obrita de cuidado.

A mí un besito me ha dado
Mi novia con gran salero.
Engarzarlo en plata quiero,
Porque soy su fiel amante.

¿Qué plata será bastante?
Diga usted, señor platero.

Tell me, Mister Silversmith,
how much silver's needed
to set a little kiss
from a woman's lips?

Mister Silversmith, thinking
that you could set jewels,
I've come to give you
a little task that needs some care.

A most alluring little kiss
my sweetheart gave me,
I'd like to set it in silver,
since I'm her faithful lover.

How much silver would it take?
Pray tell me, Mister Silversmith.

El vito[1] / El vito

Una vieja vale un real[2]
y una muchacha dos cuartos[3],
y yo, como soy tan pobre
me voy a lo más barato.

Con el vito, vito, vito,
con el vito, vito, va.
No me jaga 'usté' cosquillas,
que me pongo 'colorá'.

An old woman is worth a real
and a young girl two cuartos,
but as I am so poor
I go for the cheapest.

On with the dancing,
on with the dancing, ole!
Stop your teasing, sir,
else I'll blush!

[1]*Vito*. A dance full of fire, performed in the taverns by a woman standing on a table before an audience of bullfighters.
[2]*Real*. A silver coin.
[3]*Cuarto*. A copper coin.

Canto andaluz / Andalusian song

¡Ay!
Por darle gusto a tu gente
y a mi corazón pesar,
dije que no te quería,
teniéndote voluntad.
¡Ay!

Ah!
To please your folk
and torture my heart,
I said that I did not love you,
although I held you dear.
Ah!

Polo[1] / Polo

¡Cuerpo bueno, alma divina,
qué de fatigas me cuestas!
¡Despierta si estás dormida,
y alivia por Dios mis penas!

Mira que si no fallezco,
la pena negra me acaba!
Tan solo con verte ahora,
mis pesares se acabáran.

¡Ay! ¡Qué fatigas!
¡Ay! ¡Que ya expiro!

Fine figure, heavenly soul,
oh the torment that you cause me!
Awake, if you be asleep,
and for God's sake soothe my pain!

Don't you see, if I do not die,
black torment will end my days!
Merely by seeing you now,
my sorrows themselves would end.

Ah, what torment!
Ah, I die!

[1]*Polo*. A dance, native to Andalusia but probably of Moorish origin, in a moderately fast 3/8 time and often syncopated with periodic ornamental phrases on words such as 'Ay' and 'Olé'.

from *Diez villancicos españoles* / *Ten Spanish carols*

Villancico asturiano / *Asturian carol*

(1932)

No hay tal andar como andar a la una
y vereis el Niño en la cuna
que nació en la noche ascura,
de Bethlén en un portal
que no hay tal andar.
No hay tal andar como buscar a
    Cristo,
no hay tal andar como a Cristo
    buscar,
que no hay tal andar.

No hay tal andar como andar a las dos
y vereis al Hijo de Dios
que por nos salvar a nos
sangre quiso derramar
que no hay tal andar.
No hay tal andar como buscar a
    Cristo,
no hay tal andar como a Cristo
    buscar,
no hay tal andar.

Nothing can compare with a walk at one,
when you see the Child in the cradle,
born in the dark night
at Bethlehem in a stable.
Nothing can compare.
Nothing can compare with seeking
    Christ,
with seeking Christ nothing can
    compare,
nothing can compare.

Nothing can compare with a walk at two,
when you see the Son of God,
who to save us
willingly shed his blood.
Nothing can compare.
Nothing can compare with seeking
    Christ,
with seeking Christ nothing can compare,

nothing can compare.

Villancico andaluz / *Andalusian carol*

(1932)

Campana sobre campana
y sobre compana una,
asómate a esa ventana
verás un Niño en la cuna.
Betlén campanas de Betlén
que los ángeles tocan –
¿qué nuevas me traéis?
Recogido tu rebaño –
¿a dónde vas pastorcito?
Voy a llevar al Portal
requesón manteca y vino.
Betlén campanas de Betlén
que los ángeles tocan –
¿qué nuevas me traéis?

Campana sobre campana,
y sobre campana dos;
asómate a esa ventana,
porque está naciendo Dios.

Bell upon bell
and then one more bell,
look out of the window
and you shall see a Child in the cradle.
Bethlehem, bells of Bethlehem
which the angels ring –
what tidings do you bring me?
Once your flock is gathered,
where dost thou go, little shepherd?
I am bringing to the stable
butter, curds and wine.
Bethlehem, bells of Bethlehem
which the angels ring –
what tidings do you bring me?

Bell upon bell
and then two more bells,
look out of the window,
for Christ is being born.

Betlén campanas de Betlén
que los ángeles tocan –
¿qué nuevas me traéis?
Caminando, a medianoche –
¿a dónde vas mi buen pastor?
Le llevo al Niño, que nace
como a Dios, mi corazón.
Betlén, campanas de Betlén,
que los ángeles tocan –
¿qué nuevas me traéis?

Bethlehem, bells of Bethlehem
which the angels ring –
what tidings do you bring me?
Walking at midnight,
where dost thou go, good my shepherd?
I am bringing my heart to the Child,
who is being born as God.
Bethlehem, bells of Bethlehem
which the angels ring –
what tidings do you bring me?

Villancico castellano / Castilian carol

(1933)

San José era carpintero, ¡Ay!
Y la Virgen lavandera, ¡Ay!
El Niño bajó del cielo
en una noche lunera.
El Niño vino del aire
camino del paraiso.

Saint Joseph was a carpenter. Ah!
And the Virgin a washerwoman. Ah!
The Child came down from heaven
on a moonlit night.
The Child came from the air
on the road to Paradise.

Jesús de Nazareth / Jesus of Nazareth

(1933)

¡Ay! ¡Ay! Un niño nace de flores
¡Ay! todo vestido de amores, de amores.
Es de las flores la flor
y el amor de los amores.
Es Señor de los señores
y la flor de los amores. ¡Ay!

Ah! Ah! A child is born of flowers.
Ah! All clothed in love, in love.
He is the flower of flowers
and the love of loves.
He is the Lord of Lords
and the flower of love. Ah!

IX

JOAQUÍN TURINA
(1882–1949)

At one time it was fashionable to link the names of the fellow Andalusians (and friends) Falla and Turina in the same way that the piano composers Albéniz and Granados are often spoken of in the same breath. In the light of Falla's undiminished reputation with musicians everywhere, and Turina's waning fame (albeit not with singers who continue to programme his songs) a pairing of this sort now seems untenable. Turina has of course served the song repertoire a good deal more assiduously than any of his contemporaries, and the large number of songs in this chapter, most of them more or less still holding the recital stage, is evidence of his love of the medium. But the lack of the influence of Pedrell in his life seems to have placed Turina's music on a different plane from that of his famous contemporaries. A resident of Paris for some years, he was a pupil of D'Indy; much of his musical material seems forced into the cyclic formulas of the Schola Cantorum, on top of which is laid a patina of sevillanismo – gracefully applied to the music, one sometimes feels, rather than it being the result of the deepest feeling. It is not surprising that Turina wrote film music – he found it easy to respond to visual ideas and stimuli. It cannot be denied that he had a melodic gift, a sense of humour (somewhat lacking in Falla) and an ability to charm – particularly in his piano writing.

Joaquín Turina was born in Seville on 9 December 1882. After the almost obligatory spell in Madrid attempting unsuccessfully to conquer the world of zarzuelas, Turina moved to Paris where he was a fellow pupil of Nin, and studied the piano with Moszkowski. Albéniz (also in Paris at the time) advised him to study Spanish folk music after hearing his piano quintet, a work which owes much to César Franck. Turina returned home, but more than any of his contemporaries he set his cap at composing in the accepted European forms neglected by many a Spanish composer. He thus composed the large scale *Sinfonía sevillana*, and a great deal of chamber music for strings and piano. His impressive list of songs is dwarfed by his output of solo piano music, and some of his song cycles contain movements for piano solo, notably the opening 'Dedicatorio' from the *Poema en forma de canciones* (using a theme reminiscent of one used by Falla in *Noches en los jardines de España*), and the 'Preludio', 'Noche de feria' and the closing 'Ofrenda' – the first, fourth and seventh items of the *Canto a Sevilla*. Turina makes considerable vocal demands on his singers: for sheerly practical reasons it is not unusual to find artists picking and choosing items from within the cycles, particularly when their accompanists (or the singers themselves!) do not fancy the idea of too much intermingled piano music. Among the most often performed of Turina's songs are 'La Giralda' (evoking Seville's famous bell-tower) and 'La fantasma' – both from *Canto a Sevilla* – and the 'Farruca' from *Tríptico*. 'Tu pupila es azul' (from *Tres poemas*) has a lighter touch than is often encountered with this composer, and has always been a firm favourite. Turina was a noted critic as well as professor of composition at the Madrid Conservatoire from 1930.

The songs of Turina are all published by the Union Musical Española under the following catalogue numbers:

UMV 15316	*Poema en forma de canciones*
UMV 15317	*Tres arias*
UMV 15652	*Canto a Sevilla*
UMV 16171	*Tríptico*
UMV 17103	*Tres poemas*
UMV 17301	*Homenaje a Lope de Vega*
UMV 15829	'Corazón de mujer'
UMV 16491	*Tres sonetos*

Poema en forma de canciones / *Poem in the form of songs*

RAMÓN DE CAMPOAMOR

Op. 19   (1918)

1. *Nunca olvida . . .* / *Do not forget . . .*

Ya que este mundo abandono,
antes de dar cuenta a Dios,
aquí para entre los dos,
mi confesión te diré.

Con toda el alma perdono
hasta a los que siempre he odiado.
¡A tí, que tanto te he amado,
nunca te perdonaré!

Since this world I leave,
before the final reckoning with God,
here between the two of us
I shall make my confession.

With all my soul I forgive
even those I've always hated.
But you, whom I have loved so much,
I shall never forgive!

2. *Cantares* / *Songs*

¡Ay! Más cerca de mí te siento
cuando más huyo de tí,
pues tu imagen es en mí,
sombra de mi pensamiento.

Vuélvemelo hoy a decir,
pues, embelesado, ayer,
te escuchaba sin oír
y te miraba sin ver.

Ah! I feel you closer to me,
the more I flee from you;
since I bear your likeness within me,
as a shadow of my thoughts.

Tell me again,
since yesterday, spellbound,
I listened to you without hearing
and looked at you without seeing.

3. *Los dos miedos* / *The two fears*

Al comenzar la noche de aquel día,
ella, lejos de mí,
¿por qué te acercas tanto? me decía.
Tengo miedo de tí.

Y después que la noche hubo pasado,
dijo, cerca de mí,
¿por qué te alejas tanto de mi lado?
Tengo miedo sin tí.

At nightfall on that day,
far from me she said:
why come so close?
I am afraid of you.

And after the night had passed,
close to me she said:
why move so far away?
I am afraid without you.

4. *Las locas por amor* / *Frantic for love*

'Te amaré, diosa Venus, si
　　prefieres
que te ame mucho tiempo y con cordura.'
Y respondió la diosa de Citeres:
'Prefiero, como todas las mujeres,
que me amen poco tiempo y con locura.'

'I shall love you, goddess Venus, if you
　　wish
me to love you long and wisely.'
And the goddess of Cythera¹ replied:
'I wish, like all women,
to be loved fleetingly and frantically.'

'*Cythera*. Now Kithira. An island on the coast of Laconia, sacred to the goddess
Venus, who was surnamed Cytheraea and rose, it is said, from the sea off its coast.

Tres arias / Three arias
Op. 26 (1923)

1. *Romance* / *A Romance*
DUQUE DE RIVAS

En una yegua tordilla
que atrás deja el pensamiento,
entra en Córdoba gallardo
Atarfe el noble guerrero,

On a dapple-grey mare
which beggared all description,
there entered into Cordoba
Atarfe, the noble and gallant warrior,

el que las moriscas lunas[1]
llevó glorioso a Toledo
y torna con mil cautivos
y cargado de trofeos.
Las azoteas y calles
hierven de curioso pueblo
que en él fijando los ojos
viva, viva está diciendo;
las moras en los terrados
tremolan cándidos lienzos
y agua de azahar dan al aire
y sus elogios al viento;
y entre la festiva pompa,
siendo envidia de los viejos,
de las mujeres encanto,
de los jóvenes ejemplo,
a las rejas de Daraja,
Daraja la de ojos negros
que cuando miran abrasan
y abrasan con sólo verlos,
humilde llega y rendido
el que triunfante y soberbio,
fué espanto de los cristianos,
fué gloria de sarracenos.
Mas ¡ay! que las ve cerradas
bien distintas de otro tiempo
en que damascos y alfombras
las ornaron en su obsequio.
Y al mirar tales señales,
turbado reconociendo
que mientras ganó batallas
perdió el amor de su dueño,
con gran ternura llorando
quien mostró tan duro pecho,
vuelve el rostro a sus cautivos
de esta manera diciendo:
'Id con Dios, que ya sois libres,
desde aqui podéis volveros
y llevad vuestros despojos
que a quien presentar no tengo,
pues no es razón que conserve
de sus victorias recuerdo
quien al tiempo de guardarlas
perdió de Daraja el pecho.'

he who took the Crescent
victorious to Toledo,
he who returned with a thousand captives
and laden with trophies.
Roof tops and roads
swarm with spectators,
who fixing their eyes upon him,
cry 'viva, viva!';
the moorish women on the terrace
wave white kerchiefs
and throw orange-flower water into the air
and their praises to the wind;
and amid this festive pomp
he enters – the envy of the aged,
the delight of women
and example to the young –
and draws near Daraja's window,
Daraja of the dark eyes
which, when gazing, burn,
and burn when merely gazed at,
draws near humble and submissive,
he who triumphant and proud
was feared by Christians
and glorified by Saracens.
But then alas he sees the window closed,
greatly altered from times gone by,
when rugs and damask
bedecked it in his honour.
And seeing such signs,
he realises with dismay
that while he was winning battles
he lost the love of his lady;
he wept with great tenderness,
who had shewn so hard a heart,
and turning to his captives
he spoke thus:
'Go with God, for you are free,
you may depart from hence
and take your spoils,
which I have no one to display to
since there is no reason for him
to recall victories,
who when winning them
lost the heart of his Daraja.'

[1]The Crescent was adopted as a badge or emblem by the Turkish sultans and used as a military and religious symbol. According to the OED, the attribution of the Crescent by modern writers to the Moors of Spain is an historical and chronological error.

2. *El pescador* / *The fisherman*

JOSÉ DE ESPRONCEDA

Pescadorcita mía,
Desciende a la ribera,
Y escucha placentera
Mi cántico de amor;
   Sentado en su barquilla,
Te canta su cuidado,
Cual nunca enamorado
Tu tierno pescador.

La noche el cielo encubre
Y calla manso el viento,
Y el mar sin movimiento
También en calma está:
   A mi batel desciende,
Mi dulce amada hermosa:
La noche tenebrosa
Tu faz alegrará.

De conchas y corales
Y nácar á tu frente
Guirnalda reluciente,
Mi bien, te ceñiré;
   Y eterno amor mil veces
Jurándote, cumplida
En tí, mi dulce vida,
Mi dicha encontraré.

No el hondo mar te espante,
Ni el viento proceloso,
Que al ver tu rostro hermoso
Sus iras calmarán;
   Y sílfidas y ondinas
Por reina de los mares
Con plácidos cantares
A par te aclamarán.

Pescadorcita mía,
Desciende a la ribera,
Y escucha placentera
Mi cántico de amor;
   Sentado en su barquilla,
Te canta su cuidado,
Cual nunca enamorado
Tu tierno pescador.

Fishermaiden mine,
come down to the shore
and listen with delight
to my song of love;
   seated in his little bark,
your affectionate fisherman –
like no lover has ever done –
pours out his heart to you in song.

Night conceals the sky
and the gentle wind is hushed
and the motionless sea
is likewise becalmed:
   come down to my boat,
my sweet, my fair, my love,
the sombre night
shall be brightened by your face.

A gleaming garland
of coral, shell and mother-of-pearl
I'll wind, my love,
about your brow;
   and pledging eternal love
a thousand times, I'll find,
fulfilled in you, my sweet,
my happiness.

Let the deep sea not fright you
nor the tempestuous winds:
seeing your beautiful face
they shall quell their fury.
   And sylphs and water-sprites,
as queen of the ocean,
with peaceful song
shall acclaim you in concert.

Fishermaiden mine,
come down to the shore
and listen with delight
to my song of love;
   seated in his little bark,
your affectionate fisherman –
like no lover has ever done –
pours out his heart to you in song.

3. *Rima* / *Rima*

GUSTAVO ADOLFO BÉCQUER

Te vi un punto y flotando ante mis
    ojos
la imagen de tus ojos se quedó,
como la mancha oscura orlada en fuego
que flota y ciega si se mira al
    sol.

Y dondequiera que la vista clavo
torno a ver sus pupilas llamear;
mas no te encuentro a tí, que es tu mirada,
unos ojos, los tuyos, nada más.

De mi alcoba en el ángulo los miro
desasidos fantásticos lucir:
cuando duermo los siento que se ciernen
de par en par abiertos sobre mí.

Yo sé que hay fuegos fatuos que en la
    noche
llevan al caminante a perecer:
yo me siento arrastrado por tus ojos,
pero adónde me arrastran no lo sé.

I glimpsed you, and floating before my
    eyes
the image of your eyes remained,
like the dark spot fringed with fire
that hovers and blinds if you look at the
    sun.

And wherever I direct my gaze
I see again her glowing eyes;
but it is your gaze, not you that I see,
two eyes, your own, but nothing more.

From the corner of my room I see them
floating, phantom-like, gleaming;
when I sleep I feel them hovering
wide open there above me.

I know that will-o'-the wisps at
    night
take the traveller to his death:
I feel myself borne away by your eyes,
but whither they bear me I do not know.

Canto a Sevilla / *Song to Seville*

JOSÉ MUÑOZ SAN ROMÁN

Op. 37 (1927)

1. *Semana Santa* / *Holy Week*

Semana Santa:
penitentes y encapuchados nazarenos[1].
Perfume a rosa y manzanilla
y un rebrillar en los cielos.
Explosión de primavera,
claveles rojos y bellos.
Sobre los pasos los Cristos
y las Vírgenes luciendo.
Un ávido gentío
por las calles tortuosas
y llenas de misterio;
gritos de vendedores
y dolientes y líricas saetas[2]
por el viento.
'Miraslo por donde viene
er Señó der Gran Podé.

Holy Week:
Penitents and hooded nazarenes.
Scent of rose and camomile
and a brightness in the skies.
Explosion of spring,
carnations red and beautiful.
On tableaux held aloft
Christs and Virgins shine.
An eager crowd
along the winding streets
full of mystery;
street-vendors' cries
and mournful, melodious saetas
borne on the wind.
'See where he comes,
our Mighty Lord.

Por cada paso que dá	At his every step
nase un lirio y un clavé.'	a lily and carnation burst forth.'
Pasan Jesús del Amor,	Jesus, Lord of Love,
el Cristo de Montañés[3],	The Montañes Christ,
la Virgen de la Esperanza,	the Virgin of Hope
y Jesús de Nazaret.	and Jesus of Nazareth pass by.
Sobre Calvarios floridos	On flower-strewn calvaries
bajo palios filigranas,	beneath fine embroidered canopies
terciopelo y pedrería.	of velvet and precious stones.
Nubes de incienso inflamadas.	Burning clouds of incense.
Una morena con ojos	A dusky girl with eyes
como la noche cerrada,	as black as night
abre sus labios de mieles	opens her honeyed lips
y sollozando les canta.	and sings to them, sobbing.
Se acerca entre mil luceros,	Amidst a thousand stars
nuestra Madre Dolorosa	Our Lady of Sorrows draws near,
se acerca entre mil luceros.	amidst a thousand stars.
Viene derramando gracias	Granting favours she approaches
bajo el azúl de los cielos.	beneath the blue of heaven.
Semana Santa:	Holy Week:
armonías de clarines y tambores.	the sound of trumpets and drums.
Las calles llenas de encanto	The streets full of enchantment,
y de risas y de sones.	laughter and noise.
La noche del Jueves Santo	The night of Maundy Thursday
es claro día y no es noche.	has a brightness of day, not night.
Tiene una luna de plata	There is a silver moon
que es más clara que los soles.	brighter than any sun.
De la Macarena[4] sale	From the Macarena comes
la Esperanza, amor de amores,	Our Lady of Hope, love of loves,
y entre el gentío florece	and in the crowd
un renacer de oraciónes.	people are moved anew to prayer.
'Madre de la Macarena	'Mother of the Macarena,
por nuestro amor dolorosa,	suffering for love of us,
para alivio de las penas	that our sorrows be assuaged
tienes la cara de rosa.'	thou hast the face of a rose.'

[1]*Nazarenos*. The penitents who process during Holy Week, wearing violet clothes.

[2]*Saeta*. An unaccompanied devotional song, sung during a pause in Holy Week processions in Andalusia. 'Saeta' = arrow.

[3]*Montañés*. Juan Martinez Montañés (1568–1649) was perhaps the greatest Spanish master of polychrome sculpture. The Christ of Clemency, to which Muñoz San Román's poem probably refers, is a crucifix which hangs in Seville cathedral. He was active in Andalusia, producing works for palaces, convents and churches.

[4]*Macarena*. La Macarena, the Virgin of the Macarena, is the patron saint of Seville.

2. *Las fuentecitas del parque* / *The little fountains in the park*

Como besos solares	Like the sun's kisses
En la arena dorada;	on the golden sand;

Como tiernas caricias
De la luna de plata,
Son las fuentes del Parque
En la dulce mañana,
O entre el mago silencio
De la noche estrellada.

like the tender caresses
of the silver moon
are the fountains of the Park
in the sweet morning,
or in the magic silence
of the starry night.

Entre el bello boscaje
Donde luce la acacia,
El naranjo aromoso,
Y la altísima palma
Son las fuentes del Parque
De Sevilla la amada,
Como oasis, milagros
De frescura y de gracia.

Amid the lovely grove
where the acacia gleams,
amid fragrant orange-tree
and lofty palm
are the fountains in the Park
of beloved Seville,
oases, miracles
of freshness and grace.

¡Oh, el amor que se mira
Al espejo del agua,
De sus senos tranquilos
En la fúlgida entraña!

Oh Love, gazing at itself
in the water's mirror,
on the calm bosom
of the resplendent depths!

¡Oh, el amor que suspira
A la música grata
De las aguas que surgen
Cantarinas y cándidas!

O Love, sighing
to the sweet music
of these waters, welling up
clear and singing!

Dulce amor peregrino
Por las sendas doradas
De este Parque de ensueños.
De este edén de las almas.
Como goza el misterio
De las horas más plácidas,
Al frescor de estas fuentes
Rumorosas y mágicas.
¡Ah!

Sweet Love, wandering
through the golden paths
of this Park of dreams,
this Eden of souls –
How it revels in the mystery
of these such tranquil hours,
in the cool of these fountains,
murmuring and magical.
Ah!

3. *El fantasma* / *The phantom*

Por las calles misteriosas
ronda de noche un fantasma,
dejando un rumor de ayes
y cadenas cuando pasa.

Through the mysterious streets
a phantom prowls by night,
leaving a sound of groans
and chains in his wake.

Viéndolo aullan los perros
y las cornejas se espantan,
rasgando el tul de las sombras
con el filo de sus alas.

Dogs howl when they see him,
and crows take fright,
tearing the cloak of darkness
with the edge of their wings.

Como un desgraciado augurio
se espera la su llegada
y hasta el novio más valiente
al sentirlo se acobarda.

Like an evil omen
his arrival is awaited,
and even the most noble gallant
flinches on sensing his presence.

¿Dónde va y de dónde
   viene?
De cierto no se sabe nada;
mas dicen que es el amor,
que anda vestido de máscara.

Where is he going and from where does he
   come?
Nothing is known for certain;
but they say it is Love
wandering abroad in disguise.

4. La Giralda[1] / La Giralda

De la gloriosa Sevilla
se hizo el espíritu carne
en la torre peregrina
y la llamaron Giralda,
que es nombre que tiene un eco
de repique de campanas.
La Giralda es un ensueño
y es así como un suspiro
que lanza la tierra al cielo.
Encaje de filigrana;
como una bandera al viento
tejida en oro y en plata.

The spirit of glorious Seville
became incarnate
in the exotic tower –
and they called it Giralda,
a name which echoes
the sound of pealing bells.
The Giralda is a dream
and like a sigh
which the earth raises to the sky.
Delicately woven lace;
like a banner in the wind,
woven of gold and silver.

Como un brazo de Sevilla
que se levanta a alcanzar
las gracias que Dios le envía.

Like an arm that Seville
stretches out to grasp
the gifts bestowed by God.

Como un pensamiento loco
que hable de amor infinito
hecho repique sonoro.
Oro y plata, día y noche
y coral y pedrería;
lo mismo ahora que entonces,
cuando yo la imaginaba en sueños,
como un tesoro labrado
por manos de hadas.

Like a wild thought
speaking of infinite love,
transformed into pealing bells.
Gold and silver, day and night,
coral and precious stones,
the same now as ever it was,
when I imagined it in dreams
as a treasure wrought
by fairy hands.

Gallarda como mujer,
sin tí no sería Sevilla,
lo encantadora que es.

As graceful as woman,
without you Seville would not be
as charming as it is.

[1]*Giralda*. The bell-tower, about 318 feet high, which dominates the skyline of
Seville. It takes its name from the crowning figure of Fides (Faith), whose banner
serves as a weather vane or 'giraldillo'; eventually the whole tower, originally a
minaret attached to the mosque, became known as the 'Giralda'.

Corazón de mujer / A woman's heart

CRISTINA DE ARTEAGA

(1927)

Corazón de mujer,
Que no sabe querer,
Que no sabe entregar

A woman's heart
that cannot love,
that cannot surrender

Toda el alma y el ser
A la angustia de amar,
No se puede llamar
Corazón de mujer.

Y si un día el amor
No es el vivo fulgor
Que enardece el vivir
Y hace suave el dolor
De su mismo sufrir;
Como flor sin olor
Bien merece morir.

Aunque yo lo soñé
Tan fuerte y tan dichoso,
Aunque tú lo tejiste,
Nuestro amor nació herido
Por el germen morboso
De mi espíritu inquieto,
De tu espíritu triste

Fué pálida su aurora,
No tuvo mediodía,
Cuando apenas sellaba
La ilusión de una hora,
Nuestro amor se moría.

No quisimos creer
Que era una calentura
Que se esfumó por siempre
Que partió nuestros lazos.
¡Y fué nuestra tortura
El estrechar su sombra
Disuelta en nuestros brazos!

Hoy te tienta el recuerdo
De esa esperanza muerta;
Estaba en tu memoria
Como una flor marchita.
¡No llames a mi puerta!
Cuando el amor ha muerto,
Nadie lo resucita.

¡Pobre amor! Es ya tarde.
¡Déjalo en su reposo!
En vano lo adoraba,
En balde lo quisiste.
Era el fruto forzoso
De mi espíritu inquieto,
¡De tu espíritu triste!

A veces junto las manos
Y a veces cierro los ojos
Cuando me invaden tiranos los antojos

heart and soul
to the anguish of love,
cannot be called
a woman's heart.

And if love one day
loses the intense glow
that kindles life
and soothes the pain
of its own suffering —
like a flower without fragrance
it well deserves to die.

Though I dreamt our love
was strong and happy,
and though you wove its strands,
our love was born infected
by the diseased germ
of my restless nature
and your sad soul.

Its dawn was pale
and failed to reach its noon;
hardly had one hour
of illusion gone by,
than our love was dying.

We refused to believe
it was a fever
which vanished for ever
and severed our bonds.
And it was a torment
to clasp its dissolving shadow
in our arms!

Now you are tempted by the memory
of those withered hopes,
it lingers in your mind
like a faded flower.
Do not call at my door!
When love has died,
no one can revive it.

Poor Love! It is now too late.
Leave it in peace!
Adored in vain,
in vain desired,
it was the inevitable fruit
of my restless nature
and your sad soul!

At times I clasp my hands,
at times I close my eyes,
when I am overwhelmed

De mis latidos humanos.
¡Ante su fuerza incentiva
Se dobla lánguidamente
En defensiva inconsciente
El alma, flor sensitiva!

by the throb of human desire.
Before its ondriving force,
the soul – sensitive flower! –
languidly submits
in unconscious defence.

Cierro los ojos y espero,
Junto las manos y adoro;
¡Sufro, lloro, río, lloro,
No sé si vivo o si muero!
¡En tumultuosa amalgama
Mi vida, gozo y martirio!
Se derrama como un cirio
Disuelto en su misma llama.

I close my eyes and wait,
I clasp my hands and pray;
I suffer, cry, laugh, cry,
not knowing if I live or die!
A tumultuous fusion:
my life, with its joy and torment,
overflowing like a candle,
dissolving in its own flame.

Corazón de mujer,
Que no sabe querer,
Que no sabe entregar
Toda el alma y el ser
A la angustia de amar,
No se puede llamar
Corazón de mujer.

A woman's heart
that cannot love,
that cannot surrender
heart and soul
to the anguish of love,
cannot be called
a woman's heart.

Tríptico / Triptych

Op. 45 (1929)

1. Farruca[1] / Farruca

RAMÓN DE CAMPOAMOR

Está tu imagen, que admiro,
Tan pegada a mi deseo,
Que si al espejo me miro,
En vez de verme te veo. ¡Ah!

Your image, which I admire,
is so fused with my desire
that when I gaze into the mirror
I see your face, not mine. Ah!

No vengas, falso contento,
Llamando a mi corazón,
Pues traes en la ilusión
Envuelto el remordimiento. ¡Ah!

Do not come, false happiness,
calling to my heart,
for concealed beneath illusion
you bring remorse. Ah!

Ah, marcho a la luz de la luna
De su sombra tan en pos,
Que no hacen más sombra que una
Siendo nuestros cuerpos dos.

Ah! I wander in the moonlight,
pursuing your shadow so close
that there is but one shadow,
though we are two.

[1]*Farruca*. A type of flamenco, danced by gypsies in Triana; it has Galician and Celtic undertones, as originally the theme derived from the Galician *muñeira* or 'dance of the miller's wife'.

2. *Cantilena* / *Cantilena*

DUQUE DE RIVAS

Por un alegre prado
de flores esmaltado,
y de una clara fuente
con la dulce corriente
de aljófares regado,
mi dueño idolatrado
iba cogiendo flores,
más bella y más lozana
que ninfa de Diana.
Los risueños amores
en torno la cercaban,
y en su falda jugaban;
y en tanto que ella, hermosa,
ora un clavel cogía,
ora una linda rosa,
ora un tierno jacinto,
más flores producía
aquel fresco recinto
orgulloso y ufano;
pues al punto otras tantas,
como tronchó la mano
de mi dueño tirano,
brotaron a sus plantas.

Across a radiant field,
enamelled with flowers
and watered by a clear spring
with its sweet flow
and drops of dew,
my beloved mistress
passed by, gathering flowers,
more beautiful and fresh
than a nymph of Diana.
Smiling amoretti
encircled her
and frolicked in her skirt;
and while she, in her beauty,
picked now a carnation,
now a lovely rose,
now a young hyacinth,
more flowers issued
from that fresh enclosure,
proud and haughty —
for straight away as many
as the hand of my tyrannical
lover did pick,
sprang up at her feet.

3. *Madrigal* / *Madrigal*

DUQUE DE RIVAS

Tus ojos, ojos no son,
niña, sino dos navajas
con que destrozas y rajas
el más duro corazón.

Y tu boca celestial
no es boca, es un vaso lleno
de hechizos y de veneno,
entre perlas y coral.

Por experiencia lo sé:
vi tus ojos, y al instante
con un hierro penetrante
roto mi pecho encontré.

Tu suave voz me encantó,
bebí tu sonrisa, y luego
de ardiente ponzoña el fuego
por mis venas circuló.

Your eyes are not eyes,
my love, but two knives
with which you tear and slice
the toughest heart.

And your heavenly mouth
is no mouth but a glass
brimming with sorcery and venom
amid pearls and coral.

I know from experience:
I saw your eyes and at once
by a steely weapon
I found my heart broken.

Your soft voice bewitched me,
I drank in your smile, and then
with burning venom the fire
coursed through my veins.

Tres sonetos / Three sonnets

FRANCISCO RODRÍGUEZ MARÍN

(1930)

1. *Anhelos* / *Cravings*

Agua quisiera ser, luz y alma mía,
que con tu transparencia te brindara,
porque tu dulce boca me gustara,
no apagara tu sed: la encendería.
Viento quisiera ser; en noche umbría
Callado hasta tu lecho penetrara,
Y aspirar por tus labios me
    dejara,
Y mi vida en la tuya infundiría.
Fuego quisiera ser para abrasarte
En un volcán de amor, ¡oh, estatua inerte,
Sorda a las quejas de quien supo amarte!
Y después para siempre poseerte,
Tierra quisiera ser y disputarte,
Celoso a la codicia de la muerte.

I'd fain be water, my dearest love,
to celebrate your mirrored image;
that your sweet lips might taste me,
I would not quench your thirst, but fire it.
I'd fain be wind; on sombre nights
I'd silently enter your bed
and allow myself to breathe through your
    lips
and immerse myself in yours.
I'd fain be fire to consume you
in a volcano of fire, ah, lifeless statue,
deaf to the desires of one who loved you.
And then, in order to hold you always,
I'd fain be earth and compete for you,
jealous of death's cupidity.

2. *Vade retro!* / *Get behind me!*

Amaste á Pedro, á Ignacio, á
    Marcelino,
Á Casto, á Gil, á Justo, á Pepe, á Diego,
Á Antón después, á Restituto luego,
Y á Lúcas, y á Ginés, y á Juan, y á Lino.
    Y amaste á Cleto, á Félix, á Faustino,
É inextinguible tu amoroso fuego,
Amaste á Blas el sordo, á Luis el ciego,
Y al Pancho aquel que de las Indias vino.
    Hoy, vieja, pobre y fea, – iguarda,
    Pablo! –
Te hace exhalar interminable queja
El insufrible solteril achaque.
    Mas ¿quién te ha de querer ¡llévete el
    diablo!
Si, además de ser fea, pobre y vieja,
Tienes, en vez de un *alma*, un
    almanaque?

You loved Pedro, Ignacio,
    Marcelino,
Casto, Gil, Justo, Pepe, Diego,
then Antón, afterwards Restituto,
and Lúcas and Ginés and Juan and Lino.
    And you loved Cleto, Félix, Faustino –
your amorous ardour's unquenchable –
you loved Blas the deaf, Luis the blind
and Pancho who hailed from the Indies.
    Today, old, poor and ugly, – take care,
    Pablo! –
the intolerable affliction of celibacy
makes you moan incessantly.
    But who shall love you, devil take
    you,
if, besides being ugly, poor and old,
you have, instead of an *alma* – an
    almanac?

3. *A unos ojos* / *To a pair of eyes*

¡Ah! Luceros radiantes,
Luceros hermosos,

Ah! Radiant bright stars,
beautiful bright stars,

Sois ojos graciosos:	such lovely eyes you are:
Mas ¿qué fuisteis antes?	but what did you use to be?
Tenéis de estudiantes	You have a student's
El ser revoltosos;	rebelliousness,
Mas por lo alevosos	but through your perfidy
Parecéis matantes.	you appear murderous.
Alegres ojillos,	Happy eyes,
Ojillos traviesos,	mischievous eyes,
Cómo sois tan sabios,	how wise you are,
Cómo sois tan pillos,	how roguish you are –
Qué sabéis de besos	you who know about kisses,
Cual si fueseis labios. ¡Ah!	as though you were lips. Ah!

Saeta[1] en forma de Salve a la Virgen de la Esperanza / Saeta in the form of a Salutation to the Virgin of Hope

SERAFÍN AND JOAQUÍN ÁLVAREZ QUINTERO

(1930)

¡Dios te salve, Macarena[2],	God protect thee, Macarena,
Madre de los sevillanos,	mother of Sevillians,
paz y vida!	peace and life!
¡La que alivia toda pena;	Thou who dost assuage all sorrow
la que cura con sus manos	and heal with thine hands
toda herida!	all wounds!
¡Dios te salve, luz del cielo,	God protect thee, light of heaven,
siempre estrella y siempre aurora	eternal star and eternal dawn
de bonanza!	of fair weather!
¡La que ampara todo anhelo;	Thou who dost soothe all longing,
la divina sembradora	divine sower
de esperanza!	of hope!

———   ———

¡Dios te salve, María,	God protect thee, Mary,
Madre de gracia llena;	mother full of grace,
alma de Andalucía,	soul of Andalusia,
sol de la Macarena!	sun of Macarena!

[1]Saeta. An unaccompanied devotional song, sung during a pause in Holy Week processions in Andalusia. 'Saeta' = arrow.
[2]Macarena. La Macarena, the Virgin of the Macarena, is the patron saint of Seville.

Tres poemas / *Three poems*

GUSTAVO ADOLFO BÉCQUER

Op. 81

1. *Olas gigantes* / *Vast waves*

Olas gigantes que os rompéis bramando
en las playas desiertas y remotas,
envuelto entre la sábana de espumas,
¡llevadme con vosotras!

Vast waves, breaking with a roar
on deserted and distant strands,
shroud me in a sheet of foam,
bear me away with you!

Ráfagas de huracán que arrebatáis
del alto bosque las marchitas hojas,
arrastrado en el ciego torbellino,
¡llevadme con vosotras!

Hurricane gusts, snatching
the tall wood's withered leaves,
dragging all along in dark turbulence,
bear me away with you!

Nubes de tempestad que rompe el rayo
y en fuego ornáis las desprendidas orlas,
arrebatado entre la niebla oscura,
¡llevadme con vosotras!

Storm clouds rent by lightning,
with your edges bordered in fire,
snatch me up in a dark mist,
bear me away with you!

Llevadme por piedad a donde el vértigo
con la razón me arranque la memoria.
¡Por piedad! ¡Tengo miedo de quedarme
con mi dolor a solas!

Bear me away, I beg, to where vertigo
eradicates my memory and reason . . .
Have mercy . . . I dread being left
alone with my grief!

2. *Tu pupila es azul*[1] / *Your eyes are blue*

Tu pupila es azul y cuando ríes
su claridad suave me recuerda
el trémulo fulgor de la mañana
que en el mar se refleja.

Your eyes are blue and when you laugh
their gentle radiance reminds me
of the trembling glow of dawn
reflected in the sea.

Tu pupila es azul y cuando lloras
las trasparentes lágrimas en ella
se me figuran gotas de rocío
sobre una vïoleta.

Your eyes are blue and when you weep
their transparent tears
seem to me like dew-drops
on a violet.

Tu pupila es azul y si en su fondo
como un punto de luz radia una idea
me parece en el cielo de la tarde
una perdida estrella.

Your eyes are blue and if in their depths
like a point of light a thought gleams
they seem to me in the evening sky
like stars adrift.

[1]Originally entitled 'Imitación de Byron', this poem was inspired by Byron's 'I saw thee weep'. See Appendix.

3. *Besa el aura* / *The breeze, softly moaning, kisses*

Besa el aura que gime blandamente
las leves ondas que jugando riza;
el sol besa a la nube en occidente
y de púrpura y oro la matiza;
la llama en derredor del tronco ardiente
por besar a otra llama se desliza
y hasta el sauce inclinándose a su
    peso
al río que le besa, vuelve un beso.

The breeze, softly moaning, kisses
the gentle waves it ripples in jest;
the sun kisses the cloud in the west,
tingeing it with purple and gold;
the ardent flame slips round the tree
to kiss another flame
and even the willow, bowing beneath its
    weight,
returns the river's kiss.

Homenaje a Lope de Vega / *Homage to Lope de Vega*

LOPE DE VEGA
Op. 90 (1935)

1. *Cuando tan hermosa os miro* / *When I gaze on thy great beauty*

(from *La discreta enamorada*)

Cuando tan hermosa os miro,
De amor suspiro,
Y cuando no os veo,
Suspira por mí el deseo.
Cuando mis ojos os ven,
Van á gozar tanto bien;
Mas como por su desdén
De los vuestros me retiro,
De amor suspiro;
Y cuando no os veo,
Suspira por mí el deseo.

When I gaze on thy great beauty,
I sigh with love,
and when I do not see thee,
desire sighs for me.
When my eyes see thee,
they revel in such delight;
but since because of their disdain
I avoid thine eyes,
I sigh with love;
and when I do not see thee,
desire sighs for me.

2. *Si con mis deseos* / *If with my desires*

(from *La Estrella de Sevilla*)

Si con mis deseos
los tiempos caminaran,
al sol aventajaran
los pasos giganteos,
y mis dulces empleos
celebrara Sevilla,
sin envidiar celosa,
amante venturosa,
la regalada y tierna tortolilla
que con arrullos roncos
tálamos hace de los huecos troncos.
Ah!

If with my desires
time would walk apace,
the sun would be outstripped
by their giant steps,
and my sweet employments
would be celebrated by Seville,
without her envying jealously,
fortunate lover,
the delicate and tender turtle dove,
who with husky cooings
makes bridal beds from hollow trunks.
Ah!

3. *Al Val de Fuente Ovejuna . . . / Into the Vale of Fuente Ovejuna . . .*

(from *Fuente Ovejuna*)

Al val de Fuente Ovejuna	Into the Vale of Fuente Ovejuna
la niña en cabellos baja;	a maiden with flowing hair descends;
el caballero la sigue	the knight of Calatrava
de la Cruz de Calatrava[1].	is following her there.
Entre las ramas se esconde,	She hides behind the branches,
de vergonzosa y turbada;	bashful and in turmoil;
fingiendo que no le ha visto,	feigning not to have seen him,
pone delante las ramas.	she moves the branches in front of her.
«¿Para qué te escondes,	'Why dost thou hide,
niña gallarda?	charming maid?
Que mis linces deseos	My keen desire
paredes pasan.»	Can pass through walls!'
Acercóse el caballero,	The nobleman drew near,
y ella, confusa y turbada,	and she, confused and in turmoil,
hacer quiso celosías	tried to fashion a screen
de las intrincadas ramas;	from the entangled branches;
mas como quien tiene amor	but since whoever loves
los mares y las montañas	can cross with ease
atraviesa fácilmente,	oceans and mountains,
la dice tales palabras:	he addresses her thus:
«¿Para qué te escondes,	'Why dost thou hide,
niña gallarda?	charming maid?
Que mis linces deseos	My keen desire
paredes pasan.»	can pass through walls!'

[1]*Calatrava*. Spain's military orders were modelled partially on the monastic orders of the Holy Land. The Templars had obtained extensive rights in Spain, and when their empire waned, the Spanish orders flourished. The Order of Calatrava sprang up when the Templars abandoned the convent-fortress of Calatrava, near Ciudad Real. The order was given papal sanction in 1164.

X

JESÚS GURIDI
(1886–1961)

Like a number of other Spanish song composers, Jesús Guridi is known to song recital audiences for one work – his *Seis canciones castellanas* (UMV 17468) – although he wrote three sets of songs in his native Basque language, and a good many other vocal works. He was born of an extremely musical family in Vitoria, south-west of San Sebastian in the Alava province of north-eastern Spain. Guridi studied with Grovlez and d'Indy – the link between the Schola Cantorum and Spain was a particularly strong one it seems – as well as with Joseph Jongen in Brussels. He achieved considerable fame as an organist and improviser, and as the conductor of the Bilbao Choral Society; he also quickly established himself as one of the relatively few successful Basque composers (Juan Crisóstomo de Arriaga – after whom the main theatre in Bilbao is named – and José Maria Usandiziga are others). From the beginning Guridi put his cards on the table as a composer willing to write in his own language: he composed two successful Basque operas, *Mirentxu* (1910) and *Amaya* (1920), as well as a popular zarzuela, *El caserío*. It is significant that the one vocal work published by the state publishing company, the Union Musical Española, is a set of Castilian songs. The high musical quality and charm of the *Seis canciones castellanas* and the success of the early Basque operas suggest that some of the composer's other works might have been better known abroad if the conditions of Franco's Spain had not discouraged the dissemination of Basque culture.

Seis canciones castellanas / *Six Castilian songs*

1. *Allá arriba, en aquella montaña* / *High up on that mountain*

Allá arriba, en aquella montaña,	High up on that mountain
yo corté una caña, yo corté un clavel.	I picked a cane, I picked a carnation.

Labrador ha de ser,
labrador,
que mi amante lo es.
No le quiero molinero,
que me da con el maquilandero.
Yo le quiero labrador,
que coja las mulas y se vaya a arar
y a la medianoche me venga a rondar.
Entra labrador si vienes a verme.
Si vienes a verme ven por el
    corral,
sube por el naranjo, que seguro vas.
Entra labrador si vienes a verme.

A ploughman,
a ploughman
must my lover be.
I do not want a miller
who treats me like his corn.
I want a ploughman
to take his mules to plough
and at midnight serenade me.
Enter, ploughman, if you come to see me.
If you come to see me, come through the
    yard,
climb the orange tree and you'll be safe.
Enter ploughman, if you come to see me.

2. ¡Sereno! / Nightwatchman

¡Sereno! En mi casa hay un hombre
durmiendo con un capotón.
En la mano llevaba un reloj
y un puñal de plata.
¡Ay! Sereno, este hombre me
    mata.

Nightwatchman, in my house a man
with a large cloak is sleeping.
In his hands he was holding a watch
and a silver dagger.
Ah, nightwatchman, this man is killing
    me!

3. Llámale con el pañuelo / Call him with your kerchief

Llámale con el pañuelo,
llámale con garbo y modo.
Echale la escarapela
al otro lado del lomo.
Llámale majo al toro.
Torero tira la capa;
torero tira el capote[1];
mira que el toro te pilla,
mira que el toro te coge.
Majo, si vas a los toros,
no lleves capa pa torear;
que son los toros muy bravos
y a algún torero le van a matar.

Call him with your kerchief,
call him with grace and style.
Toss your pennant
over its shoulder.
Majo, call out to the bull.
Torero, fling down your cape[1];
torero, fling down your capote;
Take care, lest the bull seize you,
take care, lest the bull catch you.
Majo, if you go to the bulls,
don't wear a cape to fight;
for the bulls are most brave
and will kill some toreros.

[1]Capote. The coloured cloak used by bullfighters.

4. No quiero tus avellanas / I do not want your hazelnuts

No quiero tus avellanas,
tampoco tus alhelíes,
porque me han salido vanas
las palabras que me diste,
yendo por agua a la fuente.
Como eran palabras de amor,
se las llevó la corriente
de las cristalinas aguas,

I do not want your hazelnuts,
nor your gillyflowers –
for they've turned out to be empty,
the promises you made,
as I fetched water from the fountain.
Since they were words of love,
the water bore them away,
the crystal-clear water,

hasta llegar a la fuente,
donde me diste palabra
de ser mía hasta la muerte.

down to the fountain,
where you gave me your word
to be mine unto death.

5. *¡Cómo quieres que adivine!* / *How do you expect me to guess*

¡Cómo quieres que adivine
si estás despierta o dormida,
como no baje del cielo
un ángel y me lo diga!
¡Cómo quieres que adivine!
Alegría y más alegría,
hermosa paloma,
¡cuándo serás mía!
cuándo vas a ser,
hermosa paloma,
ramito laurel!
Cuándo voy por leña al monte,
¡olé ya, mi niña!
y me meto en la espesura
y veo la nieve blanca,
¡olé ya, mi niña!
me acuerdo de tu hermosura.
Quisiera ser por un rato
anillo de tu pendiente,
para decirte al oído
lo que mi corazón siente.
Las estrellas voy contando,
¡olé ya, mi niña!
por ver la que me persigue.
Me persigue un lucerito,
¡olé ya, mi niña!
pequeñito, pero firme.

How do you expect me to guess
if you are awake or asleep,
since no angel descends
from heaven to tell me!
How do you expect me to guess!
Joy and more joy shall we have,
pretty dove,
when you are mine,
when you come to be mine,
pretty dove,
my bouquet!
When I go to the forest for firewood,
ah my love,
when I am caught in a thicket
and see the white snow,
ah my love,
I think of your beauty.
I'd like for a while to be
the link in your earring,
to whisper in your ear
what I feel in my heart.
I count the stars,
ah my love,
to see which one pursues me.
It is a morning star,
ah my love,
small but steadfast.

6. *Mañanita de San Juan*[1] / *Early on St John's day*

Mañanita de San Juan,
levántate tempranito
y en la ventana verás
de hierbabuena un poquito.
Aquella paloma blanca
que pica en el arcipiés,
que por dónde la cogería,
que por dónde la cogeré;
si la cojo por el pico
se me escapa por los pies.
Coge niño la enramada,
que la noche está serena
y la música resuena
en lo profundo del mar.

Early on St John's day,
be up with the lark,
and in the window you'll see
a little sprig of mint.
That white dove
which pecks the you know what,
where might I catch it,
where shall I catch it?
If I grasp it by the beak
its feet are still free to run.
Pick up the garlands, my lad,
for the night is clear
and music resounds
from the depths of the sea.

[1]St John's day is 24 June, Midsummer day.

XI

OSCAR ESPLÁ
(1886–1976)

Not at all attracted to composing music with local colour (he considered this kitsch and limiting), Esplá nevertheless invented an original scale which derived from the folksong of his home region, and which is the basis of much of his music. This oblique and intellectual approach to folk music places him in the same category as Alan Bush in England – both composers preferred to revise their entire harmonic idiom to incorporate the folksong modes of their countries, and then to compose large-scale music which, to the casual ear, sounds unrelated to the folk idiom. The *Canciones playeras*, UMV 18658, derive slightly more obviously from his native Alicante (they are fishermen's songs) than most of Esplá's work. They were composed in 1929, and exist also in an orchestral version. His other song cycle *Soledades* dates from 1927. Esplá's output was very large and includes operas, ballets, symphonic poems, and a good deal of chamber and piano music.

Esplá was born on 5 August 1886. He was destined for a career as an engineer, and throughout his musical life he retained scientific and philosophical interests – he obtained a doctorate of philosophy in later life. After an engineering course at Barcelona University (1903–11), he studied with Reger in Munich and Saint-Saëns in Paris. He held many distinguished posts including director of the Madrid Conservatoire and membership of the international council of UNESCO. The Conservatoire of music in Alicante is named in his honour.

Cinco canciones playeras españolas / Five Spanish songs of the seashore

RAFAEL ALBERTI

(1930)

1. *Rutas* / *Routes*

Por allí, por allá,
a Castilla se va.
Por allá, por allí,
a mi verde país.
    Quiero ir por allí,
quiero ir por allá.
A la mar, por allí,
a mi hogar, por allá.

This way or that
is the road to Castille.
That way or this
to my green native land.
    I want to go this way,
I want to go that.
This way to the sea,
that way to my home.

2. *Pregón* / *Street-cry*

¡Vendo nubes de colores:
las redondas, coloradas,
para endulzar los calores!

Coloured clouds for sale,
red round ones
to cool the burning heat!

¡Vendo los cirros morados
y rosas, las alboradas,
los crepúsculos dorados!

Cirrus clouds, purple
and pink, dawns,
golden twilights!

¡El amarillo lucero,
cogido a la verde rama
del celeste duraznero!

The yellow morning star,
tied to the green branch
of the celestial peach tree!

¡Vendo la nieve, la llama
y el canto del pregonero!

For sale! Snow, flame
and the song of the street vendor!

3. *Las doce* / *Twelve o'clock*

(Las doce, en la aldea.)
¡Sal a tu azotea!
(¡El ángel la dió!)
¡Sal, que salgo yo!

Twelve rings out in the village.
Come out on to your rooftop!
The angel struck twelve –
come out, for I come too!

Tu verde sombrilla,
mi negro sombrero,
la flor del romero,
clavada en tu horquilla.

You with your green parasol,
me with my black hat,
rosemary
fastened to your hair-pin.

¡Oh, qué maravilla
tan lejana, oh!

Oh, what a miracle
so far away!

Cierra tu sombrilla.
¡Sal, que salgo yo!

Close your parasol,
come out, for I come too!

4. *El pescador sin dinero* / *The penniless fisherman*

Pez verde y dulce del río,
sal, escucha el llanto mío:
  Rueda por el agua, rueda,
que no me queda moneda,
sedal tampoco me queda . . .
Llora con el llanto mío.
  No me queda nada, nada,
ni mi cesta torneada,
ni mi camisa bordada,
con un ancla, por mi amada . . .
Llora con el llanto mío.
    ¡Sí, llorad, sí, todos, sí!

Sweet green fish of the river,
jump out, listen to my lament:
  turn in the water, turn,
for I have no money
and I have no line . . .
Weep with my lament.
  Nothing, nothing have I left,
neither well-turned basket
nor shirt embroidered
with an anchor by my love . . .
Weep with my lament.
    Yes, weep! All of you, weep!

5. *Coplilla* / *Ditty*

Un duro[1] me dió mi madre,
antes de venir al pueblo,
para comprar aceitunas
allá en el olivar viejo.

My mother gave me a duro,
before I came to the town,
to buy olives there
in the old olive-grove.

Y yo me he tirado el duro
en cosas que son del viento:
un peine, una redecilla
y un moño de terciopelo.

And I threw the duro away
on empty trifles:
a comb, a hair-net
and a velvet chignon.

    [1]*Duro*. Silver coin worth five pesetas.

XII

FREDERIC MOMPOU
(1893–1987)

Mompou was a petit maître, and unashamedly – almost determinedly – so. Inspired by the understatement and pudeur of Fauré, a composer he admired from his youth, and subsequently by the minimalism of Satie, Mompou succeeded in creating a body of works in miniature forms, songs and piano pieces which in their ability to weave a magical spell quite out of proportion to their technical complexity recall the music of Francis Poulenc. Much of the Mompou magic consists in the fact that more than any other Catalan composer he was in touch with his roots. He was concerned to capture in music the intimate and transcendental nature of Catalan poetry, and to experience the rebirth (he termed it 'Recomença-ment') of a state of unsullied musical innocence. As Lionel Salter has written, Mompou seems at times to approach the ideal of silence in the 'static, incantatory quality [of] his poetic evocations'. It is surprising that in filtering his gifts through French muslin rather than Castilian or Andalusian gauze, he lost none of his Iberian individuality –rather is the specifically Catalan flavour of his creations preserved and intensified.

Frederic Mompou was born on 16 April 1893. His mother was of French descent, and his earliest enthusiasms were for French music, so that after initial studies at the Conservatorio del Liceo in Barcelona, all paths led to Paris. He lived there between 1911 and 1914 and again between 1921 and 1941, returning to Barcelona with the fall of France. Most of the Mompou songs are published by the French firm of Salabert. The exceptions are 'Cançoneta incerta', and 'L'hora grisa' (Union Musical Española), and 'Sant Martí' which is published by Edicions Tenora, Barcelona. *Charmes*, settings of Paul Valéry, was published by Max Eschig. Mompou seemed happy to melt the barriers between mélodie and canción – his perspicacious choice of Valéry, a poet otherwise all but ignored in the French song repertoire, matched the perfume of his improvisatory style. Both sets of *Comptines* (children's miniatures that simultaneously recall the faux-naif, faux-medieval miniatures of Satie and the 'Louise Lalanne' and Max Jacob songs of Poulenc) essay a deliberately bilingual format, with the second song in each set sandwiched between two Catalan ones. The first set of *Comptines* is dedicated to Jane Bathori who created Ravel's *Schéhérazade* and *Histoires naturelles*. In the *Quatre mélodies* Mompou sets his own poems, but his best-known set of songs, the *Combat del somni*, are by the Catalan publisher and poet Josep Janés. Another song has a text by Janés's daughter Clara, who was also one of the composer's biographers. Unlike his contemporary Toldrà, Mompou did not embrace the modernisme movement which romanticised Catalan urban life. Mompou was, if anything, a noucentista – an adherent of *noucentisme* (named after the style of the 1900s), which supplanted modernisme in the same way that the rigours of Cézanne succeeded the vagaries of the French Impressionists. Mompou did not altogether eschew Spanish poets: he set the Andalusian Nobel prize-winner Juan Ramón Jiménez, and his last set of songs, published in 1980, is to the poems of another Sevillian, the celebrated Gustavo Adolfo Bécquer. In this work, entitled *Bécquerianas*, some critics detected a new direction in the 87-year-old composer's literary taste.

L'hora grisa / The grey hour

MANUEL BLANCAFORT
(1915)

¡Tot dorm a l'hora grisa,
els arbres, les muntanyes, els ocells, el vent!
Solament el fum fa son camí lentament,
amunt, amunt, com l'oració.
Més tard, quan el cel s'apagui,
sortirà una estrelleta d'or.
¡Tot dorm a l'hora grisa,
els arbres, les muntanyes, els ocells, el vent!

All is asleep in the grey hour,
the trees, the mountains, the birds, the wind!
Only the smoke moves slowly
upwards, upwards like a prayer.
Later, when the sky grows dark,
a tiny golden star will appear.
All is asleep in the grey hour,
the trees, the mountains, the birds, the wind!

Charmes / Charms

PAUL VALÉRY
(1920)

La fausse morte / The woman falsely dead

Humblement, tendrement, sur le tombeau charmant,
Sur l'insensible monument,

Humbly, tenderly, on the enchanting tomb,
over the insensate monument

Que d'ombres, d'abandons, et d'amour
    prodiguée,
Forme ta grâce fatiguée,
Je meurs, je meurs sur toi, je tombe et je
    m'abats,
Mais à peine abattu sur le sépulcre
    bas,
Dont la close étendue aux cendres me
    convie,
Cette morte apparente, en qui revient la
    vie,
Frémit, rouvre les yeux, m'illumine et me
    mord,
Et m'arrache toujours une nouvelle mort
Plus précieuse que la vie.

which, with a wealth of shadow, abandon
    and love,
your exhausted grace forms,
I die, I die above you, I fall and
    subside;
but scarce have I slumped on the low
    sepulchre
whose narrow confines beckon me to the
    ashes,
than this seeming dead woman, regaining
    life,
quivers, opens again her eyes, illuminates
    and bites me,
and wrests me for another death,
more precious than life.

L'insinuant / The hinter

O courbes, méandre,
Secrets du menteur,
Est-il art plus tendre
Que cette lenteur?

O curves, o meanders,
secrets of the liar,
is there an art more tender
than this slow pace?

Je sais où je vais,
Je t'y veux conduire,
Mon dessein mauvais
N'est pas de te nuire . . .

I know where I go,
I shall take you there;
my evil design
is not to harm you . . .

(Quoique souriante
En pleine fierté,
Tant de liberté
La désoriente!)

(Though smiling
in her full pride,
she is thrown
by so much freedom!)

O courbes, méandre,
Secrets du menteur,
Je veux faire attendre
Le mot le plus tendre.

O curves, o meanders,
secrets of the liar,
I shall make her wait
for that most tender word.

Le sylphe / The sylph

Ni vu ni connu
Je suis le parfum
Vivant et défunt
Dans le vent venu!

Neither seen nor known
I am the perfume
living and dead
that came on the wind!

Ni vu ni connu,
Hasard ou génie?
A peine venu
La tâche est finie!

Neither seen nor known,
Fate or Genius?
Scarce arrived,
my task is done!

Ni lu ni compris?
Aux meilleurs esprits
Que d'erreurs promises!

Ni vu ni connu
Le temps d'un sein nu
Entre deux chemises!

Neither read nor understood?
To the finest of spirits
how many promised errors!

Neither seen nor known
the moment for a naked breast
between two shirts!

Le vin perdu / Lost wine

J'ai, quelque jour, dans l'océan,
(Mais je ne sais plus sous quels cieux),
Jeté, comme offrande au néant,
Tout un peu de vin précieux . . .

One day, into the ocean
(but under which skies I no longer know)
I threw, as an offering to the void,
a sprinkling of precious wine . . .

Qui voulut ta perte, ô liqueur?
J'obéis, peut-être au devin?
Peut-être au souci de mon coeur,
Songeant au sang, versant le vin?

Who willed this waste, o liquor?
Did I perhaps obey the soothsayer?
Or perhaps my heart's anxiety,
dreaming of blood, spilling the wine?

Sa transparence accoutumée
Après une rose fumée
Reprit aussi pure la mer . . .

Its usual transparence –
later a pink spread of cloud –
was assumed as purely by the sea . . .

Perdu ce vin, ivres les ondes! . . .
J'ai vu bondir dans l'air amer
Les figures les plus profondes . . .

Lost this wine, drunken the waves! . . .
I saw hurtling through the bitter air
the profoundest figurations . . .

Les pas / The steps

Tes pas, enfants de mon silence,
Saintement, lentement placés,
Vers le lit de ma vigilance
Procèdent muets et glacés.

Your steps, children of my silence,
with slow and saintly tread,
towards my vigil's bed
are advancing mute and frozen.

Personne pure, ombre divine,
Qu'ils sont doux, tes pas
    retenus!
Dieux! . . . tous les dons que je devine
Viennent à moi sur ces pieds nus!

Pure person, divine shadow,
your constrained steps, how sweet they
    are!
Gods! . . . all the gifts that I surmise
come to me on those naked feet!

Si, de tes lèvres avancées,
Tu prépares, pour l'apaiser
A l'habitant de mes pensées
La nourriture d'un baiser,

If, with your proffered lips,
you prepare, to appease
the inhabitant of my thoughts,
the nourishment of a kiss,

Ne hâte pas cet acte tendre,
Douceur d'être et de n'être pas,
Car j'ai vécu de vous attendre,
Et mon coeur n'était que vos pas.

do not hasten this tender act,
sweetness of being and being not,
for I have lived off awaiting you,
and my heart was naught but your steps.

Cançoneta incerta / Uncertain song

JOSEP CARNER

(1926)

¿Aquest camí tan fi, tan fi,
qui sap on mena?
És a la vila o és al pi
de la carena?

Un lliri blau color de cel
diu 'vine, vine';
però 'no passis' diu un vel
de teranyina.

¿Serà drecera del gosat,
rossola ingrata
o bé un camí d'enamorat
colgat de mata?

¿Es un recer per a dormir
qui passi pena?
¿Aquest camí tan fi, tan fi,
qui sap on mena?

¿Qui sap si trist o somrient
acull a l'hoste?
Qui sap si mor sobtadament
sota la brosta?

¿Qui sabia mai aquest camí,
a què em convida?
I és camí incert cada matí,
n'és cada vida.

This path so narrow,
who knows where it leads?
To the town or to that pine
on the mountainside?

A sky-blue lily
says 'Come, come';
but 'Do not pass',
says a spider's web.

Is this a short cut for the daring,
a slippery descent,
or is it a lover's path,
covered with brush?

Is it a shelter to sleep
for one in pain?
This path so narrow,
who knows where it leads?

Who knows whether sad or smiling
it greets the traveller?
Who knows if it dies of a sudden
beneath the thicket?

Who would ever know this path,
know to what it invites me?
Every morning is an uncertain path,
and every life is too.

Quatre mélodies / Four mélodies

FREDERIC MOMPOU

(1925)

Incertitud / Uncertainty

Incertitud del meu camí.
Del meu amor tot l'infinit,
d'estrelles n'està escrit.
Claror dels camps, claror de nit.
Claror de cel, sobre un desig.

Uncertainty of my path.
The utter infinity of my love
is written in the stars.
Light of the fields, splendour of night.
Splendour of the sky over a wish.

Rosa del camí / Rose of the path

En dolç desmai
durant la nit
a sobre del bosc
ha caigut una estrella.
De bon matí
jo trobaré una rosa
sobre el meu camí.

In a sweet swoon
during the night,
upon the forest
a star has fallen.
At early morn
I shall find a rose
on my path.

Neu / Snow

No és neu, són flors de cel.
Cor meu com te desfulles.
Són fulls de ma vida esquinçats.
Plugeta de paper blanc.
No és neu, són flors de cel.
Dolor, com te desfulles.
¡Ai! Quina tristesa fa.

Not snow but flowers from the sky.
O my heart, how you are unleaving!
Lacerated pages from my life.
Fine rain of white paper.
Not snow but flowers from the sky.
O suffering, how you are unleaving!
Ah, how sad!

Cortina de fullatge / Curtain of leaves

Encara veig al lluny
els llums de ma ciutat.
I el nostre petit niu
Amagat entre el ramatge.

Still I see in the distance
the light of my city.
And our little nest
concealed between branches.

Sé que la lluna
és al darrera d'aquests arbres.
I en la penombra d'aquest bosc
jo puc fer entrar
una carícia de llum tendra sobre els teus
    ulls
tan sols obrint una cortina de fullatge.

I know that the moon
is behind these trees.
And in the shadow of this forest
I can let in
a tender caress of light upon your
    eyes,
purely by parting a curtain of leaves.

Tres comptines / Three ditties
(1926)

1. Dalt d'un cotxe / On a buggy

Dalt d'un cotxe n'hi ha una nina
que en repica els cascabells.
Trenta, quaranta,
l'ametlla amarganta,
el pinyol madur:
ves-te'n tu.

On a buggy there's a girl
ringing little bells.
Thirty, forty,
the almond is bitter,
the kernel ripe.
Be off with you!

2. *Margot la pie* / *Margot the magpie*

Margot la pie a fait son nid
dans la cour à David.
David l'attrape,
lui coupe la patte;
ric-rac, ric-rac,
comme une patate.

Margot the magpie built her nest
in David's courtyard.
David catches her,
cuts off her leg,
snip-snip, snip-snip,
like a potato.

3. *He vist dins la lluna* / *I saw in the moon*

He vist dins la lluna
tres petits conills
que menjaven prunes
com tres desvergonyits.
La pipa a la boca
i la copa als dits,
tot dient: 'Mestressa,
poseu-nos un got
ben ple de vi.'

I saw in the moon
three little rabbits
eating plums
like three naughty boys.
Pipe in mouth,
cup in hand,
they all say: Mistress!
Pour us a glass
brimming with wine.

Tres comptines / *Three ditties*
   (1943)

1. *Aserrín, Aserrán* / *Sawing song*

Aserrín, aserrán,
los maderos de San Juan.
Los de arriba sierran bien
y los de abajo también.
Al milano, ¿qué le dan?
Bellotitas con el pan.
Por la noche pan y pera,
y otra noche pera y pan.
Aserrín, aserrán,
los maderos de San Juan.

Saw away, saw away
at the logs of Saint John.
Those on top saw well
and those on bottom too.
What do they feed the kite?
Little acorns with bread.
Bread with pears at night,
and the next night pears with bread.
Saw away, saw away
at the logs of Saint John.

2. *Petite fille de Paris* / *Little Parisian girl*

Petite fille de Paris,
prête-moi tes souliers gris.
Prête-moi tes souliers gris
pour aller en Paradis.
Nous irons un à un
dans le chemin des Saints,
deux à deux
dans le chemin des cieux.

Little Parisian girl,
lend me your grey shoes,
lend me your grey shoes
to go to Paradise.
We'll go one by one
on the pathway of the saints,
and two by two
on the pathway in the sky.

3. *Pito, pito, colorito* / *Pito, pito, full of colours*

Pito, pito, colorito,
¿dónde vas tú tan bonito?
Pito, pito, colorito,
¿dónde vas tú tan bonito?
A la acera
verdadera.
Pim, pom, fuera.

Pito, pito, full of colours,
where are you going, my pretty one?
Pito, pito, full of colours,
where are you going, my pretty one?
To the pavement –
I swear I am.
Pim, pom, out!

Llueve sobre el río / *It rains on the river*

JUAN RAMÓN JIMÉNEZ

(1945)

Llueve sobre el río . . .

It rains on the river . . .

El agua estremece
los fragantes juncos
de la orilla verde . . .
¡Ay, qué ansioso olor
a pétalo frío!

The water stirs
the fragrant reeds
on the green shore . . .
Ah, what an uneasy scent
of cold petals!

Llueve sobre el río . . .

It rains on the river . . .

Mi barca parece
mi sueño, en un vago
mundo. ¡Orilla verde!
¡Ay, barca sin junco!
¡Ay, corazón frío!

My boat seems to be my dream
in a hazy
world. Green shore!
Ah, boat adrift!
Ah, cold heart!

Llueve sobre el río . . .

It rains on the river . . .

Pastoral / *Pastorale*

JUAN RAMÓN JIMÉNEZ

(1945)

Los caminos de la tarde
se hacen uno, con la noche.
Por él he de ir a tí,
amor que tanto te escondes.

The paths of evening
merge into one at night.
Upon that path I must go to you,
my love, who always hides.

Por él he de ir a tí,
como la luz de los montes,
como la brisa del mar,
como el olor de las flores.

Upon that path I must go to you,
like the light of the mountains,
like the breeze of the sea,
like the scent of the flowers.

Combat del somni / Dream combat

JOSEP JANÉS

1. Damunt de tu només les flors / Above you naught but flowers
(1942)

Damunt de tu només les flors.
Eren com una ofrena blanca:
la llum que daven al teu cos
mai més seria de la branca;

tota una vida de perfum
amb el seu bes t'era donada.
Tu resplendies de la llum
per l'esguard clos atresorada.

¡Si hagués pogut ésser sospir
de flor! Donar-me, com un llir,
a tu, perquè la meva vida

s'anés marcint sobre el teu pit.
I no saber mai més la nit,
que al teu costat fóra esvaïda.

Above you naught but flowers.
They were like a white offering:
the light they shed on your body
will nevermore belong to the branch.

An entire life of perfume
was given you with their kiss.
You were resplendent in the light,
treasured by your closed eyes.

Could I have been the sigh
of a flower! Given myself as a lily,
that my life might

wither over your breast,
nevermore to know the night,
vanished from your side.

2. Aquesta nit un mateix vent / Tonight the same wind
(1946)

Aquesta nit un mateix vent
i una mateixa vela encesa
devien dur el teu pensament
i el meu per mars on la tendresa

es torna música i cristall.
El bes se'ns feia transparència
– si tu eres l'aigua, jo el mirall –
com si abracéssim una absència.

¿El nostre cel fóra, potser,
un somni etern, així, de besos
fets melodia, i un no ser
de cossos junts i d'ulls encesos

amb flames blanques, i un sospir
d'acariciar sedes de llir?

Tonight the same wind
and the same gleaming sail
are bearing your thoughts
and mine across seas where tenderness

turns to music and crystal light.
Our kiss became transparent –
if you were the water, I was the mirror –
it was as though we embraced a void.

Is our heaven, perhaps,
an eternal dream of kisses
made melody – an incorporeal
union, with burning eyes

and white flames and a sigh
as if caressing silken lilies?

3. *Jo et pressentia com la mar* / *I sensed you were like the sea* (1948)

Jo et pressentia com la mar
i com el vent, immensa, lliure,
alta, damunt de tot atzar
i tot destí. I en el meu viure,

com el respir. I ara que et tinc
veig com el somni et limitava.
Tu no ets un nom, ni un gest. No
   vinc
a tu com a la imatge blava

d'un somni humà. Tu no ets la mar,
que és presonera dins de platges,
tu no ets el vent, pres en l'espai.

Tu no tens límits; no hi ha, encar,
mots per a dir-te, ni paisatges
per ser el teu món – ni hi seran
   mai.

I sensed you were like the sea,
and like the wind, immense, free,
towering above all hazard
and all destiny. And in my life

like breathing. And now that I have you,
I see how limiting my dream had been.
You are neither name nor gesture. Nor do
   I come
to you as to a hazy image

of a human dream. You are not the sea,
which is confined between beaches,
you are not the wind, caught in space.

You are boundless; there are as yet
no words to express you, nor landscapes
to form your world – nor will there ever
   be.

4.[1] *Fes-me la vida transparent* / *Make my life transparent* (1951)

Fes-me la vida transparent,
com els teus ulls;
torna ben pura la mà meva,
i al pensament
duu-m'hi la pau.
Altra aventura no vull,
sinó la de seguir
l'estela blanca que neixia
dels teus camins.
I no llanguir
per ser mirall d'uns ulls.
Voldria ser com un riu oblidadís
que es lliura al mar,
les aigües pures de tota imatge
amb un anhel de blau.
I ser llavors feliç
de viure lluny d'amors obscures
amb l'esperança del teu cel.

Make my life transparent,
like your eyes;
make my hand wholly pure,
and to my thoughts
bring peace.
I desire no other adventure
than to follow
the white wake created
by your passage,
nor to languish
for being the mirror of your eyes.
I would wish to be like an oblivious river
that abandons itself to the sea,
the pure waters of every image,
yearning for the blue.
And to be happy then,
living far from dark loves
with hope for your heaven.

[1]This song, although originally part of the cycle *Combat del Somni*, is now very
frequently performed on its own.

Cançó de la fira / Song of the fair

TOMÀS GARCÉS

(1949)

Els seus tresors mostra la fira	The fair displays its wonders
perquè els agafis amb la mà.	for you to grasp in either hand.
Jo sóc cansat de tant mirar	I am weary with so much gazing
i la meva ànima sospira.	and my soul sighs.
Cotó de sucre, cavallets,	Candy-floss, merry-go-round,
càntirs de vidre i arracades	jugs of glass and earrings
lluen i salten fent ballades	gleam and dance as they quiver
entre el brogit dels platerets.	amid the clamour of cymbals.
El teu esguard ple d'avidesa	Your gaze, brimming with eagerness,
un immortal desig el mou.	craves an immortal wish.
¿Cerques un espectacle nou	Are you seeking a new spectacle
més amunt de la fira encesa?	beyond the glowing fair?
Els estels punxen tot el cel.	The stars pierce the whole expanse of sky.
L'oreig escampa espurnes. Mira:	The breeze scatters the sparks. Look:
cam poc a poc es mor la fira	how gradually the fire dies
sota la llum d'aquell estel.	beneath the light of that star.
Glateixes per copsar l'estrella?	Do you yearn to catch the star?
Ai, que el desig t'estreny el cor!	Ah, desire clutches your heart!
Mai més voldràs la joia d'or	Never again will you crave golden jewel
ni la rialla del titella.	or a clown's laughter.

Le nuage / The cloud

MATHILDE POMÈS

(1951)

S'embarquer, ô lente nef,	To embark, o languid ship,
à ton bord sans capitaine;	on your deck devoid of captain;
s'embarquer, ô blanc vaisseau,	to embark, o white vessel,
à ton bord sans gouvernail,	on your deck devoid of helmsman,
rompues les amarres du souvenir	the mooring ropes of memory itself
même,	broken,
perdu le sextant du désir concret.	the sextant of concrete desire lost.
Aller voguer dans une douce dérive,	To sail in a sweet drift,
sur une mer sans couleur	on a sea devoid of colour
vers des îles sans contour.	toward islands devoid of shape,
Voguer, aller, aller . . .	to sail, to go, to go . . .
Le silence diaphane	The diaphanous silence
tenant lieu pour espace,	in lieu of space,
le coeur ne martelant plus	the heart now hammering
la scansion des secondes	the scansion of seconds
qu'en battements étouffés.	with mere stifled beats.
Aller voguer, voguer	To sail, sail,
à chaque coup de roulis	with every roll
perdre un peu de sa figure,	losing a fraction of one's form,
perdre un peu de sa substance.	losing a fraction of one's substance.
Voguer, aller	To sail, to go

jusqu'à ce point idéal
où la mer du ciel se comble
pour baigner le clair visage
d'une terre plus fleurie;
mon esquif plus frêle
que neige en avril,
fondue au soleil la haute misaine,
l'étrave rongée par les alizés,
du beau port en vue
mollement couler . . .

to that ideal point
where the sea fills with sky
to bathe the bright face
of a more blossoming land;
my skiff more frail
than April snow,
the high foresail melted in the sun,
the stem-post gnawed by trade winds,
with the beautiful port in sight,
gently gliding . . .

Aureana do Sil[1] / *Aureana of Sil*

RAMÓN CABANILLAS

(1951)

As arenas de ouro,
Aureana do Sil,
son asbagoas acedas
que me fas chorar ti.
Si queres ouro fino,
Aureana do Sil,
abre o meu corazón
tés de a topalo a li.

The golden sands,
Aureana of Sil,
are the bitter tears
you make me cry.
If you want fine gold,
Aureana of Sil,
open up my heart –
you shall find it there.

Co que collas no rio,
Aureana do Sil,
mercaras cando moito
un amor infeliz.
Para dar c' un cariño
verdadero has de vir
enxoitar os meus ollos,
Aureana do Sil.

With what you glean from the river,
Aureana of Sil,
you will buy, at most,
an unhappy love.
To find a true love
you must come
to bewitch my eyes,
Aureana of Sil.

[1]*Sil*. The most important river in Galicia.

Cantar del alma / *Song of the soul*

SAN JUAN DE LA CRUZ

(1951)

Aquella eterna fuente está escondida,
que bien sé yo dó tiene su manida,
aunque es de noche.

That eternal spring is hidden,
but well I know where it rises,
though it is night.

Su origen no lo sé, pues no le tiene,
mas sé que todo origen de ella viene,
aunque es de noche.

I do not know its source, for it has none,
but I know that all things stem from it,
though it is night.

Sé que no puede ser cosa tan bella
y que cielos y tierra beben de ella,
aunque es de noche.

I know there is nothing more beautiful
and that sky and earth drink from it,
though it is night.

Sé ser tan caudalosas sus corrientes
que infiernos, cielos riegan y las gentes,
aunque es de noche.

El corriente que nace de esta fuente,
bien sé que es tan capaz y tan potente,
aunque es de noche.

Aquesta viva fuente que yo deseo,
en este pan de vida yo la veo,
aunque es de noche.

I know its streams to be so full
that they water hell, heaven and mankind,
though it is night.

The stream that rises from this spring
is, well I know, so broad and so mighty,
though it is night.

This living spring that I desire
I see as the bread of life,
though it is night.

Sant Martí / Saint Martin

PÈRE RIBOT

(1962)

Pedra ferma entre muntanyes.
Ull de serp, olor de pi.
Sant Martí,
rei de les teves entranyes,
la ploma, l'aire i el vi.

Respira la teva imatge
caritat pel pelegrí.
Sant Martí,
la intimitat del paisatge,
tu i jo pel mateix camí.

Cavaller del Crist, l'espasa
mati el serpent i el verí.
Sant Martí,
vetlli la flama la casa
i la veu del Sinaí.

Firm stone amid mountains.
Granite stone, pine fragrance.
Saint Martin,
King in your very being,
quill, air and wine.

Your image breathes
compassion for the pilgrim.
Saint Martin,
the intimate landscape . . .
you and I on the same path.

Knight of Christ, with your sword
kill the monster and its poison.
Saint Martin,
let your flame guard the house
and the voice of Sinai.

Primeros pasos / First steps

CLARA JANÉS

(1964)

Tu cuerpo como un árbol,
tus ojos como un lago,
y yo soñaba hundirme
debajo de tu abrazo.
Tu tiempo no era tiempo,
tu ser era un milagro
y te busqué hasta hallarte
debajo de tu abrazo.
El sol murió en el cielo,
tus pasos se alejaron
y se quedó mi sueño
debajo de tu abrazo.

Your body like a tree,
your eyes like a lake,
and I dreamed I was drowning
in your embrace.
Your time was not time,
your existence was a miracle,
and I sought you till I found you
in your embrace.
The sun died in the sky,
your steps faded away,
and my dream was left
in your embrace.

Bécquerianas / Bécquer songs

GUSTAVO ADOLFO BÉCQUER

(1971)

Hoy la tierra y los cielos me sonríen / Today the earth and heavens smile on me

Hoy la tierra y los cielos me
   sonríen,
hoy llega al fondo de mi alma el
   sol,
hoy la he visto . . ., la he visto y me ha
   mirado . . .
¡hoy creo en Dios!

Today the earth and heavens smile on
   me,
today the sun reaches the depth of my
   soul,
today I saw her . . . saw her and she
   looked on me . . .
today I believe in God!

Los invisibles átomos del aire / The invisible atoms of the air

Los invisibles átomos del aire
en derredor palpitan y se inflaman,
el cielo se deshace en rayos de oro,
la tierra se estremece alborozada.
Oigo flotando en olas de armonías
rumor de besos y batir de alas;
mis párpados se cierran . . . ¿Qué
   sucede?
¿Dime? . . . ¡Silencio! ¡Es el amor
   que pasa!

The invisible atoms of the air
around me throb and flare,
the sky dissolves in rays of gold,
the earth shivers in ecstasy.
Floating on waves of harmony, I hear
the sound of kisses and fluttering wings;
my eyelids close . . . What is
   nigh?
Tell me? . . . Hush! It is love that
   passes by!

Yo soy ardiente, yo soy morena / I am fiery, I am dark

  – Yo soy ardiente, yo soy morena,
yo soy el símbolo de la pasión,
de ansia de goces mi alma está llena.
¿A mí me buscas?
  – No es a ti: no.

   I am fiery, I am dark,
I am the symbol of passion,
my soul is filled with a thirst for pleasure.
Is it me you seek?
   No it is not you. No.

  – Mi frente es pálida, mis trenzas de
   oro,
puedo brindarte dichas sin fin.
Yo de ternura guardo un tesoro.
¿A mí me llamas?
  – No: no es a ti.

   My brow is pale, my tresses
   gold,
I can offer you boundless joy.
A wealth of tenderness I hold.
Is it me you call?
   No: no it is not you.

  – Yo soy un sueño, un imposible,
vano fantasma de niebla y luz;
soy incorpórea, soy intangible:
no puedo amarte.
  – ¡Oh, ven; ven tú!

   I am a dream, an impossibility,
a futile phantom of mist and light;
I have no body, I am intangible:
I cannot love you.
   Oh come! Come!

Yo sé cuál el objeto / *I know the reason*

Yo sé cuál el objeto	I know the reason
de tus suspiros es.	for your sighs.
Yo conozco la causa de tu dulce	I know the cause of your sweet,
secreta languidez.	secret languor.
¿Te ríes . . .? Algún día	You laugh . . .? Some day,
sabrás, niña, por qué:	my love, you'll know why:
Tú lo sabes apenas	you scarcely sense it
Y yo lo sé.	and I know it.
Yo sé cuándo tú sueñas,	I know when you dream,
y lo que en sueños ves;	and what in your dreams you see;
como en un libro puedo lo que callas	Like a book I can read on your brow
en tu frente leer.	what you conceal.
¿Te ríes . . .? Algún día	You laugh . . .? Some day,
sabrás, niña, por qué:	my love, you'll know why:
Tú lo sabes apenas	you scarcely sense it
y yo lo sé.	and I know it.
Yo sé por qué sonríes	I know why you smile
y lloras a la vez:	and weep in one:
yo penetro en los senos misteriosos	I can fathom the mysterious declivities
de tu alma de mujer.	of your woman's soul.
¿Te ríes . . .? Algún día	You laugh . . .? Some day,
sabrás, niña, por qué;	my love, you'll know why;
mientras tú sientes mucho y nada	while you feel many things and know
sabes,	none,
yo que no siento ya, todo lo sé.	I, who can no longer feel, know all.

Volverán las oscuras golondrinas / *The darkling swallows will return*

Volverán las oscuras golondrinas	The darkling swallows will return
en tu balcón sus nidos a colgar,	to hang on your balcony their nests,
y otra vez con el ala a sus	and brush again your windows with their
cristales	wings
jugando llamarán.	as they playfully call.
Pero aquéllas que el vuelo refrenaban	But those that lingered in their flight
tu hermosura y mi dicha a contemplar,	to behold your beauty and my joy,
aquéllas que aprendieron nuestros	those that learned our
nombres . . .	names . . .
ésas . . . ¡no volverán!	those . . . will not return!
Volverán las tupidas madreselvas	The dense honeysuckle will return
de tu jardín las tapias a escalar	to climb again your garden walls
y otra vez a la tarde aún más hermosas	and again at evening, lovelier still,
sus flores se abrirán.	their flowers will unfold.

Pero aquellas cuajadas de rocío
cuyas gotas mirábamos temblar
y caer como lágrimas del día . . .
ésas . . . ¡no volverán!

But those that hung bedecked with dew,
whose dewdrops we saw tremble
and fall like tears of day . . .
those . . . will not return!

Volverán del amor en tus oídos
las palabras ardientes a sonar,
tu corazón de su profundo sueño
tal vez despertará.

Upon your ears will fall again
the sound of ardent words of love;
your heart from its deep sleep
will then perhaps awake.

Pero mudo y absorto y de rodillas
como se adora a Dios ante su altar,
como yo te he querido . . . desengáñate,
así . . . ¡no te querrán!

But mute and rapt and kneeling,
as God before His altar is adored,
as I loved you, you may be sure,
– none shall ever love you so!

Olas gigantes / Vast waves

Olas gigantes que os rompéis bramando
en las playas desiertas y remotas,
envuelto entre la sábana de espumas,
¡llevadme con vosotras!

Vast waves, breaking with a roar
on deserted and distant strands,
shroud me in a sheet of foam,
bear me away with you!

Ráfagas de huracán, que arrebatáis
del alto bosque las marchitas hojas,
arrastrado en el ciego torbellino,
¡llevadme con vosotras!

Hurricane gusts, snatching
the tall wood's withered leaves,
dragging all along in dark turbulence,
bear me away with you!

Nubes de tempestad que rompe el rayo
y en fuego ornáis las desprendidas orlas,
arrebatado entre la niebla oscura,
¡llevadme con vosotras!

Storm clouds rent by lightning
with your edges bordered in fire,
snatch me up in a dark mist,
bear me away with you!

Llevadme, por piedad, adonde el vértigo
con la razón me arranque la memoria.
¡Por piedad! Tengo miedo de quedarme
con mi dolor a solas!

Bear me away, I beg, to where vertigo
eradicates my memory and reason . . .
Have mercy . . . I dread being left
alone with my grief!

XIII

EDUARDO TOLDRÀ
(1895–1962)

Toldrà was born on 7 April 1892. Like Mompou he was Catalan (he studied in Barcelona), but unlike Mompou his compositions stemmed from the active part he played in the everyday musical life of Catalonia, rather than in introspection and French exile. Also in contrast to Mompou, he was influenced by modernisme (see p. 146). He was best known in his early years as first violin of the Renaixement string quartet, and then as a conductor (he was the founder conductor of the Barcelona Municipal Orchestra from 1944). He was later professor of the violin at Barcelona Music School. His first opera (in Catalan) *El giravolt de Maig* dates from 1928, and he also composed orchestral and chamber music, particularly works involving his own instrument, the violin.

The songs of Toldrà included in this volume are original compositions in both Catalan and Spanish. They show a resourceful choice of texts and a variety of poetic styles. The music entertains and never outstays its welcome; it eschews sophistication and is undemanding to the listener – all of which may seem the damnation of faint praise, but Toldrà's virtues do not preclude genuine imagination and sensitivity. In a song like 'Maig', a miracle of expressive simplicity in the right voice and hands, Toldrà earns his place among the most sympathetic song writers of his generation. Like almost all his contemporaries, he also arranged a book of folksongs (*Doce canciones populares españolas*, UMV 20649), which is a wide-ranging anthology of music from various Spanish regions from north to south.

Maig / May

TRINITAT CATASÚS

(1920)

Terra qui floreix,	Burgeoning earth,
mar qui s'hi encanta,	enchanting sea,

suavíssim bleix
de vida triomfanta.

softest breath
of exultant life.

Pluges cristallines,
aigües reflexant
tendrors infantines
qui riuen brillant.

Crystal raindrops,
waters reflecting
gentle children
brightly laughing.

Claredat sonora,
núvol qui s'hi perd,
aura qui eixamora
la tendror del verd.

Sonorous brightness,
vanishing cloud,
breeze which dries up
the tender green.

Bordoneig suau
d'abelles, profunda,
silenciosa pau
d'una hora fecunda.

Soft humming
of bees, deep
silent peace
of a fertile time.

Món rejovenit,
amor que hi esclata,
deliciós oblit
de les nits de plata.

World made young again,
burgeoning love,
exquisite oblivion
of silvery nights.

Quan el pleniluni,
de Maig, silenciós,
de qualque infortuni
sembla dir a les flors.

When the full moon
of May silently
seems to tell the flowers
of some misfortune.

A l'ombra del lledoner . . . / *In the shade of the nettle-tree*

TOMÀS GARCÉS
(1924)

A l'ombra del lledoner / *In the shade of the nettle-tree*

A l'ombra del lledoner
una fadrineta plora.
La tarda mor dalt del cim
i llisca per la rossola,
l'esfilagarsen els brucs,
la tenebra se l'emporta.
La noia plora d'enyor:
el lledoner no fa ombra.
Fadrina, l'amor és lluny;
enllà, la carena fosca.

In the shade of the nettle-tree
a young maiden weeps.
The afternoon dies on the peak,
glides over the slope,
is frayed by the heather
and darkness bears it away.
The girl weeps with longing,
the nettle-tree gives no shade.
Maiden, love is far –
beyond the dark mountain ridge.

Si passava un cavaller . . .
Du el cavall blanc de la brida.
L'arbre li dóna repòs,
l'oratge, manyac, arriba.
Al cel la llum de l'estel
és la rosada del dia.

A knight went by . . .
leading a white steed by the reins.
The tree gives him rest,
a gentle breeze springs up.
In the sky the star's light
is the dew of the day.

– Cavaller, l'amor és lluny;
amb l'ombra i el cant fugia.
– Fadrina, l'amor és lluny;
per l'ampla plana camina.

La nit sospira, la nit,
el bosc, la riera clara.
Les branques del lledoner
són fines i despullades;
fulla i ocell n'han fugit,
però hi crema l'estelada.
Fadrina, l'amor és lluny;
demana'l a punta d'alba
quan l'ombra del lledoner
s'allargui com un miracle.

Knight, love is far,
with shade and song it fled.
Maiden, love is far,
moving across the wide plain.

The night sighs, the night,
the forest, the clear brook.
The branches of the nettle-tree
are thin and bare;
leaf and bird have gone
but the starry sky is ablaze.
Maiden, love is far;
implore it at the break of day,
when the shade of the nettle-tree
lengthens like a miracle.

Cançó de comiat / Farewell song

«Adéu, galant terra, adéu!»
Adéu-siau, vinya verda,
flor seca del caminal,
lledoner de bona ombreta.
Ja no m'assec al pedrís
ni me bressa la riera.
Adéu, galant terra, adéu.

'Farewell, dear land, farewell!'
Farewell, green vineyard,
dry flower of the path,
nettle-tree of welcome shade.
No more do I sit on the seat of stone
nor does the stream embrace me.
Farewell, dear land, farewell.

Les lloses d'aquell bancal
són ombrejades i fresques.
Els lledoners de la font
han tret una fulla tendra
i els ceps faran bon raïm
quan els oregi el setembre.
Adéu, galant terra, adéu.

The flagstones of this seat
are shady and cool.
The nettle-trees of the fountain
have grown tender leaves
and the vines will yield good grapes
when the September wind sways them.
Farewell, dear land, farewell.

Els ceps faran bon raïm
i llum viva les estrelles.
Vindran les nits de l'estiu,
la mar quïeta i estesa
llambrant sota el cop dels rems,
tallada per la carena.
Adéu, galant terra, adéu.

The vines will yield good grapes
and the stars vivid light.
Summer nights will come
and the sea calm and spread,
gleaming beneath the beat of the oars,
cut by the keel.
Farewell, dear land, farewell.

Vindran les nits de l'estiu,
la tardô i la primavera,
les boires que baixa el cim,
el crit de les orenetes.
I sempre el respir del mar
i el batec de les estrelles.
Adéu, galant terra, adéu.

Summer nights will come,
Autumn and Spring,
mists descending the peaks,
swallow cries
and always the breathing of the sea
and the throb of the stars.
Farewell, dear land, farewell.

Adéu, muntanya, pedrís,
paret blanca de l'església,
aigua clara de la font,

Farewell, mountain, and seat of stone,
white wall of the church,
clear water of the fountain,

plata de les oliveres,
olor mullada dels horts,
estrella, riera, vela.
Adéu, galant terra, adéu!

silver olive trees,
moist scent of the orchard,
star, brook, sail.
Farewell, dear land, farewell!

Cançó de grumet / The cabin-boy's song

Adéu, turons de Marsella,
ja s'en van els mariners.
Tot just hem hissat la vela
es gira un oratge fresc.
Aquell pinar de la costa
deu ser ple de cants d'ocell;
si no sentim l'ocellada
ens du romaní l'oreig.
Quin goig, de bon dematí,
seguir la darrera estrella:
«no hi ha lliri sense flor
ni barco sense bandera.»

Farewell, hills of Marseilles,
the sailors are now departing.
The sails have just been hoisted,
a fresh wind is blowing.
That pine-wood by the shore
must be loud with birdsong;
we hear no more the birds in flight
but catch the rosemary on the wind.
What joy at dawn
to follow the last star!
'There's no lily without a flower,
nor boat without a banner!'

Infla't vela, llisca vela!
Com s'allunya la ciutat!
Guaita l'or clar de la platja
i a dalt de tot el cel clar.
Timoner, potser sospires?
l'enyorança t'ha punxat?
El gallaret llengoteja
i enjoia tota la nau.
Quin goig, cremant sobre els
        pals,
el gallaret de la festa:
«no hi ha lliri sense flor
ni barco sense bandera.»

Swell, sail; glide, sail!
How the city dwindles!
Behold the pale gold of the beach
and the clear blue sky above.
Helmsman, can it be that you are sighing?
Has homesickness seized you?
The pennant sticks out its tongue
and brightens the whole ship.
What joy it brings, gleaming over the
        masts,
that festive pennant!
'There's no lily without a flower,
nor boat without a banner.'

¡Adéu, turons de Marsella!
¡Adéu, la noia i el pi!
No ens espanten les ventades
ni la boira de la nit.
Si el vent xiula entre les cordes,
demà el mar serà ben llis.
A cada port ens espera,
amorós, un llavi fi.
Quin goig, tornant de la mar,
el petó d'una donzella:
«no hi ha lliri sense flor
ni barco sense bandera.»

Farewell, hills of Marseilles!
Farewell maidens and pines!
Neither winds
nor night mists scare us.
If the wind howls through the rigging,
tomorrow the sea will be calm.
In every port there waits for lovers
like us a pair of lovely lips.
What joy, returning from the sea,
to be kissed by a maiden's lips!
'There's no lily without a flower,
nor boat without a banner.'

Cançó de bressol / Cradle-song

«Sant Jordi del Corredor
feu-me dormî aquesta nina,

'Saint George of the Corridor,
send this girl to sleep for me,

que son pare n'és al camp
a collir menta florida.»

De bon matí se n'ha anat;
tot just despuntava el dia
i l'estrella de l'amor
era un brot de tarongina.
La rosada del matí
era un plor de pedres fines.
    Dorm, infant,
que ton pare n'és al camp
a collir menta florida.

Apartarà els esbarzers
quan el punxin les espines.
Espines, feu-vos enllà;
vina, la menta florida.
Quan passa el seu cavall blanc
l'ocell tremola i refila.
    Dorm, infant,
que ton pare n'és al camp
a collir menta florida.

La selva s'aclarirà,
que la lluna l'il·lumina.
Sota la llum de la nit
l'herba florida fugia,
però els ulls del cavall blanc
en la fosca l'endevinen.
    Dorm, infant,
que ton pare n'és al camp
a collir menta florida.

Dorm, infant, que el son és dolç
i l'oratjol hi convida.
Demà, de bon dematí,
ton pare serà a la llinda.
Que et trobi dintre el bressol
com una estrella dormida.
    Dorm, infant,
que ton pare n'és al camp
a collir menta florida.

for her father has gone to the fields
to gather the blossoming mint.'

He went early in the morning
as day was just dawning
and the star of love gleamed
like a sprig of orange blossom.
The morning dew
was a weeping of precious stones.
    Sleep, child,
for your father has gone to the fields
to gather the blossoming mint.

He will push aside the brambles
when the thorns prick him.
Away with you, thorns!
Come, blossoming mint!
When his white horse goes by,
the bird trembles and warbles.
    Sleep, child,
for your father has gone to the fields
to gather the blossoming mint.

The wood will brighten,
for the moon will light it.
Beneath the gleam of the night
the flowering grasses fled,
but the eyes of the white horse
discerned it in the dark.
    Sleep, child,
for your father has gone to the fields
to gather the blossoming mint.

Sleep, child, for sleep is sweet
and the breeze invites it.
Tomorrow, at break of day,
your father will be at the door.
Let him find you in the cradle
like a sleeping star.
    Sleep, child,
for your father has gone to the fields
to gather the blossoming mint.

Romanç de Santa Llúcia[1] / *The ballad of Saint Lucy's day*

JOSÉ DE SAGARRA

(1924)

Perquè avui és Santa Llúcia
dia de l'any gloriós,
pels volts de la Plaça Nova
rondava amb la meva amor.

Since today is Saint Lucy's day,
the most glorious of the year,
around the Plaça Nova
I went walking with my love.

Anem tots dos a la fira,
amiga anem-hi de jorn,
que una mica de muntanya
alegri nostra tristor.

Let us both go to the fair,
my friend, let us go this morning,
for a morsel of mountain
will lighten our grief.

Comprarem grapats de molsa
i una enramada d'arboç
i una blanca molinera
i una ovella i un pastor.

We'll buy handfuls of moss
and a branch of evergreen,
and a white milleress
and a ewe and a shepherd.

Ho posarem a migdia
dins el nostre menjador
i abans de seure a la taula
ens ho mirarem tots dos;
que una mica de muntanya
ens faci el menjar més dolç.

We'll arrange them at noon
in our dining room,
and before sitting down at table,
we'll look at them together;
for a morsel of mountain
will sweeten our meal.

Perquè avui és Santa Llúcia
dia de l'any gloriós,
tals paraules m'acudien
quan he vist la meva amor.

Since today is Saint Lucy's day,
the most glorious of the year,
such words occurred to me
when I saw my love.

'The Christmas crèche fair in Barcelona is held on St Lucy's day. The chapel of Santa Llúcia in Barcelona cathedral actually looks out on to the Plaça Nova, where artisans sell statues of the Holy Family, bushes, branches etc., which the people buy to decorate the manger at home.

Anacreòntica / Anacreontic lines

CLEMENTINA ARDERIU

(1927)

Un dia Amor, ai trist,
Per tot sempre ja no s'és distret.
No havia vist l'abella entre les roses
I al dit va ser fiblat.
Perquè amb barroeria l'havia despertat
Amor enfolleit pica de peus i plora,
No veu ningú a la vora.
I vola i corre prest a la gentil Cítera
Que sempre Amor espera.
Oh, mare, só perdut! li diu: ai, las, jo em
    moro!
No em renyis perquè ploro.
Que m'ha picat al dit
Aquell ser ben petit
Armat de fibló i ales,
Que abella, per mon dol, ne diu el
    camperol.
Amor, això no és res, ella respon,
I què, aquest fiblar d'abella,
Si penses en aquella ferida que sofreix
Qui ton dardell fereix.

One day, alas, Cupid
was distressed as never before.
He had not seen the bee among the roses,
and his finger was stung –
for clumsily he had woken it.
Cupid, maddened, writhes and cries,
sees no one nigh
and flees running to gentle Cythera,
who always waits for him.
'O mother, I am lost!' said he. 'Alas, I
    die!
Do not scold me for my weeping –
he pricked my finger,
that tiny creature
armed with sting and wing,
in a way he'd treat no
    peasant.'
'Cupid', she replied, 'it is nothing,
and what is such a sting
compared with the wound you inflict
with your fierce little dart?'

Cançó incerta / Uncertain song

JOSEP CARNER
(1927)

¿Aquest camí tan fi, tan fi,
que sap on mena?
És a la vila o és al pi
de la carena?

Un lliri blau color de cel
diu 'vine, vine';
però 'no passis' diu un vel
de teranyina.

¿Serà drecera del gosat,
rossola ingrata
o bé un camí d'enamorat
colgat de mata?

¿Es un recer per a dormir
qui passi pena?
Aquest camí tan fi, tan fi,
qui sap on mena?

¿Qui sap si trist o somrient
acull a l'hoste?
¿Qui sap si mor sobtadament
sota la brosta?

¿Qui sabia mai aquest camí,
a què em convida?
I és camí incert cada matí,
n'és cada vida.

This path so narrow,
who knows where it leads?
To the town or to that pine
on the mountainside?

A sky-blue lily
says 'Come, come';
but 'Do not pass',
says a spider's web.

Is this a shortcut for the daring,
a slippery descent,
or is it a lover's path,
covered with brush?

Is it a shelter to sleep
for one in pain?
This path so narrow,
who knows where it leads?

Who knows whether sad or smiling
it greets the traveller?
Who knows if it dies of a sudden
beneath the thicket?

Who would ever know this path,
know to what it invites me?
Every morning is an uncertain path,
and every life is too.

Seis canciones / Six songs

La zagala alegre / The merry shepherdess

PABLO DE JÉRICA
(1940)

A una donosa zagala
su vieja madre reñía
cuando pasaba las horas
alegres, entretenidas;
y ella, su amor disculpando,
con elocuencia sencilla,
cantando al son del pandero,
así mil veces decía:

A pretty shepherdess
was scolded by her old mother
for spending her time
in pleasure and mirth;
and she defended her love
with simple eloquence,
singing to the tambourine
a thousand times over:

Ahora que soy niña, madre,
ahora que soy niña,
déjeme gozar ahora,
sin que así me riña.

while I am still a girl, mother,
while I am still a girl,
let me enjoy myself
without scolding me so.

¿Qué mal nos hace Salicio
si cuando pasa me mira,
y me tira de la saya
o en el brazo me pellizca?
No piense, madre, que busca
mi deshonra; no lo diga:
mi gusto sólo, y su gusto,
queriéndome así codicia.

What harm does Salicio cause us
if he looks at me as he passes
and tugs at my skirt
or pinches my arm?
Do not think, mother, that he seeks
to dishonour me; do not say so:
he craves my pleasure only, and his own,
by loving me like this.

Ahora que soy niña, madre,
ahora que soy niña,
déjeme gozar ahora,
sin que así me riña.

While I am still a girl, mother,
while I am still a girl,
let me enjoy myself
without scolding me so.

Cuando casada me vea,
hecha mujer de familia,
me sobrarán mil cuidados,
me faltará mi alegría.
Por eso quisiera, madre,
pasar alegres los días
que me restan de soltera
en bailes, juegos y risas.

When you see me wed
with a family,
I shall have a thousand worries
and be deprived of joy.
That is why, mother,
I wish to enjoy
my remaining days as a maiden
with dancing, games and laughter.

Ahora que soy niña, madre,
ahora que soy niña,
déjeme gozar ahora,
sin que así me riña.

While I am still a girl, mother,
while I am still a girl,
let me enjoy myself
without scolding me so.

Madre, unos ojuelos vi / *Mother, I saw two sparkling eyes*

LOPE DE VEGA

(1941)

Madre, unos ojuelos vi,
verdes, alegres y bellos.
¡Ay, que me muero por ellos,
y ellos se burlan de mí!

Mother, I saw two sparkling eyes,
green, happy and lovely!
Ah, I die for them
and they mock me!

Las dos niñas de sus cielos
han hecho tanta mudanza,
que la color de esperanza
se me ha convertido en celos.
Yo pienso, madre, que vi
mi vida y mi muerte en vellos.
¡Ay, que me muero por ellos,
y ellos se burlan de mí!

Those two sweet stars
have changed so much
that the colour of hope
has turned to jealousy.
I think, mother, that in them
I saw my life, my death.
Ah, I die for them
and they mock me.

¡Quién pensara que el color
de tal suerte me engañara!

Who would think the colour
of such fortune would deceive me?

Pero ¿quién no lo pensara,
como no tuviera amor?
Madre, en ellos me perdí,
y es fuerza buscarme en ellos.
¡Ay, que me muero por ellos,
y ellos se burlan de mí!

But he who thinks not so,
knows not love.
Mother, I lost myself in them,
and in them I must find myself.
Ah, I die for them
and they mock me!

Mañanita de San Juan[1] / Dawn on St John's day

(1940)

Mañanita de San Juan,
mañanita de primor,
cuando damas y galanes
van a oír misa mayor,
allá va la mi señora,
entre todas la mejor;
viste saya sobre saya,
mantellín de tornasol,
camisa con oro y perlas,
bordada en el cabezón;
en la su boca muy linda
lleva un poco de dulzor;
en la su cara tan blanca
un poquito de arrebol
y en los sus ojuelos garzos
lleva un poco de alcohol;
así entraba por la iglesia
relumbrando como el sol.
Las damas mueren de envidia
y los galanes de amor;
el que cantaba en el coro
en el credo se perdió;
el abad que dice misa
ha trocado la lición;
monacillos que le ayudan
no aciertan responder, non:
por decir amén, amén,
decían amor, amor.

Dawn on St John's day,
dawn of exquisite beauty,
when ladies and gentlemen
go to high mass
and my lady is among them –
the most beautiful of all.
Behold her skirts,
her mantilla of sunflowers,
her blouse of pearls and gold
embroidered on the collar;
on her lovely mouth
lies a touch of sweetness,
on her pallid face
a little rouge
and on her blue eyes
a hint of kohl.
She entered the church so,
radiant as the sun.
The ladies die of envy,
the gentlemen of love;
the chorister lost
his way in the credo,
the abbot saying mass
read the wrong lesson,
the acolytes serving him
fail to respond:
instead of amen, amen,
they say amor, amor.

[1] St John's day is 24 June, Midsummer day.

Nadie puede ser dichoso / None can be happy

GARCILASO DE LA VEGA

(1941)

Nadie puede ser dichoso,
señora, ni desdichado,
sino que os haya mirado.

None can be happy,
my lady, nor unhappy,
if he has not looked on thee.

Porque la gloria de veros
en ese punto se quita
que se piensa mereceros.

For the joy of seeing thee
vanishes as soon as
one thinks to deserve thee.

Así que, sin conoceros,
nadie puede ser dichoso,
señora, ni desdichado,
sino que os haya mirado.

Thus it is, that without knowing thee,
none can be happy,
my lady, nor unhappy,
if he has not looked on thee.

Cantarcillo / A little carol

LOPE DE VEGA

(1941)

Pues andáis en las palmas,
ángeles santos,
¡que se duerme mi Niño,
tened los ramos!

Since you hover about the palms,
holy angels,
hold back the boughs,
for my Child is sleeping!

Palmas de Belén,
que mueven airados
los furiosos vientos
que suenan tanto,
no le hagáis ruido,
corred más paso:
¡que se duerme mi Niño,
tened los ramos!

Palms of Bethlehem,
tossed angrily
by the raging winds
that roar so loud,
do not bluster so,
blow more gently:
hold back the boughs,
for my Child is sleeping!

El Niño divino,
que está cansado
de llorar en la tierra,
por su descanso,
sosegar quiere un poco
del tierno llanto:
¡que se duerme mi Niño,
tened los ramos!

The holy Child,
who is weary
of weeping on earth
for peace,
craves a little respite
from his piteous weeping:
hold back the boughs,
for my Child is sleeping!

Rigurosos hielos
le están cercando,
ya veis que no tengo
con qué guardarlo;
ángeles divinos
que vais volando,
¡que se duerme mi Niño,
tened los ramos!

Bitter frosts
surround him;
see, I have nothing
with which to shield him.
Blessed angels
flying by,
hold back the boughs,
for my Child is sleeping!

Después que te conocí / Since meeting thee

FRANCISCO DE QUEVEDO

(1941)

Después que te conocí,
todas las cosas me sobran:
el sol para tener día,
abril para tener rosas.

Since meeting thee
all else is superfluous:
the sun to bring day,
April to bring roses.

Por mí, bien pueden tomar
otro oficio las auroras,
que yo conozco una luz
que sabe amanecer sombras.
Bien puede buscar la noche
quien sus estrellas conozca,
que para mi astrología
ya son oscuras y pocas.

Después que te conocí,
todas las cosas me sobran:
el sol para tener día,
abril para tener rosas.

Ya no importunan mis ruegos
a los cielos por la gloria,
que mi bienaventuranza
tiene jornada más corta.
Bien puede la margarita
guardar sus perlas en conchas,
que búzano de una risa
las pesco yo en una boca.

Después que te conocí,
todas las cosas me sobran:
el sol para tener día,
abril para tener rosas.

Dawn could take on
another task,
since I know a light
that can bring shadows at dawn.
Well might the stargazer
search night for stars,
but in my book
they are faint and few.

Since meeting thee
all else is superfluous:
the sun to bring day,
April to bring roses.

No longer do I burden the heavens
with pleas for Paradise,
since my happiness
enjoys a much shorter lease.
Well might the oyster
guard its pearls in shells,
but I, diving in search of a smile,
find them in a mouth.

Since meeting thee
all else is superfluous:
the sun to bring day,
April to bring roses.

XIV

ROBERTO GERHARD
(1896–1970)

The career of Gerhard, and indeed his music, does not fit into the mould of that of his compatriots. He was born in Catalonia (Valls) on 25 September 1896, and studied briefly with Granados. Later, he had the distinction of being the last pupil of Felip Pedrell. He then moved to Berlin and Vienna where he studied with Schoenberg (1923–8), which equipped him to use atonal and serial techniques, although his music always retains a distinctly Spanish flavour. He was against the facile nationalism of much Spanish music, a trend which was no doubt exacerbated by the length of Franco's control over all aspects of Spanish life – one could not easily envisage a thriving musical avant-garde in fascist Spain. A number of distinguished composers with impeccable republican credentials as young men, later made accommodations with the powers-that-be in their country, but not Gerhard. He had something of Falla's formidable integrity, and like Victor Hugo in Jersey, he preferred exile to political compromise. He left Spain at the end of the Civil War and lived in Cambridge until his death, regarding himself as an English composer despite a decade of neglect by the musical establishment of the country of his adoption. He preserved a tough and individual voice which is perhaps the prerogative of an uncompromised political exile.

Although most of the large-scale music in Gerhard's considerable output avoids the conscious use of Spanish colour, he seems to have been happy for his songs to exude an earthy Spanish simplicity, where the vocal line is considerably easier to master than the demanding accompaniments. The *Sis cançons populars de Catalunya* date from his student years in Austria, but it seems strange that the anthologies *Cantares* and the *Cancionero de Pedrell*, based on folk tunes collected by Felip Pedrell (1841–1922) and published in four volumes in 1922, were written in the most English of university towns. Like the celebrated folksong arrangements of Falla, to which the *Cancionero* is a worthy and underestimated successor, the composer has selected an anthology of folksongs from all over Spain. This work is published by Boosey and Hawkes.

Sis cançons populars de Catalunya / Six Catalan folksongs
(1928)

1. La calàndria / The lark

No't recordes, amor meu,
d'aquella matinada,
que ens estàvem conversant
a la soca d'un arbre,
a la sombra d'un xipré;
parlàvem del nostre bé,
que de l'amor parlàvem.
Ai trist de mi,
quina enyorança!

De la lluna la claror
ta cara illuminava.
Mentre estàvem conversant
va passa una calàndria.
La calàndria va cantant
i per tot va declarant
que el dia ja arribava.
Ai trist de mi,
l'han castigada!

Quan sa mare ho va saber
ja lan' ha renyadeta,
ja l'ha tancadeta
amb clau a dins d'una cambreta,
que no'n veu sol ni claror.
Jo tampoc la resplandor
veig de la seva cara.
Ai trist de mi,
quina enyorança!

Don't you remember, my love,
that morning,
when we talked
by the trunk of a tree
beneath the shade of a cypress;
we talked of our good fortune,
we talked of love.
Woe is me!
What longing!

Moonlight
lit your face.
While we were talking
a lark went by.
The lark sang,
announcing to the world at large
that day had dawned.
Woe is me,
she was punished!

When her mother discovered it,
she scolded her,
locked her
in a little room
where she could see no sun nor light.
I too cannot see
the light of her face.
Woe is me!
What longing!

2. La mort i la donzella / Death and the maiden

Desperteuvos el meu pare,
desperteuvos si dormiu;
que jo veig una tal cara,
que és una figura rara
que n'apar un encantament.

Donzelleta, sóc la mort,
si mai l'heu vista pintada.
Fuig-me d'aquí cuca fera,

Wake up, father,
wake up if you sleep;
for I see such a face,
so strange a figure,
like an apparition.

Young maiden, I am Death,
in case you never saw my likeness.
Away with you, wild creature,

que jo'n porto la bandera
de les nines principals.

for I bear the banner
of the fairest beauties.

3. *El petit vailet* / *The little farm-hand*

El petit vailet
de matí
se'n va 'gafa
la relleta per aná
a llaurar.
Lairum, laireta,
lairum, lairum, lairà.

The little farm-hand
in the morning
goes and takes
the plough to till
the land.
Lairum, laireta,
lairum, lairum, lairà.

La petita jove
li duu l'esmorzar,
un tupí de sopes
i un crostó de pa.
Lairum, laireta,
lairum, lairum, lairà.

The little maiden
brings him his lunch,
a mug of soup
and crust of bread.
Lairum, laireta,
lairum, lairum, lairà.

Al mig de la vila
una font hi ha,
el que hi vulgue
beure s'ha d'agenollar.
Lairum, laireta,
lairum, lairum, lairà.

In the middle of the town
there is a spring,
he who wants
to drink must kneel.
Lairum, laireta,
lairum, lairum, lairà.

Jugarem a córrer
qui més correrà,
tu per la costeta,
jo pel camí plà.
Lairum, laireta,
lairum, lairum, lairà.

Let's play a game to see
who can run the faster,
you along the uphill path,
me along the plain.
Lairum, laireta,
lairum, lairum, lairà.

4. *El Cotiló* / *Old Cotilo*

Si'n soc fill de Montagut
d'on tinc el sant Baptisme,
on tinc el meu pare estimat,
la mare que m'ha criat
tots els dies de ma vida.

I am a son of Montagut,
where I was christened
and where I have my dear father
and my mother, who's cared for me
every day of my life.

Si me'n soc anat a Olot
sols per apendre d'ofici.
Al carrer de Sant Bernat
si me'n soc acomodat
amb una tal Margarida.

I went to Olot
merely to learn a trade.
In Sant Bernat street
I found lodgings
with a certain Margarida.

Sempre m'estava dient
la pobra de Margarida:
'Posa te'n a treballar

She was always telling me,
poor Margarida:
'You must get a job

aquest mon deixa'l estar!'
Per mi remei no hi havida.

and give up this way of life!'
But for me there was no remedy.

Quan jo corria pel mon
tot hom Cotilo'm cridava;
mes ara que soc en preso
tot hom em crida traidor
per ferme'n més grossa causa.

When I travelled the world,
everyone called me Cotilo;
but now that I'm in prison
everyone calls me traitor
to increase my notoriety.

5. *Enemic de les dones* / *The misogynist*

De casarme, mare,
ho havia pensat.

To marry, mother,
I had a mind.

Més discorro ara
treure m'ho del cap.

But after discussion
I had other thoughts.

Car totes les dones
són plenes de verí.

For all women
are full of poison.

Val més que no'm casi,
m'estiga fadrí.

Better I should not marry,
but stay a bachelor.

Val més que no'm casi,
m'estiga tot sol,

Better I should not marry,
but live all alone,

a l'estiu a l'ombra,
a l'hivern al sol.

with shade in summer
and sun in winter.

No casantme, mare,
ho tinc arreglat.

I'll not marry, mother,
all is settled.

Sempre pa a la taula
i cap mal de cap.

Always bread on the table
and no headaches at all.

Fora, dones, les dones,
i visca el bon vi.

Away, then, with women,
and long live good wine!

Val més que no'm casi,
m'estiga fadrí.

Better I should not marry,
but stay a bachelor.

Val més que no'm casi,
m'estiga tot sol,

Better I should not marry,
but live all alone,

a l'estiu a l'ombra,
a l'hivern al sol.

with shade in summer
and sun in winter.

6. *Els ballaires dins un sac* / *The dancers in the sack*

Si n'hi havia tres o quatre
que'n ballaven dins un sac,

There were three or four
who danced in a sack,

l'un n'era el senyor batlle,
l'altre el regidor en cap.

one was the mayor,
the other the councillor.

Jo que no ballo ni trumfo
amb dones,

I neither dance nor succeed
with women,

jo que no ballo ni trumfo
amb cap.

I neither dance nor succeed
with anyone.

També hi havia el vicari
que'n ballava més que cap.

The vicar was also there,
dancing more than anyone.

Ja n'ha vingut el dimoni
i se n'ha emportat el sac.

Then the devil arrived
and took away the sack.

Jo que no ballo ni trumfo
amb dones,

I neither dance nor succeed
with women,

jo que no ballo ni trumfo
amb cap.

I neither dance nor succeed
with anyone.

Cancionero de Pedrell / The Pedrell song book
(1941)

1. Sa ximbomba[1] / The ximbomba
(Majorca)

Sa ximbomba ja és passada,
jo que volia ballar,
i ma mare em fa filar
cada vespre una fuada.

The ximbomba is worn out,
and I wanted to dance,
and my mother makes me spin
a skein each evening.

Sa ximbomba ja no sona,
ja no sona ni sonarà,
perquè té sa pell de ca
i sa canya que no és bona.
Jo que volia ballar!

The ximbomba no longer makes a sound,
nor will it ever again,
for it is made of dog's hide
and its cane is no good.
And I wanted to dance!

[1]Ximbomba. A friction drum of Moorish origin.

2. La mal maridada / The badly married one
(Catalonia)

Rossinyol, bon rossinyol,
tu que fas llarga volada,
rossinyol, bon rossinyol,

Nightingale, good nightingale,
you who fly so far,
nightingale, good nightingale,

encomana'm a la mare
d'un vol, d'un vol,
i al pare no pas gaire.

Encomana'm à la mare
i al pare no pas gaire,
rossinyol, bon rossinyol,
que m'ha mal maridada,
d'un vol, d'un vol,
que m'ha mal maridada.

M'ha casada amb un vellot,
m'ha casada amb un vellot,
rossinyol, bon rossinyol,
que no el vull ni m'agrada,
d'un vol, d'un vol,
que no el vull ni m'agrada!

send my love to my mother
without delay, without delay,
but not to my father.

Send my love to my mother
but not to my father,
nightingale, good nightingale,
for he has married me badly,
without delay, without delay,
for he has married me badly.

To an old codger he's married me,
to an old codger he's married me,
nightingale, good nightingale,
whom I neither want nor like,
without delay, without delay,
whom I neither want nor like!

3. *Laieta* / *Laieta*
(Catalonia)

Si fós ocellet aniria volant,
si fós ocellet aniria volant,
i a ca' la Laieta,
aniria a parlar.

Son pare em diria:
'¿Què voleu, l'hereu?'
'Vinc per la Laieta,
si me la doneu.'
'Torneu demà vespre
o de bon matí;
si ella us volia,
jo diré que sí.'

La noia bonica diu que sí que ho vol,
i a la matinada canta el rossinyol.
Laieta, Laieta, Laieta, Laieta,
Laieta bonica diu que sí que ho vol!

Were I a little bird I'd fly,
were I a little bird I'd fly,
and to Laieta's house
I'd go to talk.

Her father would say to me:
'What do you want, young heir?'
'I've come for Laieta,
if you'll give her me.'
'Return tomorrow evening
or early in the morning;
if she'll have you,
I'll consent.'

The pretty girl says 'yes' she will,
and at dawn the nightingale sings.
Laieta, Laieta, Laieta, Laieta,
pretty Laieta says 'yes' she will!

4. *Soledad* / *Soledad*
(Asturias)

Soledad del alma mía.
¡Ay, Soledad, Soledad!
Tanto te quiero de noche
como te quiero de día.

Mira, mira cómo corre
la cigüeña por la torre.

Soledad of my soul,
ah Soledad, Soledad!
I love you as much by night
as I love you by day.

See, see how the stork
makes for the tower,

Mira cómo va corriendo
para la ciudad de Oviedo.

Una pena quita pena,
un dolor, dolor.
Un clavo saca otro clavo,
pero amor no quita amor.

see how it makes
for the city of Oviedo.

Sorrow is relieved by sorrow,
pain by pain.
One nail can remove another,
but love is not erased by love.

5. *Muera yo . . .* / *Let me die*
(Asturias)

Si porque te quiero quieres
que yo la muerte reciba,
¡cúmplase tu voluntad!
¡Muera yo porque otro viva!

If because I love you
you wish me to die,
let your will be done!
Let me die that another may live!

¡Qué guapa vienes!
¡qué bien está la saya verde,
y el delantal!
¡y ese miriñaque negro!
¡y ese modito de andar!
¡Qué guapa vienes!
¡Qué maja estás
con los corales
y lazo atrás!

How pretty you look,
how becoming your green skirt
and apron!
And that black crinoline!
And your way of moving!
How pretty you look!
How beautiful you are
with the coral beads
and bow at the back!

No llores, niña, no llores;
no llores que yo no lloro
aunque me lleven mañana
a pelear con el moro.
No llores, niña,
niña, no llores.
¡Toma este ramito de flores!

Do not cry, my love, do not cry;
do not cry, for I would not cry,
even if they took me tomorrow
to fight against the Moors.
Do not cry, my love,
my love, do not cry.
Here, take this little bunch of flowers!

6. *Farruquiño* / *Frankie*
(Galicia)

Farruquiño, Farruquiño,
Farruquiño, meu amor,
estudia para crego;
será lo meu confesor.

Frankie, Frankie,
Frankie, my love,
is studying for the priesthood –
and my confessor he'll be.

Manoel por verme a min,
eu por ver a Manoel;
Manoel por ver a rosa,
eu por ver o caravel.

So Manuel can see me,
and I'll see Manuel;
Manuel can see the rose
and I the carnation.

Fun á fonte buscar auga
sin ter gana de beber.

I went to the fountain for water
with no wish to drink;

Fun por ver os meus amores;
¡deseiaba de os ver!

Manoel por verme a min,
eu por ver a Manoel;
Manoel por ver a rosa,
eu por ver o caravel.

I went to see my love;
I yearned to see him!

So Manuel can see me,
and I'll see Manuel;
Manuel can see the rose
and I the carnation.

7. *Alalá* / *Alala*

(Galicia)

Ay, la – le – lo,
Xaniño, Xaniño, Xan,
Xaniño traballador,
¡Xaniño, Xan!
La muller na romería,
Xaniño no seu labor.
¡Xaniño, Xan!

Ay, la, le, lo,
Johnny, Johnny, John,
Hardworking Johnny,
Johnny, John!
His wife's on a pilgrimage,
Johnny's off to work,
Johnny, John!

8. *Corrandes* / *Courant*

(Valencia)

Xiqueta recalcaeta,
per tu passaré la mar.
Que eres com la codonyeta,
que no tens res que tirar.

Remarkable young woman,
I'd cross the seas for you,
because you are like the quince,
which has nothing to waste.

L'u passa i em diu: sol;
l'altre passa i em diu: lluna;
i en el món no hi ha un gresol
per llumenar esta cuina!

One goes by and says to me: sun.
Another goes by and says to me: moon.
Yet there is no lamp in the world
that can light this kitchen!

Entre la flor de taronja
i la rosa més galana,
més fragància i hermosura
té la xica valenciana;
més fragància i hermosura
té la xica valenciana!

Compared with orange blossom
and the fairest rose,
there's more fragrance and beauty
in the Valencian girl,
more fragrance and beauty
in the Valencian girl!

Cantares / *Songs*

(1956)

1. *La indita* / *The Indian girl*

Este sonetito nuevo
De Veracruz ha venido
Y lo trajo una indita
Que lo canta de lo lindo.

This new little sonnet
has come from Veracruz
and an Indian girl brought it
who sings it perfectly.

Tai-rai-ri, tai-rai-ri, tai-rai-ri, ta-i-ró,
Mírele usté qué bonito.
Y con esta suavidad
Adormece los sentidos.

Tralali, tralali, tralarli, trarlala
look how pretty it is.
And with this softness
it lulls all senses to sleep.

La indita en su chinampa
Estaba cogiendo flores
Y un indito la miraba
Y cantaba sus amores.

The Indian girl in her lagooned garden
was gathering flowers
and an Indian boy watched her
and sang of his love.

Tai-rai-ri, tai-rai-ri, tai-rai-ri, ta-i-ró,
Mírele usté qué bonito.
Y con esta suavidad
Adormece los sentidos.

Tralali, tralali, tralarli, trarlala
look how pretty it is.
And with this softness
it lulls all senses to sleep.

El indito la decia
Cariñosa a su malinche:
'Por vida tuya, Soapile,
Báilame et Toticoniche'.

The Indian boy spoke
tenderly to his love:
I beseech you, Soapile,
dance for me the Toticoniche.

Tai-rai-ri, tai-rai-ri, tai-rai-ri, ta-i-ró,
Mírele usté qué bonito.
Y con esta suavidad
Adormece los sentidos.

Tralali, tralali, tralarli, trarlala
look how pretty it is.
And with this softness
it lulls all senses to sleep.

2. *El toro* / *The bull*

Ya está el torito en la plaza
Y el torero en la barrera,
Con banderillas[1] de fuego
Diciendo que el toro muera.

Already the bull's in the ring
and the bullfighter at the barrier,
with fiery banderillas
that say the bull will die.

Y otro toro,
Y otro toro,
Y otro torito más bravo,
Y otro torito más bravo.

And another bull,
and another bull,
and another braver little bull,
and another braver little bull.

Toda la plaza está llena
Que no se cabe,
Peró como no estás tú,
Como si no hubiera nadie.
Ya está el torito en la plaza
Dando locas carreras,
Ya se quedan los mozos descoloridos.

The entire ring is filled
to overflowing,
but as you are absent,
it's as though no one were there.
Already the bull's in the ring
careering wildly around,
and the boys look on pale.

Yo otro toro,
Y otro toro,
Y otro torito más bravo,
Y otro torito más bravo.

And another bull,
and another bull,
and another braver little bull,
and another braver little bull.

[1]*Banderilla*. A small dart, ornamented with a banderole, which bullfighters
plunge into the neck and shoulders of the bull.

3. *La ausencia* / *Absence*

Baldomero se llama mi novio,
Hace un mes que se fue para Francia,
Hace un mes que se fue para Francia,
Y olé, olé, olé, solita quedo yo!

My love is called Baldomero,
a month ago he left for France,
a month ago he left for France,
olé, olé, and I am left alone.

Me embarco y me desembarco,
Pom, pom, ay, ay, ay,
En una lancha penosa,
Pom, pom,
El agua no me consiente,
Pom, pom, ay, ay, ay,
A las orillas me echa,
Pom, pom,
Baldomero se fue para Francia,
Y olé, olé, olé, solita me quedo yo!

I embark and I disembark
pom, pom, la, la, la,
from a troublesome boat,
pom, pom,
the water rejects me,
pom, pom, la, la, la,
it casts me ashore,
pom, pom,
Baldomero left for France,
olé, olé, olé, and I am left alone!

A la Bartola
Cuando está sola,
Qué bien le cuadra la farandola[1],
Mira, mira, qué bien le cuadra la
    farandola,
A la Bartolina, Bartola
Cuando está sola.

Bartola
when left alone –
how well the farandola becomes her,
see how well the farandola becomes
    her,
becomes Bartolina, Bartola,
when she is alone.

Baldomero ha escrito una carta
A Bartola con letra amorosa,
Y anoche a las once y media,
Y olé, olé, olé, cantaba el sereno.

Baldomero wrote a letter
to Bartola in a loving hand,
and last night at half past eleven,
olé, olé, olé, the nightwatchman sang.

Me embarco y me desembarco,
Pom, pom, ay, ay, ay,
En una lancha penosa,
Pom, pom,
El agua no me consiente,
Pom, pom, ay, ay, ay,
A las orillas me echa,
Pom, pom,
Bartola estaba en brazos de Pedro,
Y olé, olé, olé, que ya no está sola.

I embark and I disembark,
pom, pom, la, la, la,
from a troublesome boat,
pom, pom,
the water rejects me,
pom, pom, la, la, la,
it casts me ashore,
pom, pom,
Bartola lay in Pedro's arms,
olé, olé, olé, and she's no longer alone!

A la Bartola
Cuando está sola,
Qué bien le cuadra la farandola,
Mira, mira, qué bien le cuadra la
    farandola,
A la Bartolina, Bartola
Cuando está sola.

Bartola
when left alone –
how well the farandola becomes her,
see how well the farandola becomes
    her,
becomes Bartolina, Bartola,
when she is alone.

Baldomero ha escrito una carta,
Y olé, olé, olé, con letra amorosa.

Baldomero wrote a letter,
olé, olé, olé, in a loving hand.

[1]*Farandola*. An ancient dance in 6/8 time.

4. *Un galán y su morena* / *A lover and his dusky girl*

Ay, un galán de esta villa,
Ay, un galán de esta casa,
Ay, diga lo que buscaba,
Ay, diga lo que quería.
Buscaba la su morena.

Adonde fué mi morena,
Adonde la resalada,
Adonde fué mi morena,
A la fuente fué por agua,
A la fuente fué por agua.
Y un galán me la detiene,
Y aquí la estoy aguardando,
Por ver si viene o no viene.

Ay, diga, diga el galán,
Ay, diga lo que buscaba,
Ay, diga lo que buscaba,
¡Ay, diga lo que quería!

Ah, a lover from this town,
ah, a lover from this house,
ah, let him say what he was seeking,
ah, let him say what he desired.
He was seeking his dusky girl.

Where has my dusky girl gone,
my graceful girl,
my dusky girl gone?
She went to the spring for water,
she went to the spring for water.
And a lover took her from me,
and here am I waiting
to see if she comes or not.

Ah, let the lover say,
let him say what he was seeking,
let him say what he was seeking,
let him say what he desired!

5. *La lobada* / *The pack of wolves*

Estando en la mía choza,
Estando en la mía choza,
Estando en la mía choza,
Labrando la mi cayada,
    La mi cayada.
Por lo alto de la sierra,
Por lo alto de la sierra,
Por lo alto de la sierra,
Vi venir una lobada!
Por lo alto de la sierra,
¡Vi venir una lobada!

Dónde va lobo maldito,
Dónde va lobo maldito,
Dónde va lobo maldito,
Dónde va lobo malvado,
    Lobo malvado.
Voy por una tu cordera,
Voy por una tu cordera,
Voy por una tu cordera,
Que tienes en tu manada.

Aquí mis siete cachorros,
Aquí mis siete cachorros,
Aquí mis siete cachorros
Y mi perra trujiyana.

In my little hut,
in my little hut,
in my little hut,
toiling with my shepherd's crook,
    my shepherd's crook,
from high in the mountains,
from high in the mountains,
from high in the mountains
I saw a pack of wolves draw near!
From high in the mountains
I saw a pack of wolves draw near!

Where are you going, wicked wolf,
where are you going, wicked wolf,
where are you going, wicked wolf,
where are you going, wicked wolf,
    wicked wolf.
I'm after one of your ewes,
I'm after one of your ewes,
I'm after one of your ewes,
from your flock.

Come my seven dogs,
come my seven dogs,
come my seven dogs
and my bitch from Trujillo.

Si me matáis ese lobo,   If you kill this wolf,
Si me matáis ese lobo,   if you kill this wolf,
Si me matáis ese lobo,   if you kill this wolf,
Tenéis cena ganada,   you'll have earned your supper,
        Cena ganada.   earned your supper.
Siete calderos de leche,   Seven bowls of milk,
Siete calderos de leche,   seven bowls of milk,
Siete calderos de leche   seven bowls of milk
Y otrotantos de cuajada.   and another seven of curd.
Y si no me lo matáis   And if you kill it not
Os daré con la mi cayada.   I'll beat you with my crook.

6. *La muerte y la donzella* / *Death and the maiden*

Qué hermosa noche,   What a lovely night,
Cuántas estrellas en el cielo,   how many stars in the sky,
Madre,   mother,
Abreme la ventana   Open the window,
Que quiero verlas.   for I wish to see them.

No, hija, no, no, no,   No daughter, no, no, no,
Que estás enferma,   for you are ill
Y el aire de la noche   and the night air
Dañarte podría,   could harm you,
No, hija, no.   no, daughter, no.

Ay, madre mía,   Ah mother,
Ya a nuestra puerta   already at our door
Un perro aúlla.   a dog is howling.
Madre, cuando amanezca   Mother, when dawn breaks
Ya estaré muerta.   I shall be dead.
Abreme la ventana.   Open the window.

7. *Reinas de la baraja* / *The Queens in the pack*

Si tu mare quiere una reina   If your mother wants a queen,
La baraja tiene cuatro,   the pack of cards has four,
La de copas, la de oros,   one of hearts, one of diamonds,
La de espadas, la de bastos.   one of spades and one of clubs.

    Corre que te pillo,   Run, else I'll catch you,
corre que te agarro,   run, else I'll snatch you,
mira que te lleno   look out, or I'll cover
la cara de barro.   your face in mud.

    Del olivo   The olive
me retiro,   I'll leave,
del esparto   the grass
yo me aparto,   I'll shun,
del sarmiento   by the vine
me arrepiento   I regret
de haberte querido tanto.   having loved you so.

XV

ALBERTO HEMSI
(1896–1975)

Hemsi, an Italian national of Turkish birth, is an all but forgotten composer and musicologist. His life-work was in one particular corner of Spain's musical history. It is perhaps appropriate that in 1992 we should remember Hemsi's abiding passion, which was the Sephardic music of Spain. Five hundred years ago, in 1492 – the year of Columbus's discovery of the Americas – Ferdinand and Isabella, intoxicated with righteous bigotry after their successful expulsion of the Arabs from their kingdoms, decided to do the same thing to a group of their own defenceless citizens, the Jews of Spain. This fact has cast a shadow over the present celebrations of the discovery of the Americas. The Jews, unlike the Arabs, had been an established and peaceful part of the Spanish community for fifteen centuries, but their expulsion was executed with savage cruelty. Many of these Jewish exiles made their way to the eastern Mediterranean, and threw themselves on the mercy of the Turkish Sultans in the lands of the Ottoman Empire. These potentates received them with mercy and tolerance – a medieval counterpoint to the intransigent Jewish–Islamic problems of the present time.

The depth of Sephardic culture is amply illustrated by their musical heritage. From his song-gathering headquarters on the island of Rhodes, and later in Alexandria, Hemsi made ten books of Sephardic song arrangements – *Coplas Sefardíes* – between 1932 and 1973. It seems that the music of fifteenth-century Jewish Spain was miraculously preserved in Asia Minor by the stringent measures taken by generation after generation of eastern Mediterranean Jews (particularly the women) to safeguard the Iberian heritage of which they were proud. Hemsi was both indefatigable collector and arranger of these songs. The *Coplas Sefardíes* were published by the Edition Orientale de Musique in Alexandria, a publishing house which Hemsi founded. I inherited three volumes of the collection from the library of the late Gerald Moore, and they show an admirable passion for their subject, with ample annotations in the manner of Joaquín Nin. Hemsi's piano accompaniments are far from negligible in effect, and no less a luminary in Spanish musicology than José Subira contributed an introduction to his editions. Hemsi contributed a good deal to the musical life of Egypt and was active in ethnomusicology in France to the end of his life. The Sephardic song arrangements are only part of Hemsi's large catalogue of music in every form, the majority of it inspired by Jewish themes.

Popular Sephardic songs of the fifteenth century

Una hija tiene el rey / The king has a daughter

Una hija tiene el rey,	The king has a daughter,
una hija regalada,	a daughter greatly fair,
la metió en altas torres,	in a high tower he confined her,
por tenerla bien guardada.	to keep her well guarded.
Un día por los calores	One day in the burning heat
aparóse en la ventana,	she appeared at the window
vido venir un segador	and saw a reaper draw near,
segando trigo y cebada.	reaping wheat and barley.

Una matica de ruda / A little bunch of rue

Una matica de ruda,	A little bunch of rue,
una matica de flor,	a little bunch of flowers,
hija mía mi querida,	my darling daughter –
dime a mí quién te la dió.	who gave it, pray?

Una matica de ruda,	A little bunch of rue,
una matica de flor,	a little bunch of flowers,
me la dió un mancevino	a young man gave it,
que de mí se enamoró.	who fell in love with me.

Como la rosa en la güerta / Like the rose in the garden

Como la rosa en la güerta	Like the rose in the garden
y las flores sin avrir	and the flowers yet to bloom –
ansí es una doncella	such is a maiden
a las horas del murir.	at the hour of her death.

Tristes horas en el día	These are the sad hours of the day
que harina ya cayó	when the flower as dust has fallen,
como la reyna en su lecho	like the queen in her bed
ya cayó y se desmayó.	it drooped and swooned away.

Estavase la mora[1] en su bel estar / The Moorish girl felt much at ease

La moxca

Estavase la mora en su bel estar,
venía la moxca por hazerle mal.
    La moxca a la mora,
    la mora a la moxca;
    ¡Mezquina la mora
    que en los campos mora!

The fly

The Moorish girl felt much at ease,
when along came a fly to harm her.
    The fly and the girl,
    the girl and the fly;
    poor Moorish girl
    that in the fields must dwell!

La abezba

Estavase la moxca en su bel estar,
venía la abezba por hazerle mal.
    La abezba a la moxca,
    la moxca a la mora;
    ¡Mezquina la mora
    que en los campos mora!

The bee

The fly was feeling much at ease,
when along came the bee to harm her.
    The bee and the fly,
    the fly and the girl;
    poor Moorish girl
    that in the fields must dwell!

La araña

Estavase la abezba en su bel estar,
venía la araña por hazerle mal.
    La araña a la abezba,
    la abezba a la moxca,
    la moxca a la mora;
    ¡Mezquina la mora
    que en los campos mora!

The spider

The bee was feeling much at ease,
when along came a spider to harm her.
    The spider and the bee,
    the bee and the fly,
    the fly and the girl;
    poor Moorish girl
    that in the fields must dwell!

[1]*La mora* means blackberry, mulberry, or Moorish girl.

Aquel rey de Francia / That King of France

Aquel rey de Francia
tres hijas tenía,
La una cortava
y la otra cuzía;
La más chiquitica
bastidor hazía.
Lavrando lavrando
el sueño le venía
La madre con ravia
harvarla quería.

That King of France,
three daughters had he,
one cut cloth,
and the other sewed;
the youngest of all
embroidered.
She toiled and toiled
till sleep came upon her;
her mother in a rage
sought to drive her on.

Ah, el novio no quiere dinero / Ah, the groom does not want money

Ah, el novio no quiere dinero,
Quere a la novia de mazal
  bueno.
  Yo vengo a ver

Ah, the groom does not want money,
he wants a bride with a good field of
  maize.
  I come to see

que gozen y logren
y tengan mucho bien.
Ah, el novio no quiere ducados,
Quere a la novia de mazal alto.
  Yo vengo a ver
  que gozen y logren
  y tengan mucho bien.

Ah, el novio no quere manillas,
Quere a la novia de cara de alegría.
  Yo vengo a ver
  que gozen y logren
  y tengan mucho bien.

that they prosper and flourish
and enjoy great fortune and wealth.
Ah, the groom does not want ducats,
he wants a bride whose maize grows tall.
  I come to see
  that they prosper and flourish
  and enjoy great fortune and wealth.

Ah, the groom does not want bracelets,
he wants a bride of happy mien.
  I come to see
  that they prosper and flourish
  and enjoy great fortune and wealth.

Aquel Conde y aquel Conde / That Count, ah that Count

Aquel Conde y aquel Conde,
que en la mar sea su fín,
armó naves y galeas
para Francia quiso ir.
Armólas de todo punto
echólas adientro del sangí.

That Count, ah that Count,
who was to meet his end at sea,
armed ships and galleons,
for he wished to sail for France.
He armed them to the hilt
and hurled them into the bloody fray.

Con pavor recordó el moro / With dread the Moor remembered

Con pavor recordó el moro
y empeçó a gritos dar
mis arreos son las armas
mi descanso es pelear.

Mi cama las duras peñas
mi dormir siempre es velar,
mis vestidos son pesares
que no se pueden rasgar.

With dread the Moor remembered
and began to shout:
my clothing is armour,
my rest is combat.

My bed is hard rock,
my sleep eternal vigil,
my garments are sorrows
that cannot be cut asunder.

XVI

FERNANDO OBRADORS
(1897–1945)

Obradors is the Spanish song writer par excellence for our times, which is to say his music unfailingly provides what many of today's English-speaking singers demand of the canción when they want to close their recitals with a 'bang'. The music of Joaquín Turina, with its dramatic Sevillian fantasy, fulfilled this role for an earlier generation, but the neo-classicism of Obradors, everything deriving from folksong and tonadilla, has a lighter, less portentous flavour, and is every inch as Spanish. The songs, or more accurately arrangements, are tuneful and immediately 'ethnic', they can be both charming and exciting, and they offer reasonable (though not excessive) vocal and pianistic challenges; they sound harder than they actually are. For this reason the name of Obradors is seen everywhere (in the United States even more than here) on concert programmes, but sadly usually at the head of the same group of four or five songs. It would be churlish to deny that singers and pianists are often wise to take populist considerations into account when planning the closing groups of their programmes, but a broader knowledge of Spanish song on the part of performers would place Obradors's achievements in a more realistic perspective.

It is astonishing that the name of such an often performed composer is not to be found in any of the musical reference books in English. Gilbert Chase, the great American authority on Spanish music, has written that the songs of Obradors 'appear frequently on concert programmes every-where, while very little is known of the composer himself.' He was born in Barcelona and studied the piano with his mother Julia at the Municipal Music School. He was self-taught in harmony, counterpoint and composi-tion, and was conductor of the Liceo and Radio Barcelona Orchestras, as well as the Philharmonic Orchestra of Gran Canaria. Obradors wrote a number of zarzuelas and symphonic works including *Reply to the Farandole of Bizet*. His main claim to fame, however, rests on the

Canciones clásicas españolas which are published in four volumes by the Unión Musical Española, the contents of the first of which (UMV 34070) is identical with the American edition, *Obradors – Classical Spanish Songs*, published by the International Music Company (No. 1748). The remaining three volumes of the Spanish edition (UMV 16455, 17433 and 17434) all contain delightful songs, much less often encountered, and with the same mixture of lyricism and manageable display which characterise the overworked first volume.

La mi sola, Laureola / *My only Laureola*

JUAN PONCE

La mi sola, Laureola	My only Laureola,
La mí sola, sola, sola,	my only, only, only one,
Yo el cautivo Leriano	I, the captive Leriano,
Aunque mucho estoy ufano	am so proud
Herido de aquella mano	to be wounded by the hand,
Que en el mundo es una sola.	the only hand in the world.
La mi sola Laureola	My only Laureola,
La mi sola, sola, sola.	my only, only, only one.

Al Amor[1] / *To Love*

CRISTÓBAL DE CASTILLEJO

Dame, Amor, besos sin cuento	Give me, Love, kisses without number,
Asido de mis cabellos	your hands seizing my hair,
Y mil y ciento tras ellos	give me eleven hundred of them,
Y tras ellos mil y ciento	and eleven hundred more,
Y después . . .	and then . . .
De muchos millares, tres!	many more thousands, and three more!
Y porque nadie lo sienta	And so that no one may know,
Desbaratemos la cuenta	let's forget the tally
Y . . . contemos al revés.	and . . . count backwards.

[1] See Appendix for original Catullus poem.

¿Corazón, porqué pasáis . . . / *Oh heart . . .*

Corazón, porqué pasáis	O heart, why do you lie awake
Las noches de amor despierto	during the nights made for love,
Si vuestro dueño descansa	when your mistress rests
En los brazos de otro dueño?	in the arms of another lover?

El majo[1] celoso / The jealous majo

Del majo que me enamora	From the majo who's courting me
He aprendido la queja	I've learned this plaintive song
Que una y mil veces suspira	which he sighs a thousand and one times
Noche tras noche en mi reja:	night after night at my window:
Lindezas, me muero	My darling, I am dying
De amor loco y fiero	of a wild and fierce love –
Y quisiera olvidarte	would that I could forget you,
¡Mas quiero y no puedo!	but I try and cannot!
Le han dicho que en la Pradera[2]	They told him that in the Pradera
Me han visto con un chispero[3]	I was seen with a dandy,
Desos de malla de seda	who was dressed in a silk shirt
Y chupa de terciopelo.	and a velvet vest.
Majezas, te quiero,	My handsome boy, I love you,
No creas que muero	do not think I am dying
De amores perdida	with rakish love
Por ese chispero.	for that dandy.

[1]*Majo*. The word, and its feminine form maja, was used to describe the working-class population of Madrid in such areas as Lavapiés at the end of the eighteenth century. At the other end of the social scale from Señor, a majo is usually stereotyped as boisterous, ostentatious, physically attractive and a little arrogant.
[2]*Pradera*. A park near Madrid.
[3]*Chispero*. A rough character from the Maravillas quarter of Madrid.

Con amores, la mi madre / With love in my heart, mother

Con amores, la mi madre,	With love in my heart, mother,
Con amores m'adormí.	with love in my heart, I fell asleep.
Así dormida soñaba	While sleeping I dreamed
Lo qu'el corazon velaba,	of what my heart was hiding,
Qu'el amor me consolaba	and love consoled me
Con más bien que merecí.	more than I deserved.
Adormeciome el favor	I was lulled to sleep by the token
Que Amor me dió con amor:	Love bestowed on me:
Dió descanso a mi dolor	my pain was soothed
La fe con que le serví.	by the faith with which I served her.

Del cabello más sutil / From the finest hair

Del cabello más sutil	From the finest hair
Que tienes en tu trenzado	in your tresses
He de hacer una cadena	I wish to make a chain
Para traerte a mi lado.	to draw you to my side.
Una alcarraza en tu casa,	In your house, young girl,
Chiquilla, quisiera ser,	I'd fain be a pitcher,
Para besarte en la boca,	to kiss your lips
Cuando fueras a beber. ¡Ay!	whenever you went to drink. Ah!

Chiquitita la novia / A tiny bride

Chiquitita la novia,	A tiny bride,
Chiquitito el novio,	a tiny groom,
Chiquitita la sala	a tiny room
Y er dormitorio,	and a bedroom,
Por eso yo quiero	that's why I want
Chiquitita la cama	a tiny bed
Y er mosquitero.	and a mosquito net.

Consejo / Counsel

MIGUEL DE CERVANTES

Es de vidrio la mujer;	A woman is made of glass;
Pero no se ha de probar	but no one should attempt
Si se puede o no quebrar,	to see if she breaks,
Porque todo podría ser.	since anything might come to pass.
Y es más fácil el quebrarse,	Breaking is easier,
Y no es cordura ponerse	and it is not wise
A peligro de romperse	to run the risk of tearing apart
Lo que no puede soldarse.	what cannot be joined together again.
Y en esta opinión estén	And may everyone agree
Todos, y en razón la fundo;	for this reason:
Que si hay Dánaes[1] en el mundo,	if Danaës exist in this world,
Hay pluvias de oro también.	there'll be golden showers as well.

[1]*Danaë*. Daughter of Acrisius, King of Argos. Told by an oracle that his daughter's son would put him to death, he locked her up in a tower – in vain, since Jupiter found access to her in the form of a golden shower.

El Tumba y lé / El Tumba y lé

Aunque soy chiquilla,	Though I'm young,
si topo un marido	if I find a husband
tendré de él cada año	I'll have with him each year
dos o tres chiquillos.	two or three children.
Tumba y lé	Tumba y lé,
que me voy contigo,	I shall go with you,
tumba y lé	tumba y lé,
que luego me iré,	and then I shall leave,
tumba y lé	tumba y lé,
para ir al molino,	to go to the mill,
tumba y lé	tumba y lé,
para ir a moler.	to work the grindstone.
Aunque yo no tengo	Though I only have
más que un buey mansito,	a placid little ox,

entre él y yo haremos
más que seis novillos.

Tumba y lé . . .

Los mozos temiendo
que me embista un toro,
dicen que me quite
mi justillo rojo.

Tumba y lé . . .

Pero aunque se dice que:
tras cuernos, palos,
yo tan solo temo
a los del diablo.

Tumba y lé . . .

between us we'll make
more than six calves.

Tumba y lé . . .

The lads, fearing
that a bull will attack me,
tell me to take off
my red jerkin.

Tumba y lé . . .

But though it's said that
after horns come rods –
I only fear
those of the devil.

Tumba y lé . . .

Confiado jilguerillo / Trusting little linnet

On a theme from *Acis and Galatea* by Antonio de Literes

Confiado jilguerillo
mira como importuna
de tu estado primero
te derribó el amor y la fortuna,
y el viento que tan ufano presumiste
aún no le hallaste cuando le perdiste.

Si de rama en rama
si de flor en flor
ibas saltando, bullendo, cantando.
¡Dichoso quien ama las ansias de amor!
Ibas saltando, ibas saltando,
bullendo y cantando.
¡Dichoso quien ama las ansias de amor!
Ibas saltando, bullendo y
    cantando.
¡Dichoso quien ama las ansias de amor!

Advierte que aprisa
es llanto la risa
y el gusto dolor,
es llanto la risa
y el gusto dolor
¡Ay, Ay!
es llanto la risa
y el gusto dolor
¡Ay, Ay!

Trusting little linnet,
see how love and fortune
so untimely did unseat you
from your first high place,
and the air you once so proudly assumed
is now so lost as never to be found.

You flitted once from bough to bough,
from flower to flower,
hopping, quivering, singing –
lucky is the one who yearns for love.
You flitted hopping,
quivering and singing –
lucky is the one who yearns for love.
You flitted hopping, quivering and
    singing –
lucky is the one who yearns for love.

Notice how quickly
laughter turns to weeping
and pleasure to sorrow,
laughter to weeping
and pleasure to sorrow.
Ay, ay,
laughter turns to weeping
and pleasure to sorrow.
Ay, ay!

Tres morillas / Three Moorish maids

Tres morillas me enamoran
en Jaén:
Axa y Fátima y Marién.
Tres morillas tan garridas
iban a coger olivas,
y hallábanlas cogidas
en Jaén:
Axa y Fátima y Marién.
Y hallábanlas cogidas
y tornaban desmaídas
y las colores perdidas
en Jaén:
Axa y Fátima y Marién.

Tres morillas tan lozanas,
iban a coger manzanas
en Jaén:
Axa y Fátima y Marién.

Three Moorish maids bewitched me
in Jaén:
Axa and Fatima and Marién.
Three such graceful maids
went to pick olives
and found them gathered
in Jaén:
Axa and Fatima and Marién.
And found them gathered
and returned dismayed
and pale of face
in Jaén:
Axa and Fatima and Marién.

Three sprightly Moorish maids
went to pick apples
in Jaén:
Axa and Fatima and Marién.

La guitarra sin prima / The guitar with no first string

La guitarra sin prima
suena quejosa,
como estoy yo contigo,
por cierta cosa.
¡Ah! ¡Anda!
Como estoy yo contigo.
'¿Qué será?'

La guitarra que toco,
no tiene prima,
pero tiene bordones
de plata fina.
¡Ay! ¡Anda!
Pero tiene bordones.
'¿Qué será?'

The guitar with no first string
sounds angry,
as I am with you,
because of a certain matter.
Ah! Away!
As I am with you.
'What can it be?'

The guitar I play
has no first string,
but it has bass strings
of finest silver.
Ah! Away!
But it has bass strings.
'What can it be?'

Aquel sombrero de monte / That mountain hat

Aquel sombrero de monte,
hecho con hojas de palma,
¡ay! que me le lleva el río,
¡ay! que me le lleva el agua.

Lo siento por una cinta
que le puse colorada.
No he de tener más mi huerta
a la ribera cercana.

That mountain hat
made of palm leaves,
ah! the river snatched it from me,
ah! the water snatched it from me.

I grieve for a coloured band
I put on it.
No longer must I keep my field
by the river bank.

Se va yendo poco a poco	Little by little it was going,
y ya no me queda nada.	and now no more is left me.
¡Ay! que me le lleva el río,	Ah! the river snatched it from me.
¡Ay! que me le lleva el agua.	Ah! the water snatched it from me.

Polo[1] del contrabandista[2] / Song of the smuggler

Yo soy el contrabandista,	I am the smuggler
y campo por mi respeto.	and do as I please.
A todos los desafío,	I challenge everyone
pues a nadie tengo miedo.	and fear no one.
¡Ay! ¡Jaleo muchacha!	Ay! Jaleo! My girl!

¡Quién me compra	Who will buy from me
algún hilo negro!	some black thread!
Mi caballo esta cansado.	My horse is tired.
¡Ay!	Ay!
Y yo me marcho corriendo.	And I run beside it.

¡Ay! Que viene la ronda	Ay! The night patrol approaches
y se movió el tiroteo.	and they're starting to shoot.
¡Ay! Caballito mío,	Ay! My little horse,
caballo mío ligero.	my sprightly horse!

¡Ay! ¡Jaleo que nos cogen!	Ay! Jaleo! They're catching up with us!
¡Ay! ¡Sácame de este aprieto!	Ay! Get me out of this mess!
¡Ah! ¡Ay!	Ay! Ay!
¡Ay! ¡Jaleo muchacha! ¡Ay!	Ay! Jaleo! My girl!
¡Quién me merca	Who will buy from me
algún hilo negro!	some black thread!

> [1]*Polo*. A dance, native to Andalusia but probably of Moorish origin, in a moderately fast 3/8 time and often syncopated with periodic ornamental phrases on words such as 'Ay' and 'Olé'.
> [2]See Appendix for Geibel's translation.

El vito[1] / El vito

Una vieja vale un real[2]	An old woman is worth a real
Y una muchacha dos cuartos[3],	and a young girl two cuartos,
Pero como soy tan pobre	but as I am so poor
Me voy a lo más barato.	I go for the cheapest.

Con el vito, vito, vito,	On with the dancing,
Con el vito, vito va.	on with the dancing, olé!
No me haga 'usté' cosquillas	Stop your teasing, sir,
Que me pongo 'colorá.' ¡Ay!	else I'll blush! Ay!

> [1]*Vito*. A dance full of fire, performed in the taverns by a woman standing on a table before an audience of bullfighters.
> [2]*Real*. A silver coin.
> [3]*Cuarto*. A copper coin.

Trova / Ballad

Echame, niña bonita,
lágrimas en un pañuelo,
y las llevaré a Granada
que las engarce un platero;
con ellas quiero adornarme
la tapa de un guardapelo,
que el Jueves santo,
mi niña,
lo lucirá
el Nazareno.

Shed for me, my pretty one,
your tears in a handkerchief,
and to Granada I'll carry them
for a silversmith to set;
with them I wish to adorn
the lid of a locket,
so that on Maundy Thursday,
my pretty one,
the Christ
will wear it.

El molondrón / The lout

Desde que vino la moda
que sí, que no, que ¡ay!
de los pañuelitos blancos,
me parecen los mocitos
palomitas en el campo.
Molinero, a la hora de maquilar
ten cuidado que la rueda
no se te vaya a escapar
y te vaya a tí a coger
molinero al moler.
¡Molondrón, molondrón, molondrero!
Fui a pedir las marzas
en cá del molinero,
y perdí las sayas,
y perdí el pañuelo,
y perdí otra cosa
que ahora no recuerdo.
¡Molondrón, molondrón, molondrero!

Since the fashion began –
with a hey, and a ho, and a hey nonino –
of white kerchiefs,
youngsters seem to me
like little doves in the field.
Miller – at weighing time,
take care that your wheel
doesn't get out of control
and seize you, miller,
while you mill.
Lout, lout, boor!
I asked the young men to sing
at the miller's house;
and I lost my skirts,
and I lost my kerchief,
and I lost something else
that I can't now recall.
Lout, lout, boor!

Malagueña[1] de 'La Madrugá' / Dawn malagueña

Antes de que rompa el día,
cuando la huerta está en calma,
vengo a dar satisfacciones
a la que le dí mi alma,
el alma y la vida mía.

Before the break of day,
when the orchard is quiet,
I come to please
the one to whom I gave my soul,
my soul and very life.

[1]*Malagueña*. An Andalusian song originally from Malaga, it can also take the form of an instrumental piece.

Canción del Café de Chinitas / Song of Chinitas café

En el café de Chinitas
dijo Paquiro a su hermano;

In Chinitas café
Paquiro said to his brother;

en el café de Chinitas
dijo Paquiro a su hermano:
– Soy más valiente que tú,
más torero y más gitano;
soy más valiente que tú,
más torero y más gitano.

Sacó Paquiro el reló
y dijo de esta manera;
sacó Paquiro el reló
y dijo de esta manera:
– Este toro ha de morir
antes de las cuatro y media;
este toro ha de morir
antes de las cuatro y media.

Al dar las cuatro en la calle
se salieron del café;
al dar las cuatro en la calle
se salieron del café
y era Paquiro en la calle
un torero de cartel;
y era Paquiro en la calle
un torero de cartel.

in Chinitas café
Paquiro said to his brother:
'I'm more courageous than you,
more of a bullfighter and a gypsy;
I'm more courageous than you,
more of a bullfighter and a gypsy.'

Paquiro took out his watch
and spoke thus;
Paquiro took out his watch
and spoke thus:
'This bull must die
before half past four;
this bull must die
before half past four.'

When four struck in the street
they left the café;
when four struck in the street
they left the café
and in the street Paquiro
was a bullfighter of repute;
and in the street Paquiro
was a bullfighter of repute.

Romance de los pelegrinitos / *Romance of the little pilgrims*

Hacia Roma caminan
dos pelegrinos,
a que los case el Papa,
mamita,
porque son primos,
niña bonita,
porque son primos,
niña.

Sombrerito de hule
lleva el mozuelo
y la pelegrinita,
mamita,
de terciopelo,
niña bonita,
de terciopelo,
niña.

Le ha preguntado el Papa
cómo se llaman.
El le dice que Pedro,
mamita,
y ella que Ana,
niña bonita,
y ella que Ana,
niña.

There travel to Rome
two pilgrims,
for the Pope to marry them,
mother,
for they are cousins,
my sweet one,
for they are cousins,
my sweet.

A little hat of oil cloth
the young lad wears,
and the pilgrim lass,
mother,
a hat of velvet,
my sweet one,
of velvet,
my sweet.

The Pope asked them
their names.
He said Peter,
mother,
and she said Anna,
my sweet one,
and she said Anna,
my sweet.

Le ha preguntado el Papa
que si han pecado.
El le dice que un beso,
mamita,
que le había dado,
niña bonita,
que le había dado,
niña.

Y ha respondido el Papa
desde su cuarto:
'Cásate, pelegrina, corriendo,
que él es un santo,
y hoy no hay paredes
de cal y canto.'
¡Niña!

Las campanas de Roma
ya repicaron,
porque los pelegrinos
ya se casaron.
Un paso entre dos besos
hace el camino corto.
¡Niña!

The Pope asked them
if they had sinned.
He said just a kiss,
mother,
that he had given her,
my sweet one,
that he had given her,
my sweet.

And the Pope replied
from his chamber:
'Marry, pilgrim lass, at once,
for he is a saint,
and today there are no walls
to hold him in.'
My sweet.

The bells of Rome
rang out,
for the pilgrims
now got wed.
One step then two kisses
shortens the way,
my sweet!

XVII

FEDERICO GARCÍA LORCA
(1898–1936)

As a child Lorca was taught to play the guitar by his Aunt Isabel. Soon after his family moved to Granada, he had piano lessons with Antonio Segura, a gifted musician and composer of zarzuelas. So quick was Lorca's progress on the instrument that he neglected his school studies at the expense of hours of practice at the keyboard. Many years later he claimed that it was Segura who initiated him into the study of folk music. Under Segura's guidance, Lorca began to compose in his early university years. The history of both music and poetry might have been different if Segura had not died in 1916 at a crucial time in Lorca's development. He had lost his greatest ally and Lorca himself wrote in his *Autobiographical Note*, 'Since his parents refused to allow him to move to Paris to continue his musical studies, and his music teacher died, García Lorca turned his creative urges to poetry.'

The second stage of the story concerns Manuel de Falla, who was more than twenty years older than the poet. In 1920 Falla settled in Granada and soon became friendly with the young Lorca. As a sort of reincarnation of Segura in Lorca's life, he became the young man's musical mentor. They shared a fascination, both musical and poetic, for the cante jondo, the deep song of Andalusia, the most primitive and powerful of all Spain's musical well-springs. Both Lorca and Falla believed that cante jondo was the 'thread that joins us to the impenetrable Orient' and that it probably originated with the adoption by the Church of Byzantine chant as well as the influence of Moorish music. In 1921 Lorca also took flamenco guitar lessons, believing that it was the gypsies of the region who had given cante jondo its definitive shape. There is no doubt that his poetry was immensely enriched by these studies. He accompanied Falla on several of his song-gathering missions, and the songs published under the title *Canciones españolas antiguas* (UMV 19635)) were the fruits of these and later journeys. Lorca never lost his interest in music or piano playing, and although his simple accompaniments are not in the same league as those of Falla, the collection is a remarkable cross-over achievement. Only Robert Burns could claim a parallel status as great poet and conscientious collector of folk music.

Trece canciones españolas antiguas / *Thirteen ancient Spanish songs*

1. *Anda jaleo*[1] / *Come, clap hands*

Yo me alivié a un pino verde
por ver si la divisaba
y solo divisé el polvo
del coche que la llevaba.

    Anda jaleo, jaleo;
ya se acabó el alboroto
y vamos al tiroteo.

    No salgas, paloma, al campo,
mira que soy cazador
y si te tiro y te mato
para mí será el dolor,
para mí será el quebranto.

    Anda jaleo, jaleo;
ya se acabó el alboroto
y vamos al tiroteo.

    En la calle de los Muros
han matado una paloma.
Yo cortaré con mis manos
las flores de su corona.

    Anda jaleo, jaleo;
ya se acabó el alboroto
y ahora empieza el tiroteo.

I hastened to a green pine
to see if I could glimpse her,
but I merely glimpsed the dust
of the carriage that bore her away.

    Come, clap hands,
the tumult is over,
away to the shoot.

    Go not to the field, my dove,
for see, I am a hunter,
and if I shoot you and kill you,
the pain will be mine,
the grief will be mine.

    Come, clap hands,
the tumult is over,
away to the shoot.

    In the Calle de los Muros
they have killed a dove.
With my hands I shall cut
the flowers from its crown.

    Come, clap hands,
the tumult is over,
away to the shoot.

[1]*Jaleo.* A dance in moderate 3/8 time, accompanied by castanets. It also denotes the clapping of hands to encourage dancers. Other meanings include scuffle, quarrel, commotion.

2. *Los cuatro muleros* / *The four muleteers*

De los cuatro muleros,
mamita mía,
que van al agua,
el de la mula torda,
mamita mía,
me roba el alma.

Of the four muleteers,
o mother mine,
going to the water,
the one with the dappled mule,
o mother mine,
has stolen my heart.

De los cuatro muleros,
mamita mía,
que van al río,
el de la mula torda,
mamita mía,
es mi marío.

De los cuatro muleros,
mamita mía,
que van al campo,
el de la mula torda,
mamita mía,
moreno y alto.

¿A qué buscas la lumbre,
mamita mía,
la calle arriba,
si de tu cara sale,
mamita mía,
la brasa viva?

Of the four muleteers,
o mother mine,
going to the river,
the one with the dappled mule,
o mother mine,
is my husband.

Of the four muleteers,
o mother mine,
going to the field,
the one with the dappled mule,
o mother mine,
is dark and tall.

Why look for fire,
o mother mine,
there up the street,
if from your face,
o mother mine,
the ardour shines.

3. *Las tres hojas* / *The three leaves*

Debajo de la hoja
de la verbena
tengo a mi amante malo:
¡Jesús, qué pena!

Debajo de la hoja
de la lechuga
tengo a mi amante malo
con calentura.

Debajo de la hoja
del perejil
tengo a mi amante malo
y no puedo ir.

Beneath the leaf
of the verbena
my lover lies sick:
Lord, what anguish!

Beneath the leaf
of the lettuce
my lover lies sick
with a burning fever.

Beneath the leaf
of parsley
my lover lies sick
and I cannot go there.

4. *Lo mozos de Monleón* / *The Monleón boys*

(LEDESMA: CANCIONERO SALMANTINO) / (LEDESMA: SALAMANCAN SONGBOOK)

Los mozos de Monleón
se fueron a arar temprano,
para ir a la corrida,
y remudar con despacio.
Al hijo de la 'Velluda'
el remudo no le han dado.
– Al toro tengo de ir,
aunque vaya de prestado.

The Monleón boys
set out early to plough,
to go to the bullfight
and change their clothes at leisure.
The 'Hairy woman's' son
had no change of clothes.
'To the bull I must go,
even in borrowed clothes.'

Recitado sobre la música

– Permita Dios, si lo encuentras,
que te traigan en un carro,
las albarcas y el sombrero
de los siniestros colgando.
Se cogen los garrochones,
se van las navas abajo,
preguntando por el toro,
y el toro ya está encerrado.
A la mitad del camino
al mayoral se encontraron.
– Muchachos que vais al toro:
mirad que el toro es muy malo,
que la leche que mamó
se la dí yo por mi mano.

Recited over the music

'Pray God, that if you encounter the bull,
they carry you home in a cart,
with your sandals and hat
fatefully hanging down.'
They gather up the lances,
they move across the plain
searching for the bull,
and the bull is already caged.
Halfway there
they meet the bull's keeper.
'Boys, you are going to the bull:
beware, the bull is vicious,
for the milk it sucked
I gave him with my own hand.'

Cantado

Se presentan en la plaza
cuatro mozos muy gallardos;
Manuel Sánchez llamó al toro;
nunca le hubiera llamado,
por el pico de una albarca
toda la plaza arrastrado;
cuando el toro lo dejó,
ya lo ha dejado.

Sung

They enter the arena,
those four valiant boys;
Manuel Sánchez called out to the bull,
but should never have done so,
by the tip of one sandal
he was dragged across the arena;
when the bull dropped him,
he left him bleeding.

Recitado sobre la música

– Amigos, que yo me muero;
amigos, yo estoy muy malo;
tres pañuelos tengo dentro,
y este que meto son cuatro.
– Que llamen al confesor,
pa que venga a confesario.
Cuando el confesor llegaba
Manuel Sánchez ha expirado.

Recited over the music

'Friends, I am dying;
friends, I am very sick.
I have three handkerchiefs inside me,
and with this I have four.'
'Let them call the priest
to come and confess him.'
When the priest arrived,
Manuel Sánchez had died.

Cantado

Al rico de Monleón
le piden los bueis y el carro,
pa llevar a Manuel Sánchez,
que el torito le ha matado.
A la puerta de la 'Velluda'
arrecularon el carro.
– Aquí tenéis vuestro hijo
como lo habéis demandado.

Sung

The rich man of Monleón
was asked for oxen and cart
to take away Manuel Sánchez
whom the bull had killed.
At the 'hairy woman's' door
they backed the cart.
'Here you have your son,
just as you asked.'

5. *Las morillas de Jaén / The Moorish maids of Jaén*

CANCION POPULAR DEL SIGLO XV / 15TH-CENTURY FOLKSONG

Tres moricas me enamoran
en Jaén:
Axa y Fátima y Marién.

Three Moorish maids bewitched me
in Jaén:
Axa and Fatima and Marién.

Tres moricas tan garridas
iban a coger olivas,
y hallábanlas cogidas
en Jaén:
Axa y Fátima y Marién.

Y hallábanlas cogidas
y tornaban desmaídas
y las colores perdidas
en Jaén:
Axa y Fátima y Marién.

Tres moricas tan lozanas
iban a coger manzanas
y hallábanlas tomadas
en Jaén:
Axa y Fátima y Marién.

Díjeles: ¿Quién sois, señoras,
de mi vida robadoras?
Cristianas que éramos moras
en Jaén:
Axa y Fátima y Marién.

Three such graceful maids
went to pick olives,
and found them gathered
in Jaén:
Axa and Fatima and Marién.

And found them gathered
and returned dismayed
and pale of face
in Jaén:
Axa and Fatima and Marién.

Three sprightly Moorish maids
went to pick apples
and found them gathered
in Jaén:
Axa and Fatima and Marién.

I said to them: 'Who are you, señoras,
who rob me of my life?'
'Christian girls, once Moors
in Jaén:
Axa and Fatima and Marién.'

6. *Sevillanas del siglo XVIII / 18th-century sevillanas*

¡Viva Sevilla!
Llevan las sevillanas
en la mantilla
un letrero que dice:
¡Viva Sevilla!

¡Viva Triana!
¡Vivan los trianeros,
los de Triana!
¡Vivan los sevillanos
y sevillanas!

Lo traigo andado.
La Macarena y todo
lo traigo andado.

Lo traigo andado;
cara como la tuya
no la he encontrado.
La Macarena y todo
lo traigo andado.

Qué bien pareces,
ay río de Sevilla,
lleno de velas blancas
y ramas verdes.

Viva Sevilla!
The ladies of Seville wear
in their mantillas
a sign which reads:
Viva Sevilla!

Viva Triana!
Long live Trianans,
the people of Triana!
Long live the men
and women of Seville!

I've seen the world,
the Virgin of the Macarena and all,
I've seen the world.

I've seen the world;
but a face such as yours
I have never seen.
The Virgin of Macarena and all,
I've seen the world.

How lovely you are,
oh river of Seville,
full of white sails
and green branches.

7. *El Café de Chinitas* / *Chinitas café*

En el café de Chinitas
dijo Paquiro a su hermano:
«Soy más valiente que tú,
más torero y más gitano.»

En el café de Chinitas
dijo Paquiro a Frascuelo:
«Soy más valiente que tú,
más gitano y más torero.»

Sacó Paquiro el reló
y dijo de esta manera:
«Este toro ha de morir
antes de las cuatro y media.»

Al dar las cuatro en la calle
se salieron del café
y era Paquiro en la calle
un torero de cartel.

In Chinitas café
Paquiro said to his brother:
'I'm more courageous than you,
more a bullfighter and more a gypsy.'

In Chinitas café
Paquiro said to Frascuelo:
'I'm more courageous than you,
more a bullfighter and more a gypsy.'

Paquiro took out his watch
and spoke thus:
'This bull must die
before half past four.'

When four struck in the street
they left the café,
and in the street Paquiro
was a bullfighter of repute.

8. *Nana de Sevilla* / *Sevillian lullaby*

Este galapaguito
no tiene mare;
lo parió una gitana,
lo echó a la calle.
No tiene mare, sí;
no tiene mare, no;
no tiene mare,
lo echó a la calle.

Este niño chiquito
no tiene cuna;
su padre es carpintero
y le hará una.

This little urchin
has no mother;
a gypsy bore it,
threw it into the street.
It has no mother, yes;
it has no mother, no;
it has no mother,
she threw it into the street.

This little boy
has no cradle;
his father's a carpenter
and will make him one.

9. *Los pelegrinitos* / *The little pilgrims*

Hacia Roma caminan
dos pelegrinos,
a que los case el Papa,
porque son primos.

Sombrerito de hule
lleva el mozuelo,
y la pelegrinita,
de terciopelo.

There travel to Rome
two pilgrims,
for the Pope to marry them,
since they are cousins.

A little hat of oil cloth
the young lad wears,
and the pilgrim lass
a hat of velvet.

Al pasar por el puente
de la Victoria,
tropezó la madrina[1],
cayó la novia.

As they cross the bridge,
the Victoria bridge,
the madrina stumbled,
the bride fell.

Han llegado a Palacio,
suben arriba,
y en la sala del Papa
los desaminan.

They arrived at the Palace,
climbed the stairs,
and in the Pope's chamber
they are overawed.

Le ha preguntado el Papa
cómo se llaman.
El le dice que Pedro
y ella que Ana.

The Pope asked them
their names.
He said Peter
and she said Anna.

Le ha preguntado el Papa
que qué edad tienen.
Ella dice que quince
y él diez y siete.

The Pope asked them
their age.
She said fifteen
and he said seventeen.

Le ha preguntado el Papa
de dónde eran.
Ella dice de Cabra
y él de Antequera.

The Pope asked them
where they were from.
She said from Cabra
and he from Antequera.

Le ha preguntado el Papa
que si han pecado.
El le dice que un beso
que le había dado.

The Pope asked them
if they had sinned.
He said just a kiss
that he had given her.

Y la pelegrinita,
que es vergonzosa,
se le ha puesto la cara
como una rosa.

And the pilgrim lass,
abashed,
reddened
like a rose.

Y ha respondido el Papa
desde su cuarto:
¡Quién fuera pelegrino
para otro tanto!

And the Pope replied
from his chamber:
would that I were a pilgrim
to do the same!

Las campanas de Roma
ya repicaron
porque los pelegrinos
ya se casaron.

The bells of Rome
rang out,
for the pilgrims
now got wed.

    [1]*Madrina*. Godmother/bridesmaid.

   10. *Zorongo*[1] / *Zorongo*

Tengo los ojos azules,
tengo los ojos azules,
y el corazoncito igual
que la cresta de la lumbre.

My eyes are blue,
my eyes are blue,
and my little heart
is like a tongue of flame.

De noche me salgo al patio
y me jarto de llorar
de ver que te quiero tanto
y tú no me quieres ná.

Esta gitana está loca,
pero loquita de atar,
que lo que sueña de noche
quiere que sea verdad.

Las manos de mi cariño
te están bordando una capa
con agremán de alhelíes
y con esclavina de agua.

Cuando fuiste novio mío,
por la primavera blanca,
los cascos de tu caballo
cuatro sollozos de plata.

La luna es un pozo chico,
las flores no valen nada,
lo que valen son tus brazos
cuando de noche me abrazan.

At night I go on to the patio
and weep my heart out,
for I love you so
and you love me not at all.

This gypsy girl is mad,
as mad as mad can be,
for what she dreams at night
she wishes were true.

My loving hands
embroider you a cloak
trimmed with gillyflower,
hooded with water.

When you were my suitor
in the white springtime,
the hooves of your horse
were four sobs of silver.

The moon is a little well,
the flowers of no worth at all,
what matters are your arms
when they at night embrace me.

'*Zorongo*. An Andalusian dance.

11. *Romance de Don Boyso* / *The ballad of Don Boyso*

Camina Don Boyso
mañanita fría
a tierra de moros
a buscar amiga.
Hallóla lavando
en la fuente fría.
— ¿Qué haces ahí, mora,
hija de judía?
Deja a mi caballo
beber agua fría.
— Reviente el caballo
y quien lo traía,
que yo no soy mora
ni hija de judía.
Soy una cristiana
que aquí estoy cativa.
— Si fueras cristiana,
yo te llevaría
y en paños de seda
yo te envolvería;
pero si eres mora,
yo te dejaría.

Don Boyso rides out
in the cold early morn
to the land of the Moors
to look for a love.
He found her washing
in the cold fountain.
'What are you doing, moorish maiden,
daughter of a Jewess?
Let my horse
drink cool water.'
'May your horse perish
and he who brought it here,
for I am no Moor
nor daughter of a Jewess.
I am a Christian,
imprisoned here.'
'Were you a Christian,
I'd bear you away
and in silken weeds
envelop you,
but if a Moor you be
I'd leave you.'

Montóla a caballo	He set her on his horse
por ver qué decía;	to see what she would say;
en las siete leguas	but in seven leagues
no hablara la niña.	the girl spoke not a word.
Al pasar un campo	Passing a field
de verdes olivas,	of green olives,
por aquellos prados,	through those groves
qué llantos hacía.	how bitterly she wept.
– ¡Ay prados! ¡Ay prados!,	'Ah, olive groves,
prados de mi vida.	groves that I love!
Cuando el rey mi padre	When the King, my father,
plantó aquí esta oliva,	planted here this olive-tree,
él se la plantara,	while he planted it
yo se la tenía,	I held it;
la reina mi madre	the Queen, my mother,
la seda torcía,	spun silk,
mi hermano Don Boyso	my brother, Don Boyso,
los toros corría.	fought bulls.'
– ¿Y cómo te llamas?	'And what is your name?'
– Yo soy Rosalinda,	'I am Rosalinda,
que así me pusieron	I was given this name,
porque al ser nacida	for when I was born
una linda rosa	a beautiful rose
n'el pecho tenía.	lay on my breast.'
– Pues tú, por las señas,	'Then you, it seems,
mi hermana serías.	must be my sister.
Abra la mi madre	Fling open, mother,
puertas de alegría,	the doors of happiness,
por traerla nuera	for instead of a daughter-in-law
le traigo su hija.	I bring you your daughter.'

12. *Los reyes de la baraja* / *The kings in the pack*

Si tu madre quiere un rey,	If your mother wants a king,
la baraja tiene cuatro:	the pack of cards has four:
rey de oros, rey de copas,	king of diamonds, king of hearts,
rey de espadas, rey de bastos.	king of spades, king of clubs.
Corre que te pillo,	Run, else I'll catch you,
corre que te agarro,	run, else I'll snatch you,
mira que te lleno	look out, or I'll cover
la cara de barro.	your face in mud.
Del olivo	The olive
me retiro,	I'll leave,
del esparto	the grass,
yo me aparto,	I'll shun,
del sarmiento	by the vine
me arrepiento	I regret
de haberte querido tanto.	having loved you so.

13. *La Tarara* / *Tarara*

La Tarara, sí;	Tarara, yes,
la Tarara, no;	Tarara, no,
la Tarara, niña,	Tarara, my girl,
que la he visto yo.	for I've seen her.
Lleva mi Tarara	Tarara wears
un vestido verde	a green dress
lleno de volantes	bedecked with flounces
y de cascabeles.	and little bells.
La Tarara, sí;	Tarara, yes,
la Tarara, no;	Tarara, no,
la Tarara, niña,	Tarara, my girl,
que la he visto yo.	for I've seen her.
Luce mi Tarara	My Tarara gleams
su cola de seda	with her silken train
sobre las retamas	above the broom
y la hierbabuena.	and above the mint.
Ay, Tarara loca,	Oh, wild Tarara,
Mueve la cintura	shake your hips
para los muchachos	for the boys
de las aceitunas.	of the olive groves.

XVIII

JOAQUÍN RODRIGO
(*b*.1901)

With his *Cuatro madrigales amatorios* (published by Chester) Rodrigo had almost as much of a success on his hands with singers as with guitarists in the *Concierto de Aranjuez*, a work which for many embodies the spirit of Spanish music of our time. Listening to some of the nationally inspired music of Spain of this generation, it is difficult to tell whether it has been written as a result of deep affection for, and affinity with, the old traditions, or whether it is playing into the hands of the tourists, and giving them what they expect to hear. Although the latter is obviously not the case with an artist of the integrity of Rodrigo, there is nonetheless from time to time a suspicion that he finds it too easy to evoke picture-postcard Spain. He was, however, a prolific and hard-working artist who was seen to restore to Spain the traditional musical values disrupted by the artistic experimentation of the years leading up to the Civil War. But the stagnation of Spain's musical life in the Franco years was reflected by the safe and somewhat repetitive continuity of Rodrigo's style which underwent little development, and by his lack of distinguished younger disciples.

Joaquín Rodrigo was born in Valencia on 22 November 1901 – twelve years to the day before Benjamin Britten. Like Fuenllana he was blind from an early age. In 1927 he entered the Ecole Normale de Musique in Paris as a pupil of Dukas. In 1933 he married the Turkish pianist Victoria Kamhi whose influence, both musical and poetic, is seen in many of his songs. He lived in France during the Civil War, and returned home only in 1939. The *Concierto de Aranjuez* was premièred in 1940 and was hailed as harbinger of a new age – Carl Orff received the same sort of reception for his *Carmina Burana* in Frankfurt in 1937. Attempts to follow the success of this work with similar pieces for different concertante instruments were unsuccessful, but Rodrigo's career proceeded for the next thirty years with a substantial catalogue of orchestral music, including a ballet, a zarzuela and an opera, and many exquisite songs which show a highly discerning range of literary interest, from sixteenth-century poetry to the works of Jiménez and Machado. Rodrigo distributed his songs over a wide range of publishers in England, France and Spain. *Dos canciones españolas* were published by Schott (6238). Four works are in print with Union Musical Española: *Cantos de amor y de guerra* (UMV 21286), *Con Antonio Machado* (UMV 21748), *Dos canciones para cantar a los niños* (UMV 21798) and 'Romance del Comendador de Ocaña' (UMV 19895). One of the most interesting of the song volumes, the *Canciones para canto y piano*, a miscellaneous collection of songs from throughout the composer's career, was published under his own imprint – Edición del Autor, Madrid.

Serranilla / Serranilla

MARQUÉS DE SANTILLANA
(1928)

Moça tan fermosa non vi en la frontera, como una vaquera de la Finojosa.	So fair a lass I never saw on the frontier as a milkmaid from Finojosa.
Faziendo la vía del Calatreveño a Sancta María, vencido del sueño, por tierra fragosa perdí la carrera, do vi la vaquera de la Finojosa.	En route from Calatreveño to Sancta Maria, overcome with sleep I lost my way on the rugged terrain where I saw the milkmaid from Finojosa.
En un verde prado de rosas e flores, guardando ganado con otros pastores, la vi tan graciosa que apenas creyera que fuesse vaquera de la Finojosa.	In a verdant meadow of roses and flowers, as she tended her cows with other herders I saw her so charming I scarce could believe that she was a milkmaid from Finojosa.
Non creo las rosas de la primavera sean tan fermosas nin de tal manera (fablando sin glosa), si antes sopiera de aquella vaquera de la Finojosa.	I do not think the roses of spring would have seemed nearly so fair or of such shape (if the truth be known) if I had earlier met that milkmaid from Finojosa.

Non tanto mirara
su mucha beldad
porque me dexara
en mi libertad.
Mas dixe: «Donosa»
(por saber quién era),
«¿dónde es la vaquera
de la Finojosa?»

I did not wish to gaze long
on her great beauty,
so as not to lose
my freedom.
Yet I said: 'Fair one',
(to find out who she was),
'where is the milkmaid
from Finojosa?'

Bien como riendo,
dixo: «Bien vengades;
que ya bien entiendo
lo que demandades:
non es deseosa
de amar, nin lo espera
aquessa vaquera
de la Finojosa.»

Laughingly
she replied: 'You are welcome,
though I understand well
what you desire –
she has no wish
to love or be loved,
that milkmaid
from Finojosa.'

Cántico de la Esposa / Song of the Bride

SAN JUAN DE LA CRUZ

(1934)

¿Adónde te escondiste, Amado,
Y me dejaste con gemido?
Como el ciervo huiste,
Habiéndome ferido;
Salí tras ti clamando, y ya eras ido.

Where, Beloved, are you hiding,
leaving me to moan?
Like the stag you fled
after wounding me;
imploring I pursued, but you had flown.

Pastores los que fuéredes,
Allá por las majadas al otero,
Si por ventura viéredes
A aquel que yo más quiero,
Decidle que adolezco, peno y muero.

Shepherds high in the hills
tending your flocks,
if by chance you spy
my love whom I adore,
tell him I suffer, grieve and die.

Buscando mis amores,
Iré por esos montes y
    riberas;
Ni cogeré las flores,
Ni temeré las fieras,
Y pasaré los fuertes y
    fronteras.

To seek my love,
by those mountains and river banks I'll
    stray;
I shall not pick flowers
nor fear wild beasts,
but pass through fort and frontier on my
    way.

¡Oh, bosques y espesuras,
Plantados por la mano del Amado!
¡Oh prado de verduras,
De flores esmaltado,
Decid si por vosotros ha pasado!

O woods and thickets,
sown by my Beloved's hand!
O green fields
enamelled with flowers,
say if he has passed your way!

Coplas[1] del pastor enamorado / The song of the love-lorn shepherd

LOPE DE VEGA

(1935)

Verdes riberas amenas,	Green, enchanting river-banks,
Frescos y floridos valles,	fresh and flowering valleys,
Aguas puras, cristalinas,	pure, limpid waters
Altos montes de quien nacen.	rising from high mountains –
Guiadme por vuestras sendas,	lead me along your paths
Y permitidme que halle	and let me find
Esta prenda que perdí,	the jewel I lost,
Y me cuesta amor tan grande.	which costs me so much love.
Llevo, teñidas en sangre,	Blood-stained
Las abarcas y las manos,	are my sandals and hands,
Rotas de apartar jarales;	scratched from parting brambles;
De dormir sobre la arena	from sleeping on the sand
De aquella desierta margen.	by that deserted bank
Traigo enhetrado el cabello.	my hair is tangled.
Y cuando el aurora sale,	And when dawn breaks
Mojado por el rocío	I am soaked with the dew
Que por mi cabeza esparcen	scattered on my head
Las nubes que del sol huyen,	by clouds fleeing the sun
Humedeciendo los aires.	and moistening the air.
Verdes riberas amenas,	Green, enchanting river-banks,
Frescos y floridos valles,	fresh and flowering valleys,
Aguas puras, cristalinas,	pure, limpid waters
Altos montes de quien nacen . . .	rising from high mountains.

[1]*Coplas*. Couplets, and by extension a series of short verses held together by a
common rhythm; a popular lyric.

Canción del cucu / Song of the cuckoo

VICTORIA KAMHI

(1937)

Cuclillo, cuclillo canta,	Cuckoo, sing, my little cuckoo.
Días son de cantar,	'Tis time to sing,
Pronto el duro cierzo	soon the harsh North Wind
Corre por el pinar.	will run through the pines.
Díme si otros bosques	Tell me if one day
Un día yo veré,	I shall see other woods,
Si la lejana tierra	if very soon I shall find
Muy pronto hallaré.	the distant land.
Dí si por estos mundos	Tell me if I'll always
Vagando siempre iré,	wander through the world,
O si mi vida errante	or if very soon I'll cease
Muy pronto acabaré.	my wandering life.

Pájaro, buen pajarillo,
Díme si es verdad:
¡Ella dice que siempre,
Siempre me seguirá! . . .

Bird, sweet little bird,
tell me if it's true:
she says that always,
always she'll follow me!

Cuatro madrigales amatorios / *Four madrigals of love*
    (1948)

1.

¿Con qué la lavaré
la tez de la mi cara?
¿Con qué la lavaré,
que vivo mal penada?

Lávanse las casadas
con agua de limones:
lávome yo, cuitada,
con penas y dolores.
¿Con qué la lavaré,
que vivo mal penada?

1.

With what shall I wash
the skin of my face?
With what shall I wash it?
I live in such sorrow.

Married women wash
in lemon water:
in my grief I wash
in pain and sorrow.
With what shall I wash it?
I live in such sorrow.

2.

Vos me matastes,
niña en cabello,
vos me habéis muerto.

Riberas de un río
vi moza virgo.
Niña en cabello,
vos me habéis muerto.
Niña en cabello,
vos me matastes,
vos me habéis muerto.

2.

You killed me,
girl with hair hanging loose,
you have slain me.

By the river bank
I saw a young maiden.
Girl with hair hanging loose,
you have slain me.
Girl with hair hanging loose,
you have killed me,
you have slain me.

3.

¿De dónde venís, amore?
Bien sé yo de dónde.
¿De dónde venís, amigo?
Fuere yo testigo,
¡Ah!
Bien sé yo de dónde.

3.

Where hast thou been, my love?
I know well where.
Where hast thou been, my friend?
Were I a witness,
ah!
I know well where!

4.

De los álamos vengo, madre,
de ver cómo los menea el aire.

4.

I come from the poplars, mother,
from seeing the breezes stir them.

De los álamos de Sevilla,
de ver a mi linda amiga,
de ver cómo los menea el aire.

De los álamos vengo, madre,
de ver cómo los menea el aire.

From the poplars of Seville,
from seeing my sweet love,
from seeing the breezes stir them.

I come from the poplars, mother,
from seeing the breezes stir them.

Soneto / Sonnet

JUAN BAUTISTA DE MESA

(1950)

Dormía en un prado mi pastora
    hermosa,
Y en torno della erraba entre
    flores,
De una y otra usurpando los licores,
Una abejuela, más que yo dichosa,
    Que vió los labios donde amor reposa,
Y a quien el alba envía sus colores,
Que al vuelo refrenando los errores,
Engañada, los muerde, como a rosa.
    ¡Oh, venturoso error, discreto engaño!
¡Oh, temeraria abeja, pues tocaste
Donde aún imaginarlo no me
    atrevo!
    Si has sentido de envidia el triste daño,
Parte conmigo el néctar que robaste,
Te deberé lo que al amor no
    debo . . .

My fair shepherdess was sleeping in a
    field,
and hovering around her from flower to
    flower,
a bee sucked from each the juice,
more fortunate than I.
    It saw the lips where love reposed
and where dawn had cast her colours,
and feigning error as it flew by,
it bit them, mistakenly, like a rose.
    O happy error, wise deceit!
O bold bee – for you touched her
where, even in my dreams, I would not
    dare!
    If you have felt the sad pain of jealousy,
share with me the nectar which you stole,
and I shall owe you that which I owe not
    love . . .

Tres villancicos / Three villancicos

(1951)

Pastorcito santo / Holy little shepherd

LOPE DE VEGA

Zagalejo de perlas
hijo del alba,
¿dónde vais que hace frío
tan de mañana?
Como sois lucero
del alba mía
a traer el día
nacéis primero;
pastor y cordero,
sin choza ni lana,
¿dónde vais que hace frío,
tan de mañana?

Pearl-bright shepherd boy,
son of the dawn,
where are you bound in such cold
so early in the morning?
Since you are the morning star
of my dawn,
to bring in the day
you are the first to appear;
shepherd and lamb,
without hut or fleece,
where are you bound in such cold
so early in the morning?

Perlas en los ojos,	With pearls in your eyes
risa en la boca,	and laughter on your lips,
a placer y enojos	pleasure and anger
las almas provoca;	you bring to our souls;
cabellitos rojos,	little shock of russet hair,
boca de grana,	scarlet mouth,
¿dónde vais que hace frío,	where are you bound in such cold
tan de mañana?	so early in the morning?
¿Qué tenéis que hacer	What must you do,
pastorcito Santo,	holy little shepherd,
madrugando tanto?	to rise so early?
Lo dais a entender	You let it be known,
aunque vais a ver	even though you go forth disguised
disfrazado el alma.	to see our souls.
¿Dónde vais que hace frío	Where are you bound in such cold
tan de mañana?	so early in the morning?

Aire y donaire / Poise and grace

ANON., ADAPTED BY VICTORIA KAMHI

¡Aire y donaire!	Poise and grace!
¡Gitanillas, al baile, al baile!	Gypsy girls, to the dance, to the dance!
Aire y donaire!	Poise and grace!
¡Toca y repica,	Play and ring
sonajuelas y castañeticas!	on timbrels and castanets!
¡Gitanillas, al baile!	Gypsy girls, to the dance!
¡Ay, qué tamaño!	Ah, how superb!
No le llega Juanico al zapato.	Juanito doesn't come up to her shoe!
¡Ay, qué tamaño!	Ah, how superb!
¡Ay, qué zagala!	Ah, what a girl!
¡Cuanto va que es su madre sin falta!	I bet she's definitely his mother!
¡Ay, qué zagala!	Ah, what a girl!
¡Ande, corra, siga!	Step out, run along, follow!
¡Sonajuelas y castañeticas!	Timbrels and castanets!
¡Gitanillas, al baile!	Gypsy girls, to the dance!
¡Aire y donaire!	Poise and grace!
¡Ay qué buen viejo!	Ah, what a fine old fellow!
Que ha tenido sus flores es cierto.	He's certainly past his prime!
¡Ay qué buen viejo!	Ah, what a fine old fellow!
¡Aire y donaire!	Poise and grace!
¡Ay qué animales!	Ah, what beasts!
¡Como aquestos hay mil semejantes!	There are a thousand more like these!
¡Aire y donaire!	Poise and grace!
¡Toca y repica,	Play and ring
sonajuelas y castañeticas!	on timbrels and castanets!
¡Gitanillas, al baile, al baile!	Gypsy girls, to the dance, to the dance!
¡Aire y donaire!	Poise and grace!

Coplillas de Belén / Carols of Bethlehem

VICTORIA KAMHI

Si la palmera supiera
que al Niño en cuna tan bella
caído se le ha una estrella,
su abanico le tendiera
para que el Niño meciera.
Del monte por la ladera,
¡qué alegre va el pastorcillo,
montado en su borriquillo!
¡Corre, que el Niño te espera,
y es corta la Nochebuena!
En Belén la Virgen pura
le reza al Niño que espera.
Canta la Virgen María,
el Niño le sonreía;
¡qué triste está la Palmera!
Si la palmera supiera,
lo que espera . . .

If the palm tree knew
that for the Child in its fair cradle
a star had fallen from on high,
it would spread its fan
to rock the Child.
Down the mountainside
how happily the shepherd boy rides,
mounted on his little donkey!
Hurry, for the Child awaits you
And Christmas Eve will soon be over!
In Bethlehem the Virgin pure
prays to the waiting Child.
The Virgin Mary sings,
the Child smiled at her.
How sad the palm tree stands!
If the palm tree knew
what was nigh . . .

La espera / The wait

VICTORIA KAMHI

(1952)

Cuando llegue ay,
Yo no sé por qué
Tengo que ocultar,
¿Por qué?
¿No canta, no, el jilguero
Que regresa al tibio nido
Cuando el día ya se ha ido?
Pero yo, triste, espero.
Dímelo, ay, avecilla tú,
¿Por qué tenemos que huir,
Por qué?
Dímelo tú, la fuente,
La que brotas de la entraña
De esa árida montaña
Cristalina y transparente,
Dímelo, pues yo no lo sé.
¿Por qué tenemos que huir
Por qué?
Hijo del alborada,
Lucerito que yo ví
Dímelo si para mí
En Belén habrá esta noche posada.
Dímelo, por tu fe
¿Por qué

Alas, I do not know
when he will come,
why must I hide,
oh why?
Does not the linnet sing,
returning to its warm nest
after the day has gone?
But I sadly wait.
Tell me, ah, little bird,
why must we flee,
oh why?
Tell me, o fountain,
who spring from the heart
of this arid mountain,
crystalline and clear,
tell me, since I do not know.
Why must we flee,
oh why?
Son of the dawn,
little light that I beheld,
tell me, if for me
there be room in Bethlehem tonight?
Tell me, by your faith,
why

Tenemos que huir?	must we flee?
Escúchame, Señor,	Hear me, Lord,
No me abandonas Tú, lo sé,	Thou shalt not abandon me, I know,
Confiada caminaré	confident I shall go on,
Un portal no ha de faltar	there will be a door . . .
De Tu mano, sí, firme iré, feliz,	Guided by Thy hand I shall go, steadfast and happy.
Un Sol ha de nacer,	A Sun must rise,
Lo sé.	I know.
¡Oh, ven, Niño Divino!	O come, Holy Child!

Por mayo era, por mayo[1] / In May it was, in May

(1954)

Por mayo era, por mayo,	In May it was, in May,
Cuando hace la calor,	when the days are hot,
Cuando los trigos encallan	when the wheat ripens
Y están los campos en flor;	and the fields are in flower;
Cuando canta la calandria	when the lark sings
Y responde el ruiseñor,	and the nightingale replies,
Cuando los enamorados	when lovers
Van a servir al amor.	serve the god of Love.
Menos yo, ¡triste cuitado!	Except for me, poor wretch,
Que vivo en esta prisión,	who live in this prison,
Que no sé cuándo es de día,	unaware of daybreak
Ni cuándo las noches son,	and unaware of nightfall,
Sino por una avecica	save when a little bird
Que me cantaba al albor –	sang to me at dawn –
Matómela un ballestero . . .	An archer shot it . . .
¡Dios le dé mal galardón!	May God grant him small thanks!

[1]See Appendix for Geibel's translation.

Con Antonio Machado / With Antonio Machado

ANTONIO MACHADO

(1970)

Preludio / Prelude

Mientras la sombra pasa de un santo amor, hoy quiero	As the shade passes of a sacred love, today I wish
poner un dulce salmo sobre mi viejo atril.	to set a sweet psalm on my old music stand.
Acordaré las notas del órgano severo	I shall play the notes of the grave organ
al suspirar fragante del pífano de abril.	to match the fragrant sighing of April's fife.

Madurarán su aroma las pomas otoñales,
la mirra y el incienso salmodiarán su
  olor;
exhalarán su fresco perfume los
  rosales
bajo la paz en sombra del tibio huerto en
  flor.

Autumn's apples will ripen its scent,
myrrh and incense will chant its
  fragrance;
rosebushes will breathe forth its fresh
  aroma
beneath the shaded peace of the flowering
  warm orchard.

Al grave acorde lento de música y
  aroma,
la sola y vieja y noble razón de mi
  rezar
levantará su vuelo suave de paloma,
y la palabra blanca se elevará al
  altar.

At the sound of this slow, grave chord of
  music and scent,
the single, ancient and noble cause of my
  prayer
shall raise its soft, dove-like wing,
and the white word shall rise up at the
  altar.

Mi corazón te aguarda / My heart awaits you

Amada, el aura dice
tu pura veste blanca . . .
No te verán mis ojos;
¡mi corazón te aguarda!

The breeze, my love, heralds
your pure, white dress . . .
My eyes shall not see you;
my heart awaits you!

El viento me ha traído
tu nombre en la mañana;
el eco de tus pasos
repite la montaña . . .
No te verán mis ojos;
¡mi corazón te aguarda!

The wind has brought me
your name in the morning;
the echo of your steps
resounds on the mountain . . .
My eyes shall not see you;
my heart awaits you!

En las sombrías torres
repican las campanas . . .
No te verán mis ojos;
¡mi corazón te aguarda!

From the sombre towers
the bells are tolling . . .
My eyes shall not see you;
my heart awaits you!

Los golpes del martillo
dicen la negra caja;
y el sitio de la fosa,
los golpes de la azada . . .
No te verán mis ojos;
¡mi corazón te aguarda!

The blows of the hammer
herald the black box;
the site of the grave
the blows of the spade . . .
My eyes shall not see you;
my heart awaits you!

Tu voz y tu mano / Your voice and hand

Soñé que tú me llevabas
por una blanca vereda,
en medio del campo verde,
hacia el azul de las sierras,
hacia los montes azules,
una mañana serena.

I dreamt you were carrying me
across a white path,
in the middle of the green field,
toward the blue of the sierra,
toward the blue mountains,
one serene morning.

Sentí tu mano en la mía,
tu mano de compañera,
tu voz de niña en mi oído
como una campana nueva,
como una campana virgen
de un alba de primavera.
¡Eran tu voz y tu mano,
en sueños, tan verdaderas! . . .
Vive, esperanza: ¡quién sabe
lo que se traga la tierra!

I felt your hand in mine,
your trusted hand,
I heard your young girl's voice
like a new bell,
like the virgin bell
of a Spring dawn.
Your voice and hand,
how true they were in dreams! . . .
Live on, hope; who knows
what the earth has devoured!

Mañana de abril / April morning

Era una mañana y abril sonreía.
Frente al horizonte dorado moría
la luna, muy blanca y opaca; tras ella,
cual tenue ligera quimera,
    corría
la nube que apenas enturbia una estrella.
. . . .

It was morning and April was smiling.
Facing the golden horizon, the moon –
so white and dim – was dying; behind her,
like an insubstantial, swift chimera, a
    cloud,
scarcely obscuring a star, scudded by.

Como sonreía la rosa mañana
al sol del oriente abrí mi
    ventana;
y en mi triste alcoba penetró el oriente
en canto de alondras, en risa de
    fuente
y en suave perfume de flora temprana.

As the roseate morning smiled
at the Eastern sun, I threw open my
    window,
and the East entered my sad bedroom
in the song of larks, the laughter of
    fountains
and the sweet scent of early flowers.

Fue una clara tarde de melancolía.
Abril sonreía. Yo abrí las ventanas
de mi casa al viento . . . El viento
    traía
perfume de rosas, doblar de
    campanas . . .

It was a clear afternoon of melancholy.
April was smiling. I opened the windows
of my house to the wind . . . The wind
    carried
the perfume of roses, the tolling of
    bells . . .

Doblar de campanas, lejanas, llorosas,
süave de rosas aromado
    aliento . . .
    . . . ¿Dónde están los huertos floridos de
    rosas?
¿Qué dicen las dulces campanas al viento?
. . . .

the distant, tearful tolling of bells,
smooth with the breath of fragrant
    roses . . .
    . . . Where are the orchards abloom with
    roses?
What do the sweet bells say to the wind?

Pregunté a la tarde de abril que moría:
¿Al fin la alegría se acerca a mi
    casa?
La tarde de abril sonrió: La alegría
pasó por tu puerta – y luego,
    sombría:
Pasó por tu puerta. Dos veces no
    pasa.

I asked the dying afternoon of April:
Is happiness at last drawing near my
    home?
The April afternoon smiled: 'happiness
passed through your door.' – then, with
    sombre tone:
'passed through your door. It comes not
    twice.'

Los sueños / The dreams

El hada más hermosa ha sonreído
al ver la lumbre de una estrella pálida,
que en el hilo suave, blanco y
    silencioso
se enrosca al huso de su rubia
    hermana.

Y vuelve a sonreír, porque en su rueca
el hilo de los campos se enmaraña.
Tras la tenue cortina de la alcoba
está el jardín envuelto en luz dorada.

La cuna, casi en sombra. El niño
    duerme.
Dos hadas laboriosas lo acompañan,
hilando de los sueños los sutiles
copos en ruecas de marfil y plata.

The most beautiful fairy smiled
on seeing the light of a pale star,
which with a gentle, white and silent
    thread
entwines itself around her fair sister's
    spindle.

And smiles again, as in her distaff
the thread of fields becomes enmeshed.
Behind the bedroom's flimsy curtain
the garden is bathed in golden light.

The cradle half in shadow. The child
    asleep.
Two zealous fairies accompany him,
spinning from his dreams the fine-spun
threads with distaffs of ivory and silver.

Cantaban los niños / The children were singing

Yo escucho los cantos
de viejas cadencias
que los niños cantan
cuando en coro juegan
y vierten en coro
sus almas que sueñan
cual vierten sus aguas
las fuentes de piedra:
con monotonías
de risas eternas
que no son alegres,
con lágrimas viejas
que no son amargas,
y dicen tristezas,
tristezas de amores
de antiguas leyendas.

En los labios niños,
las canciones llevan
confusa la historia
y clara la pena;
como clara el agua
lleva su conseja
de viejos amores
que nunca se cuentan.

Jugando a la sombra
de una plaza vieja,
los niños cantaban . . .

I listen to the songs
with their ancient rhythms
which the children sing
when they play together
and pour out together
their souls which dream,
like fountains of stone
gushing with water:
with monotones
of eternal laughter
which are not happy,
with old tears
which are not bitter,
uttering sorrows,
sorrows of love
from ancient legends.

On the children's lips
the songs tell
of a confused story
and a clear pain;
like the clear water
bears tales
of old loves
that are never told.

Playing in the shade
of an old square
the children were singing . . .

La fuente de piedra
vertía su eterno
cristal de leyenda.

The fountain of stone
gushed forth its eternal
water of legend.

Cantaban los niños
canciones ingenuas,
de un algo que pasa
y que nunca llega:
la historia confusa
y clara la pena.

The children were singing
simple songs
of something that passes
and never arrives —
the story confused
and clear the pain.

Seguía su cuento
la fuente serena;
borrada la historia,
contaba la pena.

It continued its tale,
the serene fountain,
the story forgotten,
it told of the pain.

¿Recuerdas? / Do you recall?

¿Mi amor? . . . ¿Recuerdas, dime,
aquellos juncos tiernos,
lánguidos y amarillos
que hay en el cauce seco? . . .

Tell me, my love . . . Do you recall
those tender reeds,
languid and yellow
in the dry river-bed? . . .

¿Recuerdas la amapola
que calcinó el verano,
la amapola marchita,
negro crespón del campo? . . .

Do you recall the poppy
scorched by the summer,
the withered poppy,
black crepe of the field? . . .

¿Te acuerdas del sol yerto
y humilde, en la mañana,
que brilla y tiembla roto
sobre una fuente helada? . . .

Do you recall the motionless
and humble sun, in the morning,
which shines and trembles fragmented
on a frozen fountain? . . .

Fiesta en el prado / Fiesta in the field

Hay fiesta en el prado verde
– pífano y tambor – .
Con su cayado florido
y abarcas de oro vino un pastor.

There's a fiesta in the green field
– fife and drum – .
With his flower-decked crook
and golden sandals a shepherd came.

Del monte bajé,
sólo por bailar con ella;
al monte me tornaré.

Down from the mountain I came,
just to dance with her;
to the mountain I shall return.

En los árboles del huerto
hay un ruiseñor;
canta de noche y de día,
canta a la luna y al sol.
Ronco de cantar:
al huerto vendrá la niña
y una rosa cortará.

In the trees of the orchard
there is a nightingale,
it sings by night and by day,
it sings to the moon and the sun.
Hoarse with singing:
the girl will come to the orchard
and pluck a rose.

Entre las negras encinas,
hay una fuente de piedra,
y un cantarillo de barro
que nunca se llena.

Por el encinar,
con la blanca luna,
ella volverá.

Among the black oaks
there is a fountain of stone,
and an earthenware pitcher
which never fills.

Through the oak-grove,
by a white moon,
she will return.

Abril galán / Gallant April

Mientras danzáis en corro,
niñas, cantad:
Ya están los prados verdes,
ya vino abril galán.

A orilla del río
por el negro encinar,
sus abarcas de plata
hemos visto brillar.
Ya están los prados verdes,
ya vino abril galán.

While you dance in a circle,
girls, sing:
the fields are now green
and gallant April is come.

On the bank of the river,
by the black oak-grove,
its silver sandals
we have seen shine.
The fields are now green
and gallant April is come.

Canción del Duero / Song of the Duero

Molinero es mi amante,
tiene un molino
bajo los pinos verdes,
cerca del río.
Niñas, cantad:
'Por la orilla del Duero
yo quisiera pasar'.

Por las tierras de Soria
va mi pastor.
¡Si yo fuera una encina
sobre un alcor!
Para la siesta,
si yo fuera una encina
sombra le diera.

En las sierras de Soria,
azul y nieve,
leñador es mi amante
de pinos verdes.
¡Quién fuera el águila
para ver a mi dueño
cortando ramas!

¡Ay, garabí! . . .
Bailad, suene la flauta
y el tamboril.

My lover is a miller,
he has a mill
below the green pines,
near the river.
Girls, sing:
'By the banks of the Duero
I would fain pass'.

By the lands of Soria
my shepherd goes.
Were I but an oak
on a hill!
For his siesta,
if I were an oak,
I'd give him shade.

In the mountains of Soria,
blue and snowy,
my lover's a woodcutter
of green pines.
Oh to be an eagle
to see my master
cutting branches!

Olé, Olé! . . .
Dance! Play the flute
and sound the drum.

Dos canciones para cantar a los niños / Two songs to sing to children

ANON., ADAPTED BY VICTORIA KAMHI

(1973)

Corderito blanco / Little white lamb

Corderito blanco,
Que durmiendo estás,
Déjate, ben mío,
Déjate arrullar.
Si te duermes, amor mío,
Yo te quiero despertar,
Pues vinieron de Oriente
los tres Reyes a adorar.
No te duermas, mi vida;
No te duermas, mi cielo;
a-rro-rró, a-rro-rró
a-rro-rró, que te arrullo yo.

Little white lamb,
fast asleep,
let me, my love,
let me sing you to sleep.
If you are sleeping, my love,
I shall awake you,
for from the Orient have come
the three Kings to worship.
Do not sleep, my darling;
do not sleep, my sweet;
hush-a-bye, hush-a-bye,
hush-a-bye, I'll sing you asleep.

Quedito /Softly, gently

Quedito, pasito,
Silencio, chitón,
Duerme un infante,
Que tierno y constante,
Al más tibio amante
Despierta al calor.
Quedito, pasito,
Silencio, chitón,
No le despierten, no;
A la e, a la o,
A la e, a la o,
No le despierten, no.

Softly, gently,
silence, hush,
an infant is sleeping,
who tender and steadfast
kindles warmth
in the coolest lover.
Softly, gently,
silence, hush,
let them not wake him;
hush-a-bye,
hush-a-bye,
let them not wake him.

XIX

XAVIER MONTSALVATGE
(*b*.1912)

Montsalvatge represents a new direction in Spanish music – hardly avant-garde, he nevertheless acknowledged the need to look outside Spain to find a means of bringing new blood to the overworked concept of folksong and nationalism. His elegant compromise was to look to the colonial Spanish world of the Caribbean which had developed its own lively music; Montsalvatge proceeded to import this style back to the land of its very distant genesis. This West Indian manner found, in the composer's words, 'a place at the periphery of our traditions as a new, vague and evocative manifestation of musical lyricism'. The most important work for singers and accompanists in this style is the *Canciones negras* (Southern Music), the popularity of which knows no bounds on the concert platform of today. The set seems all of a piece from the poetic point of view, but it is in fact a cleverly chosen anthology, beginning with a distinguished poem by Rafael Alberti which bemoans the all-pervasive influence of the United States on the dying cultures of Central America. In a very subtle way the work addresses various issues of colonialism and racialism – a roundabout but clear message from a Catalan humanitarian living in Franco's Spain.

Xavier Montsalvatge was born on 11 March 1912, and studied in Barcelona. Too late to study with Pedrell, his first works nevertheless won the Pedrell Prize. He soon found his métier as a composer of ballets, something he shared with Stravinsky, whose music was an abiding inspiration to Montsalvatge, as were the French composers of Les Six. His West Indian style was the result of his feeling that there was a distinct affinity between that music and the music of Catalonia – he remarked on the similarity in emotional resonance of the sardana and the habanera. Another feature of his style was his sympathy for children's music and poetry. This, combined with his love of Lorca's work, resulted in the *Canciones para niños* (UMV 20507). Montsalvatge has always adopted an undogmatic and eclectic approach to style, sometimes bordering on experiment with atonality, but mostly preferring to challenge stale conventionality with oblique and ingenious musical solutions.

Cinco canciones negras / *Five Negro songs*
(1945)

1. *Cuba dentro de un piano* / *Cuba in a piano*
RAFAEL ALBERTI

Cuando mi madre llevaba un sorbete de fresa por sombrero
y el humo de los barcos aún era humo de habanero.

  Mulata vueltabajera . . .
Cádiz se adormecía entre fandangos y habaneras
y un lorito al piano quería hacer de tenor.
  . . . *dime dónde está la flor*
que el hombre tanto venera.
  Mi tío Antonio volvía con aire de insurrecto.
La Cabaña y el Príncipe sonaban por los patios de El Puerto.
(Ya no brilla la Perla azul del mar de las Antillas.
Ya se apagó, se nos ha muerto.)
  Me encontré con la bella Trinidad . . .
Cuba se había perdido y ahora era de verdad.
Era verdad,
no era mentira.
Un cañonero huído llegó cantándolo en guajira.
  La Habana ya se perdió.
Tuvo la culpa el dinero . . .
  Calló,
cayó el cañonero.
  Pero después, pero ¡ah! después
fué cuando al SÍ
lo hicieron YES.

When my mother wore a strawberry ice for a hat
and the smoke from the boats was still Havana smoke.

  Mulata from Vuelta Abajo . . .
Cadiz was falling asleep to fandango and habanera
and a little parrot at the piano tried to sing tenor.
  . . . *tell me, where is the flower*
that a man can really respect.
  My uncle Anthony would come home in his rebellious way.
The Cabaña and El Príncipe resounded in the patios of the port.
(But the blue pearl of the Caribbean shines no more.
Extinguished. For us no more.)
  I met beautiful Trinidad . . .
Cuba was lost, this time it was true.
True
and not a lie.
A gunner on the run arrived, sang Cuban songs about it all.
  Havana was lost
and money was to blame . . .
  The gunner went silent,
fell.
  But later, ah, later
they changed SÍ
to YES.

2. *Punto de Habanera*[1] / *Habanera rhythm*
NÉSTOR LUJÁN

La niña criolla pasa con su miriñaque blanco
¡Qué blanco!

The Creole girl goes by in her white crinoline.
How white!

Hola crespón de tu espuma;	The billowing spray of your crepe skirt!
¡marineros contempladla!	Sailors, look at her!
Va mojadita de lunas	She passes gleaming in the moonlight
que le hacen su piel mulata.	which darkens her skin.
Niña, no te quejes,	Young girl, do not complain,
tan solo por esta tarde.	only for tonight
Quisiera mandar al agua	do I wish the water
que no se escape de pronto	not to suddenly escape
de la cárcel de tu falda,	the prison of your skirt.
tu cuerpo encierra esta tarde	In your body this evening
rumor de abrirse de dalia.	dwells the sound of opening dahlias.
Niña, no te quejes,	Young girl, do not complain,
tu cuerpo de fruta está	your ripe body
dormido en fresco brocado.	sleeps in fresh brocade,
Tu cintura vibra fina	your waist quivers
con la nobleza de un látigo,	as proud as a whip,
toda tu piel huele	every inch of your skin is gloriously
alegre	fragrant
a limonal y a naranjo.	with orange- and lemon trees.
Los marineros te miran	The sailors look at you
y se te quedan mirando.	and feast their eyes on you.
La niña criolla pasa	The Creole girl goes by
con su miriñaque blanco.	in her white crinoline.
¡Qué blanco!	How white!

¹*Habanera*. A dance and song, introduced into Spain from Africa via Cuba, after whose capital city, Havana, it is named. It is in moderate 2/4 time, and the dancers face each other, accompanying the singing with gestures.

3. *Chévere* / *The dandy*

NICOLÁS GUILLÉN

Chévere del navajazo,	The dandy of the knife thrust
se vuelve él mismo navaja:	himself becomes a knife:
pica tajadas de luna,	he cuts slices of the moon,
mas la luna se le acaba;	but the moon is fading on him;
pica tajadas de canto,	he cuts slices of song,
mas el canto se le acaba;	but the song is fading on him;
pica tajadas de sombra,	he cuts slices of shadow,
mas la sombra se le acaba,	but the shadow is fading on him,
y entonces pica que pica	and then he cuts up, cuts up
carne de su negra mala.	the flesh of his evil black woman!

4. *Canción de cuna para dormir a un negrito* / *Lullaby for a little black boy*

ILDEFONSO PEREDA VALDÉS

Ninghe, ninghe, ninghe,	Lullay, lullay, lullay,
tan chiquito,	tiny little child,
el negrito	little black boy
que no quiere dormir.	who won't go to sleep.

Cabeza de coco,
grano de café,
con lindas motitas,
con ojos grandotes
como dos ventanas
que miran al mar.

Head like a coconut,
head like a coffee bean,
with pretty freckles
and wide eyes
like two windows
looking out to sea.

Cierra esos ojitos,
negrito asustado;
el mandinga blanco
te puede comer.
¡Ya no eres esclavo!

Close your tiny eyes,
frightened little boy,
or the white devil
will eat you up.
You're no longer a slave!

Y si duermes mucho,
el señor de casa
promete comprar
traje con botones
para ser un 'groom'.

And if you sleep soundly,
the master of the house
promises to buy
a suit with buttons
to make you a 'groom'.

Ninghe, ninghe, ninghe,
duérmete, negrito,
cabeza de coco,
grano de café.

Lullay, lullay, lullay,
sleep, little black boy,
head like a coconut,
head like a coffee bean.

5 · *Canto negro* / *Negro song*

NICOLÁS GUILLÉN

¡Yambambó, yambambé!
Repica el congo solongo,
repica el negro bien
    negro;
congo solongo del Songo
baila yambó sobre un pie.

Yambambó, yambambé!
The congo solongo is ringing,
the black man, the real black man is
    ringing;
congo solongo from the Songo
is dancing the yambó on one foot.

Mamatomba,
serembe cuserembá.

Mamatomba,
serembe cuserembá.

El negro canta y se ajuma,
el negro se ajuma y canta,
el negro canta y se va.

The black man sings and gets drunk,
the black man gets drunk and sings,
the black man sings and goes away.

Acuememe serembó,
        aé;
      yambó,
        aé.

Acuememe serembó
        aé;
      yambó,
        aé.

Tamba, tamba, tamba, tamba,
tamba del negro que tumba;
tumba del negro, caramba,
caramba, que el negro tumba:
¡Yamba, yambó, yambambé!

Bam, bam, bam, bam,
bam of the black man who tumbles;
drum of the black man, wow,
wow, how the black man's tumbling!
Yamba, yambó, yambambé!

Canciones para niños / Songs for children

FEDERICO GARCÍA LORCA

(1953)

Paisaje / Landscape

La tarde equivocada
se vistió de frío.

Detrás de los cristales,
turbios, todos los niños,
ven convertirse en pájaros
un árbol amarillo.

La tarde está tendida
a lo largo del río.
Y un rubor de manzana
tiembla en los tejadillos.

The mistaken afternoon
got dressed in cold.

Behind the windows,
misted up, all the children
see a yellow tree
turn into birds.

The afternoon is stretched
along the river.
And a red flush of apple
trembles on the rooftops.

El lagarto está llorando / Mr Lizard is crying

El lagarto está llorando.
La lagarta está llorando.

El lagarto y la lagarta
con delantalitos blancos.

Han perdido sin querer
su anillo de desposados.

¡Ay, su anillito de plomo,
ay, su anillito plomado!

Un cielo grande y sin gente
monta en su globo a los pájaros.

El sol, capitán redondo,
lleva un chaleco de raso.

¡Miradlos qué viejos son!
¡Que viejos son los lagartos!

¡Ay cómo lloran y lloran,
¡ay!, ¡ay!, cómo están llorando!

Mr Lizard is crying.
Mrs Lizard is crying.

Mr and Mrs Lizard
with little white aprons.

They have lost by mistake
their wedding ring.

Oh dear, their ring of lead,
oh dear, their little leaden ring!

A large, unpopulated sky
takes the birds up in its balloon.

The sun, that round captain,
wears a jacket of satin.

See how old they are!
How old the lizards are!

Oh dear, how they cry and cry,
oh dear, oh dear, how they are crying!

Caracola / *Conch*

Me han traído una caracola.

Dentro le canta
un mar de mapa.
Mi corazón
se llena de agua
con pececillos
de sombra y plata.

Me han traído una caracola.

They've brought me a conch.

Inside it sings
an ocean atlas.
My heart
fills with water
and little fish
of shade and silver.

They've brought me a conch.

Canción tonta / *Silly song*

Mamá.
Yo quiero ser de plata.

Hijo,
tendrás mucho frío.

Mamá.
Yo quiero ser de agua.

Hijo,
tendrás mucho frío.

Mamá.
Bórdame en tu almohada.

¡Eso sí!
¡Ahora mismo!

Mummy,
I want to be made of silver.

Son,
you'll be very cold.

Mummy,
I want to be made of water.

Son,
you'll be very cold.

Mummy,
embroider me in your pillow.

Of course!
Right away!

Canción China en Europa / *Chinese song in Europe*

La señorita
del abanico,
va por el puente
del fresco río.

Los caballeros
con sus levitas,
miran el puente
sin barandillas.

La señorita
del abanico
y los volantes,
busca marido.

The señorita
with the fan
is crossing the bridge
of the cool stream.

The caballeros
with their coats
are watching the bridge
with no rails.

The señorita
with the fan
and flounces
is seeking a husband.

Los caballeros	The caballeros
están casados,	are married
con altas rubias	to tall blondes
de idioma blanco.	who speak Whitemen's language.
Los grillos cantan	The crickets are singing
por el Oeste.	in the West.
(La señorita,	(The señorita
va por lo verde.)	walks through the grass.)
Los grillos cantan	The crickets are singing
bajo las flores.	beneath the flowers.
(Los caballeros,	(The caballeros
van por el Norte.)	are off to the North.)

Cancioncilla sevillana / Sevillian ditty

Amanecía	Day was breaking
en el naranjel.	in the orange-grove.
Abejitas de oro	Little golden bees
buscaban la miel.	were searching for honey.
¿Dónde estará	Where will
la miel?	the honey be?
Está en la flor azul,	In the blue flower,
Isabel.	Isabel.
En la flor,	In that rosemary
del romero aquel.	flower.
(Sillita de oro	(Little seat of gold
para el moro.	for the Moor.
Silla de oropel	A seat of tinsel
para su mujer.)	for his wife.)
Amanecía	Day was dawning
en el naranjel.	in the orange-grove.

AFTERWORD

SPANISH SONG OF THE FUTURE

This anthology has probably left out more Spanish composers and songs than it has been able to include. For these omissions we plead reasons of length in a book already longer than it was originally envisaged; for example, the justified charge that we have shied away from Basque poetry is answered with this excuse – we had no choice but to put all our Basques in one exit. Another of the areas not covered in our book has been the music of composers like Conrado del Campo and the Halffter family (Ernesto and Cristóbal) who have looked to Germany, rather than France, for their musical inspiration. Two of my personal regrets include the songs of my distinguished accompanist colleague Felix Lavilla, and the recent song cycle written for Montserrat Caballé by Lorenzo Martinez Palomo. Many of our readers will no doubt be disappointed by not finding all that they need in these pages, but in return we hope they will have made new friends – it is only the most knowledgeable native expert who will already know of *all* the music and poetry covered by *The Spanish Song Companion*. Such a paragon from Aragon should write his own book to the benefit of us all.

The real enthusiast may be interested in exploring works by living Spanish composers, and I am grateful to my colleague Alan Branch, who lives and works as an accompanist in Barcelona, for compiling a list of songs which appear in recitals there, but which have yet, on the whole, to find their way to concert platforms outside Spain:

Javier ALONSO (*b*.1905)   *Cinco canciones castellanas* (1957)

Miguel Asins ARBO (*b*.1916)   *6 Canciones españolas* (Machado) (1950)

Leonardo BALADA (*b*.1933)
      4 Canciones de la provincia de Madrid (1962)
      3 Cervantinas (1967)
      3 Epitafios de Quevedo (1971)

Salvador BACARISSE (*b*.1898)   *3 Canciones españolas* (1950)

Carmelo BERNAOLA (*b*.1929)   *Tríptico de canciones* (Jiménez) (1956)

Manuel BLANCAFORT (1897–1987)   *4 melodias* (1948)

Narciso BONET (*b*.1933)   *Vista al mar* (Maragall) (1948)

Juan CAMELLAS (*b*.1913)   Two series of *Lirica Catalana* (1948–51)
    Canciones de Antonio Machado (1950)
    6 Tonadas de ultramar (1953)

Manuel CASTILO (*b*.1930)   *2 Canciones de Navidad* (1954)
    3 Canciones de Juan Ramón Jiménez (1954)
    5 Poemas de Manuel Machado (1974)

Cristóbal HALFFTER (*b*.1930)
    2 Canciones sobre poemas de Vicente (1952)
    4 Canciones populares leonesas (1957)

Joaquín HOMS ALLER (*b*.1906)   *Poemas de Josep Carner* (1934)
    Cementiri de Sirena (Espriu) (1952)

Josep M. M. QUADRENY (*b*.1929)   *Cançons de bressol* (1959)

Manuel VALLS (1920–84)   *Canciones del Alto Duero* (Machado) (1950)
    Canciones sefarditas (1965)

A number of songs on this list attempt to break away from what is regarded as the typical Spanish style, and this is perhaps just as well: the endless parade of names in the music catalogues of established publishers – all offering this or that collection based on endless permutations and arrangements of folksongs, provokes an uncomfortable feeling. Do Spanish composers think we might not be interested in their music unless it *sounds* Spanish, and worse still, would they be right? Who are the other names, younger ones, who do not care about the armchair travel shop of Spanish music and who represent the real future of Spanish song – a future based on the premise that Spanish composers, inheritors of a fantastically vital and varied literary tradition, now have the right to find a musical world beyond folksong, a sound world moreover that has as much right to challenge our ears as that of the pupils of Messiaen or Elliott Carter? What has 'Greensleeves' got to do with the music of England's George Benjamin after all? The Russians have made the step beyond nationalism, and now it is the turn of the Spaniards. Who the heroes of the new Spanish music will be is still unwritten.

The Spanish Song Companion ends with Xavier Montsalvatge, a composer born in 1912. This is hardly a disgrace considering that a companion to British song with piano (considered by some to be an impossibly outmoded accompanying instrument) would probably end with Benjamin Britten (*b*.1913), *pace* a handful of distinguished younger composers who seem still to care about the medium in a conventional way. But just as Jane Manning, in the recently published *New Vocal Repertory*, has revealed a whole new range of British music with new premises and technical challenges, the same must be beginning to exist in Spain, particularly in the years since it has found once again the vitality that goes hand in hand with political freedom.

That old, enchanting Spanish garden remains as confusingly overgrown as ever. Who will be responsible for the weeding and replanting that enables new talents to grow in flower beds choked with the faded blooms of the past? The history of Spain is written in this garden – the scorched earth still tells of poverty, prejudice, suppression, wars and the terrible injustice that blighted some of the most artistically fruitful and eventful years of our century – fruitful, that is, elsewhere. But the ever resilient world of song still knocks on the door and asks a hopeful question – in the new order will there still be room for a voice without a microphone and a non-electronic keyboard? In love with its future the new Spain will perhaps be gallant enough to compromise with the best from the past and answer in the affirmative. And unlike Montsalvatge's song, this will still somehow be with a real Spanish *Sí*, rather than a Yankee *Yes*.

APPENDIX

I. *Four translations by Emanuel Geibel*

Geistliches Wiegenlied / Sacred lullaby

LOPE DE VEGA, *see* p. 170

Set by Johannes Brahms, Op. 91 No. 2 (1882)
and by Hugo Wolf, in the *Spanisches Liederbuch* (1889)

Die ihr schwebet	You who hover
Um diese Palmen	about these palms,
In Nacht und Wind,	in night and wind,
Ihr heilgen Engel,	Holy Angels,
Stillet die Wipfel!	silence their leaves!
Es schlummert mein Kind.	My child's asleep.
Ihr Palmen von Bethlehem	Palms of Bethlehem
Im Windesbrausen,	in blustering wind,
Wie mögt ihr heute	how can you today
So zornig sausen!	so angrily blow!
O rauscht nicht also!	Oh, roar not so.
Schweiget, neiget	Be still, bow
Euch leis und lind;	softly and gently;
Stillet die Wipfel!	silence the leaves!
Es schlummert mein Kind.	My child's asleep.
Der Himmelsknabe	The Son of Heaven
Duldet Beschwerde,	is suffering;
Ach, wie so müd er ward	ah, so tired has He grown
Vom Leid der Erde.	of earth's sorrows.
Ach nun im Schlaf ihm	Ah, now, in sleep,
Leise gesänftigt	gently softened,
Die Qual zerrinnt,	the pain melts away.
Stillet die Wipfel!	Silence the leaves!
Es schlummert mein Kind.	My child's asleep.
Grimmige Kälte	Fierce cold
Sauset hernieder,	comes rushing;
Womit nur deck ich	with what shall I cover
Des Kindleins Glieder!	the little child's limbs!
O all ihr Engel,	O All you Angels
Die ihr geflügelt	who, winged,
Wandelt im Wind,	travel on the wind,
Stillet die Wipfel!	silence the leaves!
Es schlummert mein Kind.	My child is asleep.

Ach im Maien wars, im Maien / Ah, in May it was, in May

See p. 216

Set by Hugo Wolf, in the *Spanisches Liederbuch* (1889)

Ach im Maien wars, im Maien,
Wo die warmen Lüfte wehen,
Wo verliebte Leute pflegen
Ihren Liebchen nachzugehen.

Ah, in May it was, in May,
when warm breezes blow,
when those in love are wont
to seek their loves.

Ich allein, ich armer Trauriger,
Lieg im Kerker so verschmachtet,
Und ich seh nicht, wann es taget,
Und ich weiß nicht, wann es nachtet.

I alone, poor, sad man,
lie so enfeebled in prison,
and I see not when it dawns,
and I know not when night falls.

Nur an einem Vöglein merkt ich's,
Das da drauß im Maien sang;
Das hat mir ein Schütz getötet –
Geb ihm Gott den schlimmsten Dank!

I could tell only by a bird
that sang out there in May;
that bird a hunter has shot –
God give him small thanks!

Der Contrabandiste / The smuggler

See p. 194

Set by Robert Schumann, Op. 74 No. 10 (1849)

Ich bin der Contrabandiste,
Weiß wohl Respekt mir zu schaffen.
Allen zu trotzen, ich weiß es,
Furcht nur, die hab' ich vor keinem.
Drum nur lustig, nur lustig!

I am the smuggler,
I know how to command respect,
and how to defy the world.
There's no one I fear.
So let's be merry!

Wer kauft Seide, Tabak!
Ja wahrlich, mein Rößlein ist müde,
Ich eil', ja eile,
Sonst faßt mich noch gar die Runde,
Los geht der Spektakel dann.
Lauf nur zu, mein lustiges Pferdchen,
Ach, mein liebes, gutes Pferdchen,
Weißt ja davon, mich zu tragen!

Who'll buy my silk, tobacco!
My little horse is tired, it's true.
I'll hurry on, hurry on,
else the patrol will catch me –
and then there'll be trouble.
Hurry on, my sprightly horse,
ah, my dear, good little horse,
you know how to carry me!

Blaue Augen hat das Mädchen / The girl has blue eyes

JUAN DEL ENCINA, see p. 33

Set by Robert Schumann, Op. 138 No. 9 (1849)

Blaue Augen hat das Mädchen,
Wer verliebte sich nicht drein?

The girl has blue eyes,
who would not fall in love with them?

Sind so reizend zum Entzücken,
Daß sie jedes Herz bestricken,
Wissen doch so stolz zu blicken,
Daß sie eitel schaffen Pein.

They charm so much that they delight
and captivate each heart,
for they can gaze with such pride
that they wantonly cause pain.

Machen Ruh und Wohlbefinden,
Sinnen und Erinnrung schwinden,
Wissen stets zu überwinden
Mit dem spielend süßen Schein.

They cause peace and happiness,
thoughts and memories to disappear,
and always know how to triumph
with their sweet and playful glow.

Keiner, der geschaut ihr Prangen,
Ist noch ihrem Netz entgangen,
Alle Welt begehrt zu hangen
Tag und Nacht an ihrem Schein.

None who has known their splendour
has ever escaped their thrall,
everyone desires to hang
night and day upon their glow.

Blaue Augen hat das Mädchen,
Wer verliebte sich nicht drein?

The girl has blue eyes,
who would not fall in love with them?

II. *Lines from the original Catullus poem (5) and Castillejo's translation, on which Obradors based his song 'Al Amor'*

See p. 189

> da mi basia mille, deinde centum;
> dein mille altera, dein secunda centum;
> deinde usque altera mille, deinde centum.
> dein, cum milia multa fecerimus –
> conturbabimus illa, ne sciamus,
> aut ne quis malus inuidere possit,
> cum tantum sciat esse basiorum.

UNA SOLA Y ES SACADA LA MAYOR PARTE DE CATULO

> Dadme, amor, besos sin cuento
> Asida de mis cabellos,
> Un millar y ciento dellos
> Y otros mill y luego ciento;
> Y mill y ciento tras ellos,
> Y después
> De muchos millares tres,
> Porque ninguno lo sienta,
> Desbaratemos la cuenta
> Y contemos al revés.

III. *La Manola*

The poem by Manuel Bretón de los Herreros which inspired Gautier's 'Séguidille', *see* p. 111

Ancha franja de velludo
En la terciada mantilla;
Aire recio, gesto crudo;
Soberana pantorrilla;
Alma atroz; sal española . . .
　　¡Alza, hola!
Vale un mundo mi Manola.

Cuando ella se pone en jarras,
¡Soleá! ¡Me río yo! . . .
Dígalo el terne de marras
Que al hospital le envió
Sin valerle la pistola.
　　¡Alza, hola!
Vale un mundo mi Manola.

De basilisco es su vista,
Cada mirada es un rayo;
No hay alma que la resista,
Y si mira de soslayo
Y pavonea la cola, . . .
　　¡Alza, hola!
Vale un mundo mi Manola.

Si algún galán abejorro
Babeando tras de ella va,
Se revuelve, tuerce el morro,
Y le responde: ¡Arre allá!,
Que no gusto de parola.
　　¡Alza, hola!
Vale un mundo mi Manola.

¡Qué caliá, y cómo cruje
Si baila jota ó fandango!
¡Y qué brio en cada empuje!
¡Y qué gloria de remango
A la más leve cabriola!
　　¡Alza, hola!
Vale un mundo mi Manola.

Con primor se calza el pié
Digno de regio tapiz:
¡Y qué dulce *no sé qué*
En aquella cicatriz
Que tiene junto á la gola!
　　¡Alza, hola!
Vale un mundo mi Manola.

Sobre el suelo, en una esquina
Ella en rábonos entiende,
Y en naranjas de la China.
Todo es fresco lo que vende . . .
Quedando aparte ella sola.
　　¡Alza, hola!
Vale un mundo mi Manola.

Roto iba yo por la calle,
Y hecho un miserable trasto,
Cuando me prendó su talle;
Y hoy faja de seda gasto,
Y luzco la guirindola.
　　¡Alza, hola!
Vale un mundo mi Manola.

Por ella en holganza eterna
Vivo como un arcediano;
Triunfo y gasto en la taberna;
Me pongo calamocano,
Y me tiendo á la bartola.
　　¡Alza, hola!
Vale un mundo mi Manola.

Como para mí trabaja,
Muchas veces se amohina,
Mas no saco la navaja,
Aunque me trate la endina
Peor que á un bozal de Angola.
　　¡Alza, hola!
Vale un mundo mi Manola.

Siempre lleva al derredor
De amantes una cohorte;
Mas toda es gente de honor . . . ,
¡Pues! Y yo, á estilo de córte,
Dejo que ruede la bola.
　　¡Alza, hola!
Vale un mundo mi Manola.

IV. *I saw thee weep*

The Byron poem which inspired Bécquer's 'Tu pupila es azul', *see* p. 136.

> I saw thee weep – the big bright tear
>   Came o'er that eye of blue;
> And then methought it did appear
>   A violet dropping dew:
> I saw thee smile – the sapphire's blaze
>   Beside thee ceased to shine;
> It could not match the living rays
>   That fill'd that glance of thine.
>
> As clouds from yonder sun receive
>   A deep and mellow dye,
> Which scarce the shade of coming eve
>   Can banish from the sky,
> Those smiles unto the moodiest mind
>   Their own pure joy impart;
> Their sunshine leaves a glow behind
>   That lightens o'er the heart.

NOTES ON THE POETS

RAFAEL ALBERTI (*b*.1902)

Poet and playwright, who originally wished to be a painter. He achieved fame in 1925 with *Marinero en tierra*, a volume of verse written in ill health, which recalled the boats on Cádiz bay and looked back nostalgically to his youth. The poems are full of delightful imagery and nonsense rhymes. The tone of his poetry is extremely varied: after his early Gongoresque manner, he went through a surrealistic phase and subsequently wrote verse of a frank realism, inspired by the Civil War, during which he aligned himself with the Communists. At its conclusion he went into exile in Argentina and returned to Spain in 1977.

ALFONSO X, KING OF CASTILE (1221–84)

Known as 'El Sabio' he was, politically speaking, anything but a successful monarch, and his reign was marked by strife and war. His failures as a statesman, however, were offset by his astonishing cultural achievements. He surrounded himself with musicians, poets, craftsmen and the best minds he could find among Christian, Moorish and Jewish scholars (he liked to call himself 'King of the Three Religions'). His native tongue was Castilian, and he not only systematised its spelling but laid the foundations of Spanish prose in his writings on history, law and science. As a poet he preferred the softer and more musical Galician-Portuguese dialect. There are some four hundred *Cantigas de Santa María* and though they all bear Alfonso's name, it is unlikely that he was author of them all. Their subject-matter deals almost exclusively with the miracles of the Virgin Mary, which range from the heavenly to the downright racy. Indeed, apart from their musical and literary value, the *Cantigas* provide us with a colourful tapestry of the Middle Ages, as kings, knights, nuns, sailors, pilgrims, merchants, peasants and vagabonds pass before us. The best verse is frequently found, not in the narrative part of the miracles, but in the 'Loores' that praise the Queen of Heaven.

SERAFÍN (1871–1938) and JOAQUÍN (1873–1944) ÁLVAREZ QUINTERO

Brothers born in Seville, who collaborated in almost two hundred plays. Their comedies and zarzuelas reflect the humour and colloquial speech of Andalusia; although the plays tend to lack dramatic intensity, they entertain in a delightful way.

CLEMENTINA ARDERIU (1889–1976)

Catalan poetess who was born and died in Barcelona. Although she came from a family of silversmiths, she soon turned to the study of music and the piano. When in 1916 she married Carles Riba, a gifted poet and the foremost literary critic of his generation, she turned from music to the world of letters. In the same year she published her *Cançons i elegies*. Other volumes include *L'alta llibertat* (1920) and *Cant i paraules* (1936). She fled her country in 1939 and finally returned in 1943.

GUSTAVO ADOLFO BÉCQUER (1836–70)

Orphaned at ten, he was brought up by his godmother and given a good education in Seville. Determined to achieve fame as a poet, he set out for Madrid in 1854 and eked out an existence in journalism, translation work and the churning out of zarzuela libretti long since forgotten. Burdened with poverty and ill health, he was compelled to accept a minor government post, as censor of novels. In 1858 he fell in love with Julia Espín, the muse of several *Rimas* – unrequitedly, as the texts of the Albéniz, Falla, Turina and Mompou songs illustrate. He married Casta Esteban Navarro in 1861, daughter of the doctor who had treated him during one of his crises, and by whom he had three children. He was later separated from her and died of consumption at the age of thirty-four. His poems have been described as 'suspiritos germánicos' ('little sighs in the German manner') – a reference to Heine's *Buch der Lieder* poems which Bécquer knew partially through Gérard de Nerval's translation of *Lyrisches Intermezzo*. The description, however, is not entirely apt, since his poems lack Heine's acidity.

MANUEL BLANCAFORT (1897–1987)

Catalan composer and author of occasional poems. Won great success with his opera *Parc d'atraccions* (*Amusement Park*). His output includes symphonic works, two string quartets and a number of art songs.

MANUEL BRETÓN DE LOS HERREROS (1796–1873)

Although he wrote poetry, adapted Golden Age plays for the contemporary stage and translated extensively from French and German, it is as a satirical dramatist that he is now remembered. He wrote over two hundred plays, mostly in verse, and his gentle satire was directed at the foibles of the middle-class Madrid society that he knew so well.

RAMÓN CABANILLAS (1873–1959)

Poet and playwright who wrote in Galician. He was born in Cambados (province of Pontevedra) and many of his poems evoke the Galician countryside. In addition to his sea poetry (*Vento mareiro*) and love lyrics (*A*

rose de cen follas), he published an important collection of oral poetry in
Antifona da cantiga.

RAMÓN DE CAMPOAMOR (1817–1901)

Poet and epigrammatist, he turned to literature having abandoned plans for a
career in the Church and dabbled in medical studies. After two unremarkable
early collections, he became famous with the publication in 1845 of *Doloras* –
concise poems, mostly short, often dramatising a universal truth with a faintly
ironic close, as in 'Los dos miedos' and 'Las locas por amor', set by Turina. His
reaction against the bombastic rhetoric of the Romantics influenced Bécquer.
His longer philosophical poems are less successful. A very rich man, he held a
number of Government posts, including the governorships of Alicante and
Valencia.

JOSEP CARNER (1884–1971)

Joined the diplomatic corps in 1920, left Spain and lived abroad for the rest of
his life. When the Spanish republic folded in 1939, he lost his consular position
and lived as an exile first in Mexico and then in Belgium, where he died. Some
of his best poems describe with gentle irony bourgeois figures from the Catalan
world.

CRISTÓBAL DE CASTRO (1880–1953)

Novelist, playwright and poet, born in the province of Cordoba. He studied
law in Granada and medicine in Madrid, before turning to literature. He is also
well known as a journalist (he has been editor of such journals as *La Epoca* and
El Liberal) and as a translator of Molière, Goldoni, Ibsen, Tolstoy, Wilde and
Pirandello.

TRINITAT CATASÚS (1887–1940)

Catalan poet born in Sitges; with Miquel Utrillo he founded *La Cantonada*
and also contributed to other journals such as *Joventut* and *El Poble Català*.
He published several volumes of poetry, including *De l'hort i de la costa*
(1915), *Poemes del temps* (1919) and *Robins de magrana* (1930), which are
characterised by a certain religiosity and a delight in landscape.

MIGUEL DE CERVANTES (1547–1616)

Born in Alcalá de Henares, the son of a poor surgeon and his wife, he served as
a soldier in Italy from 1570 to 1575, and was wounded in the battle of Lepanto
in 1571. Captured by pirates in 1575, he was sold into slavery in Algiers,
attempted to escape and was finally ransomed in 1580. He then held several
minor government positions in Spain, one of which required him to requisition
for the Armada. He was imprisoned twice for bookkeeping irregularities and
debts, and having separated from his wife, he moved with the court to Madrid

in 1606, where he eventually died in 1616. His famous novel *Don Quijote*, from which the Obradors song 'Consejo' is taken, was published in 1605 and brought him immediate fame. Less well-known, but equally fine, are his *Novelas ejemplares* (1613), a collection of twelve short stories, similar in style to the Italian novella, but with an 'exemplary' or ethical purpose – Amadeo Vives composed songs from two of these: *El celoso extremeño* and *La gitanilla*.

José de Espronceda (1808–42)

A Byronic figure in his life and poetry, he fought for the liberal cause in Holland (1828), on the Paris barricades (1830) and in Spain against Spanish Absolutism. He returned to Spain in 1833, but his radical journalism proved too much for the regime, and again he was exiled. He wrote an historical novel influenced by Scott, a splendid verse legend on the Don Juan theme (*El estudiante de Salamanca*) and some fine journalistic pieces, but he is mostly remembered for his patriotic poems calling for freedom and his poetry of social criticism.

Tomàs Garcés (b.1901)

Born in Barcelona, he studied law and philosophy at the University there, before making a career as poet, journalist and translator. *Vint cançons* was published in 1922 and was followed two years later by *L'ombra del lledoner*, from which the Toldrà songs are taken. Both collections betray the influence of Juan Ramón Jiménez. During the Civil War he lived in France, where he was greatly influenced by Verlaine's concern for musicality and form. Apart from his musical nature poetry, he is well known for his translation of Mistral.

Garcilaso de la Vega (1501–36)

He came from a noble Toledan family and introduced into Spanish literature the forms and themes of the Italian Renaissance. At the age of seventeen he joined the court of Emperor Charles V, and volunteered to fight the Turks when they besieged Vienna in 1529. He fell from favour, however, and was imprisoned on an island in the Danube. When given the choice of entering a monastery or serving Charles in Naples, he chose the latter. On a French campaign near Cannes, Garcilaso led an assault up a fortress wall and was severely wounded when French gunners dropped a rock on him – he was taken to Nice and died there eighteen days later. In his poetry he depicted a charming, artificial and stylised world.

Théophile Gautier (1811–72)

Poet, novelist and journalist, who lived in Paris. He first studied painting, with a taste for vampirism and Hoffmannesque horrors. When he began to write, he became a successful journalist, and for over forty years wrote weekly articles on literature and art. One of his most entertaining journalistic works was his

Voyage en Espagne, which includes a withering demolition of the Escorial. He is perhaps best known for his concept of 'l'art pour l'art' – the love of visual, palpable beauty, that could only be attained by the worship of form, with no interference from moral, political or social considerations. The three poems set by Falla are fine examples of this ideal.

LUIS DE GÓNGORA (1561–1627)

Perhaps the greatest poet of the late Golden Age, he was born and died in Córdoba. He came from a cultured family and was educated at the University of Salamanca, where he excelled not only in poetic activity but in wenching, gambling and duelling. In 1606 he acquired an honorary chaplaincy at the court of Philip III, and in 1617 became a priest. He was criticised by Lope de Vega and Francisco de Quevedo for his tortuous syntax and esoteric allusions. Although Gongorismo became synonymous with affected rhetoric and unnecessary embellishments, there is a brilliance about the stylised world of the *Soledades* that was of immense importance in the development of Spanish poetry.

NICOLÁS GUILLÉN (*b*.1902)

Himself a mulatto, Nicolas Guillén is the most important poet of the Afro-Cuban school, and his early poems are often written in the language and rhythm of Cuba's poor blacks. He was influenced by Lorca who visited Cuba on his way home from New York. Guillén has been a life-long revolutionary activist in Cuba and was jailed in 1936 for the publication of 'subversive material'. Exiled in 1953 by the Batista government, he returned after Castro's triumph in 1959. He is best known for his popular songs in which he introduces African rhythms and Yoruba words which are often used for their sound value, especially in refrains.

CLARA JANÉS (*b*.1940)

Daughter of Josep Janés, but unlike her father she writes in Spanish. Has published many volumes of poetry, translated Czech verse into Spanish and written a biography of Mompou, *La vida callada de Federico Mompou* (*The silent life of Frederic Mompou*).

JOSEP JANÉS (1913–59)

Catalan publisher and poet born in L'Hospitalet, near Barcelona; of his three books of poetry, the best known is *Combat del Somni* (*Dream Combat*, 1937).

GEORGES JEAN-AUBRY (1882–1949)

Jean-Aubry wrote articles on French music and became a friend of Falla's during the composer's first visit to France. He organised the first concert devoted to Spanish music to be given in France, arranged Falla's first visit to

London, in 1911, and himself lived in England from 1915 to 1930, becoming editor of the *Chesterian* in 1919.

PABLO DE JÉRICA (1781–1831?)

Born in Vitoria and educated at the University of Oñate, he entered a business firm in Cádiz. When he became involved in liberal politics, however, he was forced into exile in France. He is known as a writer of fables, and his work is mordant but humorous.

JUAN RAMÓN JIMÉNEZ (1881–1958)

Born near Huelva on Christmas Day, he met the celebrated Spanish poet Rubén Darío at eighteen and travelled to Madrid to join his circle. Often ill, he devoted his life to poetry, founding magazines and discovering new poets. In 1916 he married Zenobia Camprubí Aymar and they lived mainly in Puerto Rico during the Spanish Civil War. In 1956 he was awarded the Nobel Prize for Literature; three days later his wife died, and he survived her by eighteen months. His verse is characterised by a remarkable musicality.

SAN JUAN DE LA CRUZ (1542–91)

Born in a village near Ávila, he was the son of a weaver. He joined the Carmelite order at the age of twenty-one and studied for four years at the University of Salamanca. There he read Garcilaso de la Vega and the Bible. In 1567 he met Santa Teresa de Jesús and under her guidance devoted himself to religious reform. He was thrown in jail for eight months but managed to escape and continue the struggle. He founded many monasteries with Santa Teresa for the new Order of Discalced Carmelites, and continued his work until 1588, when he was persecuted again, stripped of all honours and exiled to Sierra Morena until his death. His poetry is inspired by his own mystical experiences and speaks of love, nature and his quest for God.

VICTORIA KAMHI (*b.*1905)

A brilliant Turkish pianist who met Rodrigo in 1928 at the Paris Conservatoire, where they were both studying. Despite parental opposition, she married him in 1933 and thereafter supported him in all aspects of his work, performing his piano music, editing his works, assisting in composition and writing texts for songs. Their daughter Cecilia was born in 1941 and later became a ballerina at the Royal School of Ballet in London.

FEDERICO GARCÍA LORCA (1898–1936)

Born in Fuentevaqueros of a well-to-do family, he studied at the University of Granada. Juan Ramón Jiménez invited him to collaborate on his literary magazine *Indice* and in 1922 he helped Manuel de Falla organise in Granada the Fiesta del Cante Jondo, which aimed to attract attention to Spain's heritage of folk poetry and folk music. He spent time in New York and on his return to Spain founded a travelling theatre group, 'La Barraca' and wrote plays until the outbreak of the Spanish Civil War, when he was executed in Granada by a Falangist firing squad. He was a prolific poet and from an early age set his own poems to music.

FERNANDEZ NÉSTOR LUJÁN (*b*.1922)

A journalist of remarkable versatility who writes on art, bullfighting, politics, sport and gastronomy. His books include the vast *Historia del toreo* (1954) and *Historia de la cocina española* (1970), written in collaboration with Joan Perucho. A man of broad cultural interests, Luján lives in Barcelona, where he is a regular contributor to *Destino*.

ANTONIO MACHADO (1875–1939)

The son of a lawyer who researched into Spanish folklore, he moved to Madrid at the age of eight and later became Professor of French at several provincial Institutos. In 1909 he married the sixteen-year-old Leonor Isquierdo Cuevas and with her spent three blissful years. Three years later she died; Machado was inconsolable and his grief surfaced intermittently in his work until his death. The uneventful life of a provincial schoolmaster came to an abrupt end at the outbreak of the Civil War, when he sided with Loyalist Spain. As the Republic collapsed, he crossed the French frontier on foot and arrived in Collioure with his mother. Almost at once he died, and three days later his mother followed him to the grave. Machado's best work reflects the Castilian landscape he knew so well, its inhabitants and their struggles. His style is terse and virtually devoid of metaphor. At the heart of his poetry lies his preoccupation with time.

GREGORIO MARTÍNEZ SIERRA (1881–1947)

Poet, playwright, novelist and journalist, who was born in Madrid. He published his first work, *Poema del trabajo*, at the age of eighteen, founded literary journals such as *Vida Moderna* and *Helios y Renacimiento*, and from 1915 to his death was one of Spain's finest theatre directors, who introduced the public to Falla, Turina, Maeterlinck, Shaw, Pirandello and others. The delicacy of his poetry owes something to his wife, María, with whom he collaborated in poems and plays.

APEL.LES MESTRES (1854–1936)

Catalan poet and playwright who translated Heine, whose irony he admired and emulated. He was a prolific poet and set many of his own 'popular' songs to music; he also wrote the libretti to three early Granados operettas: *Petrarca*, *Picarol* and *Follet*. Well known as an artist, he illustrated not only most of his own works, but also those of Andersen, Perrault, Pérez Galdos and Pereda.

José Muñoz San Román (b.1876)

Born in Camas, he spent some years as a private tutor in Seville, where he edited *El Liberal*. He wrote novels but is best remembered for his musical verse which, with its colourful imagery, recalls the school of Rueda. Turina's *Canto a Sevilla* reveals the poet's affection for his adopted home town, which is also evident in other works, including *Es una novia Sevilla* and *Sevilla la bien amada*.

Alfred de Musset (1810–57)

Poet, novelist, dramatist. His first published work was a free translation of De Quincey's *Opium Eater*. One of the foremost French Romantics, he expresses in many of his works his innermost self and sufferings. He was also capable of mocking Romanticism, and his lighter side is revealed in his *Comédies* with their wit and psychological insight; Albéniz's 'Chanson de Barberine' comes from Act III of *La Quenonille de Barberine*. In 1833 he fell passionately in love with George Sand; the tempestuous affair, which lasted on and off for two years, inspired some of his finest works.

Ildefonso Pereda Valdés (b.1899)

Uruguayan poet, essayist and short-story writer born in Montevideo. He moved to Buenos Aires where he produced his *Antología de la moderna poesía uruguaya* and *La guitarra de los negros*, which announced his interest in negro poetry, that culminated in his *Antología de la poesía negra americana* (1936). He is almost the exact contemporary of Nicolás Guillén, and like the Cuban poet, he is concerned with the position of the negro in the modern world.

Fernando Periquet (1873–1940)

Journalist, poet and librettist, whose work fostered a revival of interest in the art and customs of the past. His *Apuntes para la historia de la tonadilla y de las tonadilleras de antaño* (*Notes on the history of the tonadilla and its singers of old*) testifies to his interest in Spanish popular song, which encouraged Granados to compose his tonadillas. He wrote the libretto for Granados's opera *Goyescas*. Albéniz, López Varela and Bretón also set his poetry.

Francisco Gómez de Quevedo y Villegas (1580–1645)

Novelist, satirist, and one of the most prolific poets in world literature. His father was secretary to Princess Maria, and his mother a lady-in-waiting to the queen. Lame and short-sighted, he spent an unhappy childhood in the care of governesses and tutors. He was forced to leave the country after a duel and served the Duke of Osuna in Sicily and Naples. He was involved in the Venetian conspiracy (1618), fell into disgrace and retired to his estates in La Mancha (1621). Many years later he was employed at the court of Philip IV, but when he failed to win the approval of Olivares, the king's favourite, he slandered him and spent the next four years in an underground cell; his health broken, he died two years later. He was deeply conscious of the social and political corruption of his age which he exposed in his picaresque novel *El buscón* and his satirical verse. His occasional verse can be witty, coarse, sparkling and obscene; his sonnets on the vanity of life are unequalled; his love poems are deeply felt and highly polished. Although he ridiculed Góngora's baroquism, he himself delighted in conceits and punning.

Père Ribot i Sunyer (*b*.1908)

A Catalonian churchman who has lived a hermit-like existence in the Montseny mountains. His poetry draws inspiration from the Bible and also Paul Claudel. He has published several volumes of poetry, including *Laetare* (1935), *Epifania* (1952) and *Llevat d'amor* (1975).

Duque de Rivas (1791–1865)

Ángel de Saavedra Remírez de Baquedano was a nobleman from Córdoba who later became the Duque de Rivas. At seventeen he was an officer in the Royal Guards and distinguished himself in action against the French during the War of Independence. As a patriotic liberal in the Cortes, he was condemned to death in 1822 by Fernando VII. He fled and spent the next ten years as an exile in England, Italy, Malta and France. His most famous drama, *Don Álvaro, o la fuerza del sino*, was to inspire Verdi's *La forza del destino*. His poetry expresses a romantic glorification of the past, especially the Middle Ages and the period of the Catholic Kings.

Francisco Rodríguez Marín (1855–1943)

Born in Osuna, Seville, he was above all an academic who eventually became director of the National Library. Although best known for his definitive annotated edition of *Don Quijote* and the monumental collection *Cantos populares españoles*, he also wrote poems and short stories which reveal a concern for form and a delightful Andalusian wit.

Josep Maria de Sagarra (1894–1961)

Catalan poet, novelist, playwright and translator. He was born in Barcelona, came from an aristocratic family and was educated by the Jesuits. Having graduated in law and dabbled in the Diplomatic Service, he finally turned to literature. His output is extremely varied. The poetry can be confessional (*Cançons d'abril i de novembre*, 1918) or impressively epic (*Poema de Nadal*, 1930); and he wrote extensively for the theatre, both comedies and tragedies. During the Civil War he went into voluntary exile and on his return wrote an account of his travels, which he was obliged to publish in Castilian – the Catalan version, *La ruta blava. Viatge a les mars del sud*, was published much later in 1964. He translated the whole of Shakespeare and Dante's *Divina Commedia* into Catalan.

MARQUÉS DE SANTILLANA (1398–1458)

Íñigo Lopéz de Mendoza was given the title Marqués de Santillana by Juan II of Castile in recognition of his military triumphs at Huelva in 1436 and Olmedo in 1445. He was born near Burgos into one of the greatest families of Castile, many of whose members wrote poetry. He had a passion for politics and with the help of his remarkable mother became one of the leaders of the party of nobles in their struggle against the king. The party was successful and he became one of the most powerful men in the country. But he was first and foremost a patron of literature. An imitator of Petrarch and Dante, he was opposed to the popular poetry of his day, and his best lyrics were inspired by folk themes and forms derived from Galician poetry.

FRANCISCO DE TRILLO Y FIGUEROA (1620?–75)

A Galician by birth, he spent most of his life in Granada. After a period in Italy as a soldier he devoted himself to poetry and historical writings. He was a great admirer of Góngora and is at his best in the witty and occasionally obscene letrillas and *romances*, published in Granada in 1652. The collection includes the poem set by Vives, 'Válgame Dios, que los ánsares vuelan' – a metaphorical depiction of a girl abandoned by her lover.

ANTONIO DE TRUEBA (1819–89)

Basque poet, short-story writer and novelist, born in Biscay. He wrote in Spanish and his works often deal with his native region – he was known in Biscay as 'Antón el de los cantares', after the publication of *El libro de los cantares* (1851), which sings in simple language the everyday life and faith of his homeland. His poetry is lightly moralistic in tone, and it is as a short-story writer that he is best known.

PAUL VALÉRY (1871–1945)

Poet, critic and essayist, he was born at Sète, near Montpellier. His father was French, his mother Italian. He was influenced by Mallarmé and symbolism, and although his poetry is not as obscure as Mallarmé's, it deals with the same world of fantasy and imagery and makes a subtle, musical use of assonance and alliteration. He is well known for the twenty-nine volumes of his 'Cahiers', in which from 1894 until his death he recorded daily reflections on poetry, language, philosophy, memory and the central problem of consciousness.

LOPE DE VEGA (1562–1635)

Born in Madrid of humble origin, his full name was Lope Félix de Vega Carpio. He inherited his father's love of verse and began writing early. His life

was filled with amorous exploits and he was married twice. He was exiled from
Madrid and settled in Valencia, where he became prominent in the group of
dramatic poets. He sailed with the Armada, was ordained as a priest but still
continued his many liaisons. He died a celebrated man, and the phrase, 'es de
Lope', became a synonym for perfection. He was astonishingly prolific and
wrote some five hundred plays. His language was lyrical but simple and aimed
to please the people. He treated a universal array of themes, classical and
contemporary, sacred and profane.

SELECT DISCOGRAPHY

Many of these songs have been recorded on LP or CD, and though few are currently listed in *The Classical Catalogue*, they can usually be tracked down by the persistent collector at two remarkable shops either side of the Atlantic:

In London at GRAMEX, 84 Lower Marsh (by Waterloo Station), London SE1 7AB. Telephone: 071 401 3830. The owner is Roger Hewland whose constant turnover and knowledgeable patter attract customers from all over the world; a quarter of a million records have passed through his shop in the last decade.

In New York at Gryphon Record Shop, 251 West 72nd Street, New York, NY 10023. Telephone 0101 212 8741588. The owner is Raymond Donnell who presides over some seventy thousand LPs.

The early period

Victoria de los Angeles/Ars Musicae on Angel 35888:
Cornago: Gentil dama, non se gana
Enrique: Mi querer tanto vos quiere
Del Encina: Ay triste que vengo
Mena: No soy yo quién la descubre
Milán: Aquel caballero, madre
Fuenllana: Duélete de mí, Señora
    De Antequera salió el Moro
    De los álamos vengo, madre
Daza: Enfermo estaba Antioco
    Dame acogida en tu hato
Vasquez: Morenica, dame un beso
Valderrábano: Señora, si te olvidare
    De dónde venís, amore
Anonymous: Una hija tiene el rey
    Una matica de ruda
    Si la noche se hace oscura
    Pastorcico non te aduermas
    Pase el agua, Julieta

Victoria de los Angeles on ALP 1393
Cornago: ¿Qu'es mi vida preguntays?
Pisador ¿Porqué es dama tanto quereros?
    No me llaméis sega la erva
Anonymous: Mariam matrem

¡Ay, triste vida corporal!
¡Ay, luna que reluces!
Del Vado: Molinillo que mueles amores
Literes: Confiado jilguerillo
Plá: Seguidillas religiosas
Laserna: Jilguerillo con pico de oro
Palomino: El canapé
Anonymous: En esta larga ausencia
    Canción de cuna

Victoria de los Angeles/Ars Musicae on Angel 36468
Francisco de la Torre:
    Damos gracias a ti, Dios
Alfonso El Sabio: Rosa das Rosas
    Maravillosos e piadosos
Narváez: Paseábase el rey moro
Mudarra: Dime a do tienes las mientes
Morales: Si no's huviera mirado
Guerrero: Dexó la venda
De Morata: Aquí me declaró
Anonymous:
    Ah, el novio no quiere dinero
    Como la rosa en la güerta
    Estavase la mora
    Sobre Baça estaba el Rey
    ¡Ay! que non hay!
    Tres moricas m'enamoran
    Puse mis amores

**Teresa Berganza/Narciso Yepes on
DGG 2530 504**
Mudarra: Triste estaba el rey David
    Claros y frescos ríos
    Isabel, perdiste la tua faxa
Francisco de la Torre: Dime, triste
    coraçón
Luis Milán: Toda mi vida hos amé
Vasquez/Pisador: En la fuente del rosel
Anonymous: Dindirindín

**Teresa Berganza/Felix Lavilla on
DGG 2542 135**
De Anchieta: Con amores, la mi madre
Francisco de la Torre: Pámpano verde

Sor

Seguidillas
(Berganza/Moreno, Philips 411 030–1)

Albéniz

Seis baladas italianas
(De los Angeles/Parsons, CBS 76 833)

Rimas de Bécquer, 1 and 2
(Caballé/Zanetti, SXL 6935)

Chanson de Barberine
(Alaveda/Zanetti, Discophon 4180)

Granados

Tonadillas*
(Rodríguez de Aragón/Lavilla, London
    EL 93016
Badía/De Larrocha, Vergara L 110010
Lorengar/Lavilla, Spanish Columbia,
    CCL 32037
Caballé/Ferrer, RCA RB 6686
Lorengar/De Larrocha, Decca
    SXL 6866)

*A complete performance of the *Tonadillas*
should include the spoken text to 'La maja de
Goya', the baritone song 'El majo olvidado'
and the cor anglais obbligato in 'La maja
dolorosa 1'. No such recording exists, but those
listed above are the most complete to date.

Canciones amatorias
(Caballé/Ferrer, RCA RB 6686
Badía/De Larrocha, Everest 3237
Lorengar/De Larrocha, Decca SXL
    6866)

Elegia eterna
L'ocell profeta

La maja y el ruiseñor
(Caballé/Zanetti, SXLR 6888)

Vives

El amor y los ojos
El retrato de Isabela
¡Válgame Dios, que los ánsares vuelan!
(Caballé/Zanetti, SXL 6935)

Madre, la mi madre
(Iriarte/Lavilla, Al MC 25025)

Falla

Siete canciones populares españolas
(Barrientos/Falla, Columbia D 11701
Supervia/Marshall, HMV HQM 1220
De Ibarrondo/Sandoval, Columbia
    ML 2189
De los Angeles/Moore, HMV SLS 5012
De los Angeles/De Larrocha, Angel
    S 36896
Merriman/Moore, EX 2906543
Berganza/Lavilla, Spanish Columbia
    SCLL 14024
Gomez/Constable, Saga 5409)

Trois mélodies
(Gomez/Constable, Saga 5409)

Oración de las madres que tienen a sus
    hijos en brazos
Canción andaluza; el pan de Ronda
Dios mío, qué solos se quedan los muertos
(Alavedra, RCA SRL1 2466)

Soneto a Córdoba
(Barrientos/Falla, Columbia D11701
De los Angeles/Zanetti, ASD 2649)

Psyché
(De los Angeles/Zanetti, ASD 2649)

Tus ojillos negros
(Caballé/Zanetti, SXL 6935)

Nin

Montañesa
(Vallin/Nin, Od 188694)

Malagueña
Polo
(Vallin/Nin, Od 188695)

Granadina
Canto andaluz
(Vallin/Nin, Od 188693)

Granadina
El vito
(De los Angeles/Moore, ASD 413)

Paño murciano
Canto andaluz
(Berganza/Lavilla, Sp.C. SCLL 14024)

Villancico asturiano
Villancico andaluz
Villancico castellano
Jesús de Nazareth
(Horne/Katz, SXL 6577)

Tonada de Conde Sol
(Kareska/Thyssen-Valentin, Ducretet-
    Thomson 310 (C) 020)

Turina

Poema en forma de canciones
(Carreras/Katz, Philips 411 478
Gomez/Constable, Saga 5409)

Canto a Sevilla
(De los Angeles/Fistoulari, World
    Records F522
Lorengar/López-Cobos, Decca 410 158
Caballé/Weissenberg, EMI 16380)

Tríptico
(Richardson, World Records R 02423)

Homenaje a Lope de Vega
(Resnik, Epic BC 1384)

Saeta
(Berganza/Lavilla, DG 2542 135)

Corazón de mujer
(Murray/Johnson, Hyperion A66176)

Anhelos
(Caballé/Zanetti, Decca SXLR 6888)

Vade retro
(Resnik/Woitach, Epic BC 1384)

Tu pupila es azul
(De los Angeles/Moore, SLS 5012)

Rima
(Carreras/Zanetti, Ensayo ENY 952)

Guridi

Seis canciones castellanas
(Berganza/Alvarez Parejo, Claves
    D 8704)

Esplá

Cinco canciones playeras españolas
(De los Angeles, ASD 505)

Mompou

Combat del Somni
Aureana do Sil
Cançó de la fira
Pastoral
Dalt d'un cotxe
Margot la Pie
J'ai vu dans la lune
Aserrín, aserrán
Petite fille de Paris
Pito, pito, colorito
Cantar del alma
Sant Martí
Neu
Llueve sobre el río
(Caballé/Mompou, Vergara 701 TL)

L'hora grisa
(Supervia/Vilalta, SO 6937)

Toldrà

A l'ombra del lledoner
Maig
(Caballé/Orchestra, Vergara 110.002
    LS)

Seis canciones
(Berganza/Álvarez Parejo, Claves
    D 8704)

Cançó incerta
Anacreòntica
(De los Angeles/Patronato Orquesta,
    ASD 2517)

Romanç de Santa Llúcia
(Supervia/Gil, PMA 1058)

Gerhard

Cancionero de Pedrell
(Valente/Crone, KTC 1060)

Obradors

Del cabello más sutil
El molondrón
El vito
Aquel sombrero de monte
(Caballé/Zanetti, SXL 6935)

Al Amor
¿Corazón, por qué pasaís?
Con amores, la mi madre
Del cabello más sutil
Chiquitita la novia
(Te Kanawa/Vignoles, Decca
    425 820-2DH)

Lorca

Trece canciones españolas antiguas
(Berganza/Yepes, DGG 2530 875
De los Angeles/Zanetti, ASD 2649
La Argentinita/Lorca, Sonifolk J–105)

Rodrigo

Serranilla
(Supervia/Vilalta, OASI 504)

Cántico de la Esposa
Con qué la lavaré
De los álamos vengo, madre
(Durias/Rodrigo, Sp.C. RG 16179)

Coplas del pastor enamorado
(Durias/Rodrigo, Sp.C. RG 16176)

Pastorcito santo
(De los Angeles/Soriano, ASD 479)

Aire y donaire
Coplillas de Belén
Coplas del pastor enamorado
(Caballé/Zanetti, World records CM87)

Cuatro madrigales amatorios
(Caballé/Zanetti, SXL 6935)

Montsalvatge

Canciones negras
(Berganza/Lavilla, DGG 2530598
De los Angeles/Frühbeck de Burgos,
    ASD 505)

Canciones para niños
(Caballé/Zanetti, World Records CM 87)

INDEX OF COMPOSERS

INDEX OF POETS AND TRANSLATORS

Titles given here are those used by the composers for their settings, not necessarily the poets' own.

INDEX OF TITLES AND FIRST LINES